The US–Japan

Japan's use of soft power in its international politics is as yet understudied. Soft power presents as many challenges as promises. This book explores the way Japan uses soft power in its relationship with the United States, its Asian neighbours and Europe and aims to contribute to a deeper understanding of the role of soft power in international relations.

Hard power, on the other hand, is more tangible and has received far greater scholarly scrutiny than soft power. However, as this collection makes clear, hard power has its limitations and counterproductive consequences as an instrument of policy. This book makes it clear that hard power alone will not provide Japan with the peace and security it desires. A smart balancing or mixture of hard and soft power is required.

Is Japan up to this challenge? While this book cannot give a definitive answer to this question, the excellent contributors present their best analyses of the effectiveness of Japan's current attempt at balancing the two components of national power in meeting its bilateral and multilateral security challenges.

The US–Japan Alliance is suitable for upper undergraduates, postgraduates and academics in International Politics, Political Science, Security studies and Japanese studies.

David Arase is Associate Professor of Political Science at the Department of Government and Political Science, Pomona College, USA.

Tsuneo Akaha is Professor of International Policy Studies, Graduate School of International Policy Studies, and Director, Center for East Asian Studies, Monterey Institute of International Studies, USA.

The Nissan Institute/Routledge Japanese Studies Series

Editorial Board

Roger Goodman, Nissan Professor of Modern Japanese Studies, University of Oxford, Fellow, St Antony's College; J.A.A. Stockwin, formerly Nissan Professor of Modern Japanese Studies and former Director of the Nissan Institute of Japanese Studies, University of Oxford, Emeritus Fellow, St Antony's College; Alan Rix, Executive Dean, Faculty of Arts, The University of Queensland; Junji Banno, formerly Professor of the University of Tokyo, now Professor, Chiba University; Leonard Schoppa, Associate Professor, Department of Government and Foreign Affairs, and Director of the East Asia Center, University of Virginia

Other titles in the series:

The Myth of Japanese Uniqueness
Peter Dale

The Emperor's Adviser
Saionji Kinmochi and pre-war
Japanese politics
Lesley Connors

**A History of Japanese
Economic Thought**
Tessa Morris-Suzuki

**The Establishment of the Japanese
Constitutional System**
Junji Banno, translated by
J.A.A. Stockwin

Industrial Relations in Japan
The peripheral workforce
Norma Chalmers

Banking Policy in Japan
American efforts at reform during
the occupation
William M. Tsutsui

Educational Reform in Japan
Leonard Schoppa

**How the Japanese Learn
to Work**
Second edition
Ronald P. Dore and Mari Sako

Japanese Economic Development
Theory and practice;
Second edition
Penelope Francks

Japan and Protection
The growth of protectionist sentiment
and the Japanese response
Syed Javed Maswood

The Soil, by Nagatsuka Takashi
A portrait of rural life in Meiji Japan
Translated and with an introduction by
Ann Waswo

Biotechnology in Japan
Malcolm Brock

Britain's Educational Reform
A comparison with Japan
Michael Howarth

Language and the Modern State
The reform of written Japanese
Nanette Twine

Industrial Harmony in Modern Japan
The intervention of a tradition
W. Dean Kinzley

Japanese Science Fiction
A view of a changing society
Robert Matthew

The Japanese Numbers Game
The use and understanding of numbers
in modern Japan
Thomas Crump

Ideology and Practice in Modern Japan
Edited by Roger Goodman and
Kirsten Refsing

**Technology and Industrial Development
in Pre-war Japan**
Mitsubishi Nagasaki shipyard,
1884–1934
Yukiko Fukasaku

Japan's Early Parliaments, 1890–1905
Structure, ussues and trends
Andrew Fraser, R.H.P. Mason and
Philip Mitchell

Japan's Foreign Aid Challenge
Policy reform and aid leadership
Alan Rix

Emperor Hirohito and Shōwa Japan
A political biography
Stephen S. Large

Japan
Beyond the end of history
David Williams

Ceremony and Ritual in Japan
Religious practices in an
industrialized society
Edited by Jan van Bremen and D.P. Martinez

**The Fantastic in Modern
Japanese Literature**
The subversion of modernity
Susan J. Napier

**Militarization and Demilitarization
in Contemporary Japan**
Glenn D. Hook

Growing a Japanese Science City
Communication in scientific research
James W. Dearing

Architecture and Authority in Japan
William H. Coaldrake

**Women's *Gidayû* and the Japanese
Theatre Tradition**
A. Kimi Coaldrake

Democracy in Post-war Japan
Maruyama Masao and the
search for autonomy
Rikki Kersten

Treacherous Women of Imperial Japan
Patriarchal fictions, patricidal fantasies
Hélène Bowen Raddeker

Japanese–German Business Relations
Competition and rivalry in the
inter-war period
Akira Kudō

Japan, Race and Equality
The racial equality proposal of 1919
Naoko Shimazu

Japan, Internationalism and the UN
Ronald Dore

Life in a Japanese Women's College
Learning to be ladylike
Brian J. McVeigh

On The Margins of Japanese Society
Volunteers and the welfare of the
urban underclass
Carolyn S. Stevens

**The Dynamics of Japan's Relations
with Africa**
South Africa, Tanzania and Nigeria
Kweku Ampiah

The Right to Life in Japan
Noel Williams

The Nature of the Japanese State
Rationality and rituality
Brian J. McVeigh

**Society and the State in
Inter-war Japan**
Edited by Elise K. Tipton

**Japanese–Soviet/Russian Relations
Since 1945**
A difficult peace
Kimie Hara

**Interpreting History in
Sino-Japanese Relations**
A case study in political
decision making
Caroline Rose

Endō Shūsaku
A literature of reconciliation
Mark B. Williams

Green Politics in Japan
Lam Peng-Er

The Japanese High School
Silence and resistance
Shoko Yoneyama

Engineers in Japan and Britain
Education, training and employment
Kevin McCormick

The Politics of Agriculture in Japan
Aurelia George Mulgan

Opposition Politics in Japan
Strategies under a one-party
dominant regime
Stephen Johnson

The Changing Face of Japanese Retail
Working in a chain store
Louella Matsunaga

Japan and East Asian Regionalism
Edited by S. Javed Maswood

Globalizing Japan
Ethnography of the Japanese presence
in America, Asia and Europe
*Edited by Harumi Befu and
Sylvie Guichard-Anguis*

Japan at Play
The ludic and logic of power
*Edited by Joy Hendry and
Massimo Raveri*

The Making of Urban Japan
Cities and planning from Edo to the
twenty-first century
André Sorensen

**Public Policy and Economic
Competition in Japan**
Change and continuity in
antimonopoly Policy, 1973–95
Michael L. Beeman

Modern Japan
A social and political history
Elise K. Tipton

**Men and Masculinities in
Contemporary Japan**
Dislocating the salaryman doxa
*Edited by James E. Roberson and
Nobue Suzuki*

**The Voluntary and Non-Profit
Sector in Japan**
The challenge of change
Edited by Stephen P. Osborne

Japan's Security Relations with China
From balancing to bandwagoning
Reinhard Drifte

**Understanding Japanese Society:
Third Edition**
Joy Hendry

Japanese Electoral Politics
Creating a new party system
Edited by Steven R. Reed

The Japanese–Soviet Neutrality Pact
A diplomatic history, 1941–45
*Boris Slavinsky translated by
Geoffrey Jukes*

**Academic Nationalism in
China and Japan**
Framed by concepts of nature,
culture and the universal
Margaret Sleeboom

**The Race to Commercialize
Biotechnology**
Molecules, markets and the state
in the United States and Japan
Steve W. Collins

**Institutions, Incentives and Electoral
Participation in Japan**
Cross-level and cross-national
perspectives
Yusaka Horiuchi

Japan's Interventionist State
The role of the MAFF
Aurelia George Mulgan

**Japan's Sea Lane Security,
1940–2004**
'A matter of life and death'?
Euan Graham

The Changing Japanese Political System
The Liberal Democratic Party
and the Ministry of Finance
Harumi Hori

Japan's Agricultural Policy Regime
Aurelia George Mulgan

Cold War Frontiers in the Asia-Pacific
Divided territories in the
San Francisco system
Kimie Hara

Living Cities in Japan
Citizens' movements, machizukuri
and local environments
Andre Sorensen and Carolin Funck

**Resolving the Russo-Japanese
Territorial Dispute**
Hokkaido-Sakhalin relations
Brad Williams

Modern Japan, Second Edition
A Social and Political History
Elise K.. Tipton

The Transformation of the Japanese Left
From old socialists to new democrats
Sarah Hyde

Social Class in Contemporary Japan
*Edited by Hiroshi Ishida and
David H. Slater*

The US–Japan Alliance
Balancing soft and hard power
in East Asia
Edited by David Arase and Tsuneo Akaha

The US–Japan Alliance
Balancing soft and hard power
in East Asia

Edited by
David Arase and Tsuneo Akaha

LONDON AND NEW YORK

First published 2010
by Routledge
2 Park Square, Milton Park, Abingdon, Oxon OX14 4RN

Simultaneously published in the USA and Canada
by Routledge
711 Third Avenue, New York, NY 10017

Routledge is an imprint of the Taylor & Francis Group, an informa business

First issued in paperback 2011

© 2010 Editorial Selection and matter, David Arase and Tsuneo Akaha
Individual chapters, the contributor.

Typeset in Times New Roman by
Taylor & Francis Books

All rights reserved. No part of this book may be reprinted or reproduced or utilised in any form or by any electronic, mechanical, or other means, now known or hereafter invented, including photocopying and recording, or in any information storage or retrieval system, without permission in writing from the publishers.

British Library Cataloguing in Publication Data
A catalogue record for this book is available from the British Library

Library of Congress Cataloging in Publication Data
    p. cm. – (Nissan Institute/Routledge Japanese studies series)
  1. United States–Relations–Japan. 2. Japan–Relations–United States. 3. East Asia–Relations–United States. 4. United States–Relations–East Asia. 5. East Asia–Relations–Japan. 6. Japan–Relations–East Asia. I. Arase, David. II. Akaha, Tsuneo, 1949-
  JZ1480.A57.J37 2009b
  355'.03109730952–dc22
                    2009018029

ISBN 10: 0-415-48713-7 (hbk)
ISBN 10: 0-415-67973-7 (pbk)
ISBN 10: 0-203-86662-2 (ebk)

ISBN 13: 978-0-415-48713-9 (hbk)
ISBN13: 978-0-415-67973-2 (pbk)
ISBN 13: 978-0-203-86662-7 (ebk)

Contents

List of tables ix
List of contributors x
Series editor's preface xii
Acknowledgements xiv

Introduction: soft power, hard power, Japan, and the US–Japan Alliance 1
DAVID ARASE

PART I
Japan and the US–Japan alliance 17

1 "Soft" power, interests and identity: the future of the US–Japan alliance 19
PHILIP MEEKS

2 Japanese security policy: from soft to hard power 35
DAVID ARASE

3 Japan's soft power–hard power balancing act 58
TSUNEO AKAHA

PART II
Major powers' views of Japan and the US–Japan alliance 81

4 Chinese perspectives on the US–Japan alliance 83
JING-DONG YUAN

5 North and South Korean views of the US–Japan alliance 117
DANIEL A. PINKSTON

6 Russian perspectives on the US–Japan Security alliance 131
SERGEY SEVASTYANOV

7 European views of a changing US–Japan alliance: declining prospects for 'civilian power' cooperation? 151
CHRISTOPHER W. HUGHES

Conclusion 169
TSUNEO AKAHA

Index 174

Tables

1.1 Military expenditures and % GDP 1992–2006   22
1.2 U.S. Military aid before and after 9/11   22
1.3 Top ten recipients of ODA for 2005 for the United States and Japan   23
1.4 Global businesses as targets of terrorism   29
4.1 Power indicators: the United States, China, and Japan   86

Contributors

Tsuneo Akaha is Professor of International Policy Studies, Graduate School of International Policy Studies, and Director, Center for East Asian Studies, Monterey Institute of International Studies, USA. His current research interests include Japanese foreign and security policy, regional integration, human security, and international migration in East Asia.

David Arase teaches Politics at Pomona College. Author or editor of three books, his latest article is: "Japan in 2008: A Prelude to Change?" in *Asian Survey*. East Asian security and political economy are his interests, and currently is researching Non-Traditional Security.

Christopher W. Hughes is Professor of International Politics and Japanese at the Department of Politics and International Studies, University of Warwick, UK. He was previously a Research Fellow at the University of Hiroshima, and Asahi Shimbun Visiting Professor of Mass Media and Politics in the Faculty of Law, University of Tokyo. In 2009–10 he will be the Edwin O. Reischauer Visiting Professor of Japanese Studies at the Department of Government/Reischauer Institute, Harvard University. His publications include *Japan's Re-emergence as a 'Normal' Military Power* (Adelphi 368–69).

Philip Meeks is Associate Professor of Political Science and International Relations, Creighton University, Omaha, Nebraska, USA. His current research interests include international political economy, international security, international migration, and comparative politics.

Daniel A. Pinkston is a senior analyst and the deputy director of the North East Asia Project for the International Crisis Group in Seoul. He specializes in WMD nonproliferation and North East Asian security and political economy.

Sergey Sevastyanov is Professor of International Policy Studies at Vladivostok State University, Russia. He holds Ph.D. in Political Science from Moscow State Institute of International Relations. His current research interests have to do with exploring models of regionalism and regionalization in East Asia and Northeast Asia, and assessing Russia's possible role in them.

Jing-dong Yuan is Director of East Asia Nonproliferation Program at the James Martin Center for Nonproliferation Studies, and Associate Professor of International Policy Studies at the Monterey Institute of International Studies. An expert on Asia-Pacific security, Dr. Yuan is currently working on a book manuscript on post-Cold War Chinese security policy.

Series editor's preface

Relations between Japan and the United States in the region broadly described as East Asia are evolving along lines sharply affected by the economic growth of China. The remarkable development of China now goes back some thirty years, so that the accumulation of wealth and power in the world's most populous nation has progressed to the point where many old assumptions about the balance of power in the region hardly still apply. Japan and the United States have over more or less the same period forged a strategic and economic alliance that is surprisingly close, so that the international relations of the East Asian region in some ways look confrontational between Japan and the US on the one hand and China on the other. At the same time it seems reasonable to note that if it is a confrontational relationship it is a relatively well managed one.

The authors of this richly textured book make good use of the concepts of hard and soft power. Ever since Joseph Nye devised his serendipitous concept of 'soft power', it has proved an extremely useful addition to the vocabulary of international relations. This book demonstrates that it is of particular value in analysing relations between the states and peoples of East Asia. They do not, however, attempt to argue that manifestations of soft power have taken over, rather that the key to stability in the region is a balancing of soft power with hard power, though they agree that the balance shifts over time.

An important strength of this book is that its authors have a variety of national backgrounds, including China, Russia and Europe, so that it is not merely a familiar set of arguments from the United States and Japan but gives us a rich feast of occasionally surprising attitudes and perceptions reflecting those indigenous to China, Russia, Europe and the Koreas.

The Nissan Institute/Routledge Japanese Studies series was begun in 1986 and will soon have published its eightieth volume. It seeks to foster an informed and balanced, but not uncritical, understanding of Japanese institutions, practices and ideas. Another is to make international comparisons and see what lessons, positive or negative, can be drawn for other countries.

The present book was completed before the extraordinary results of the Japanese general elections held on 30th August 2009, which ended five decades of almost continuous rule by the Liberal Democratic Party. The new government formed following these elections has the opportunity to make much needed reforms to many aspects of the Japanese politico-economic system, including in the foreign policy-making field, though it will face severe challenges in seeking to do so. This book provides excellent analytical background towards an understanding of the possibilities and problems that lie ahead.

A.A. Stockwin
Roger Goodman

Acknowledgements

The editors thank the Japan Foundation for its grant to the Center for East Asian Studies, Monterey Institute of International Studies, which enabled the Center to organize a seminar in Monterey in March 2007, where most of the contributors to this volume presented earlier versions of their papers. The grant was made possible by the donation of Mr. Isao Sakaguchi of Tokyo and we are most grateful to him. We also wish to thank the anonymous reviewers of the earlier manuscript of this volume for their constructive comments. Thanks are also due to the individuals who offered useful comments on the papers presented at the panel on the US–Japan alliance at the annual conference of the Association for Asian Studies in Boston in March 2007.

Introduction

Soft power, hard power, Japan, and the US–Japan Alliance

David Arase

There is more attention paid today to the changing balance of power in East Asia than at anytime since the end of the cold war. China has continued to rise rapidly through three consecutive decades and could develop into a peer competitor of the US. The US has been the predominant power in the region in virtually all important respects since World War II, but its status today is changing in paradoxical ways. It has never had a larger military advantage than it has today, but its soft power and economic strength are being sapped by the burdensome wars in Iraq and Afghanistan.

Meanwhile, the Korean peninsula has seen roller-coaster events—from North Korea's test of a long-distance ballistic missile and a nuclear device in 2006 to its pledge to abandon its nuclear weapons program in 2007 in exchange for aid and normalized relations with the US. In the Taiwan Strait, the other flashpoint in the region, China's People's Liberation Army (PLA) has built a mass of missiles that threatens to pulverize Taiwan unless its people agree to be ruled by Beijing.

What has drawn less attention is the transformation of the US–Japan alliance in which Japan has changed from being a passive free rider on a US commitment to maintain stability in East Asia into a contributing alliance partner to the US. Most noteworthy has been Japan's deployment of the Self Defense Forces (SDF) to support the US in Afghanistan (2001) and Iraq (2003). These SDF deployments were non-combat missions, but they broke taboos on sending Japanese troops overseas and bore no direct relationship to the defense of Japan. With respect to its alliance role in Northeast Asia, a noteworthy development has been Japan's agreement to operate a theater-wide ballistic missile defense system with the US, only one of several moves to advance the integration of the SDF and US military forces.[1] This more robust military role means that the SDF is turning into a more substantial fighting force on its own, causing neighbors who have memories of past Japanese aggression to question Japan's motives. This volume takes up the issue of how this is happening and what lies ahead.

Soft power and hard security

Soft power enters into the picture if for no other reason than that Japan wants to develop its soft power potential into something that can support its diplomatic and strategic interests. This reflects the fact that its ultimate ambition is to become, not just militarily stronger, but also more attractive as a leader—in other words, to become a fully fledged power that others might be drawn to. Its interest in soft power also reflects concern about China's growing soft power and the declining soft power of the US, which is a dynamic that doubtless has strategic significance. For all the recent talk about soft power in East Asia, however, there has been no systematic effort to describe how soft power influences the substance and tenor of Japan's bilateral relations in the regional security context. To make a start in this direction, when authors in this volume address a particular bilateral relationship, they bring into their discussion the most salient ways in which they see soft power factors affecting, or not affecting, the strategic situation. The result is a fairly consistent overall picture of Japan's soft power, even though each bilateral relationship has its own unique aspects.

Primacy of hard power

Hard power conflict undoubtedly remains just below the surface in Northeast Asia. There are several major wars still in living memory: World War II, the civil war between the Chinese Communist Party (CCP) and the Nationalist Party (KMT), the Korean War, and the wars in Vietnam, first with the French, then the US, and lastly a civil war. These wars left a legacy of national division and mistrust, not to mention unresolved hard power confrontations in the Taiwan Strait and the Korean Peninsula that have the potential to suck the major powers into war. Also unresolved are island sovereignty issues that are a constant source of tension (i.e., the status of Taiwan, and maritime territorial disputes between Japan on the one hand, and South Korea, China, and Russia on the other). On top of all this historical antagonisms divide Japan from Korea, China, and Russia, and antipathy also exists between Russia and China, though it is covered up as both countries make common cause against the hegemonic ambitions of the US.

The newest strategic development is an emerging contest between China and the US for regional dominance. The US, with the continuing support of Japan, remains far ahead of China in military power, but China's rapidly developing military challenge to US naval predominance in East Asian waters, and its growing power to strike a lethal blow at Japan, have caused the US–Japan alliance to tighten and develop new hard power capabilities such as ballistic missile defense—which creates additional problems for China and elicits Chinese accusations of cold war thinking and revived Japanese militarism. China is seeking the ability to control its strategic environment, which brings it into conflict with the US desire to control the region's sea lanes.² The PLA has certain advantages in armed conflict on its periphery, such as proximity to combat, the ability to concentrate forces quickly, and interior lines of communication. China is thus becoming able to use speed and overwhelming force to win battles along its periphery against a foe that is superior, but distant and spread more thinly.³

The power to control the surrounding seas would give China rich maritime resources, the ability to take Taiwan by force, intimidate others in the region, block sea lanes that are vital to Japan and South Korea, and end US strategic predominance in Asia. Though it may not be China's intent, it would take only one success in a showdown with the US to cripple the alliance on which Japan relies for security. With so much at stake, the potential for an arms race and spiraling tensions between China and the US is evident, as is the rationale for a stronger US–Japan alliance as a hedge against a rising China.

The changing alliance

One could say that Japan is changing more than the US to fit a new alliance role because it has to make a larger departure from its policies of the past. Japan used to be allergic to the idea of active military cooperation with the US due to pacifist and anti-US sentiments, and Article 9 of the Constitution which forbids Japan to possess or use military forces. It is a major change to say the least when one moves from a passive, minimally armed posture to one of active partnership with the US in the operation of a missile defense system and the deployment of troops to the Indian Ocean and Persian Gulf.

The change required of the US is more a matter of reorienting an existing global security structure. The US used to stand ready to fight conventional wars using heavy conventional forces whose purpose was to destroy the massive Soviet army in any cold war theater of operation. The US today retains the ability to win a conventional war with any other state but, in addition, it seeks to take full advantage of the revolution in military affairs. New technology permits the "transformation" of its strategic doctrine and global military posture. The new goals are to command the high ground in space in wars against major states and, in unstable parts of the world, to use lighter, more versatile, and more mobile forces operating from a global network of smaller bases whose mission would be to seize or destroy strategic assets and deal quick blows against rogue states and terrorist groups.⁴

What this means for Japan is that it must continue to host US bases to serve as permanent homes for rapidly deployable US forces covering the arc of instability stretching from the Korean peninsula and Taiwan to the distant Persian Gulf. It also requires Japan to support US missions that cover the globe, and not just those that involve the defense of Japan. Even if it offers only logistical and rear area support, the burden of global interventionism is lightened for the US. Furthermore, Japan is improving its independent ability to defend its territory against conventional threats, freeing up US troops for other missions.

Implications for the region

The implications for Japan's neighbors in Northeast Asia, as well as for the trilateral security structure that includes Europe, are examined by authors in this volume. The benefits of the new relationship for Japan are mostly related to the enhancement of hard power and a more secure alliance with the US, but this comes at some cost to Japan's soft power. The renewed alliance presents China with a conundrum. Treating Japan as an enemy could be a self-fulfilling prophecy, but neither can China afford complacency when facing the changing nature of the alliance. The new strategic architecture also causes both Koreas some grave concern. The South is worried that US troops stationed there may be intended more for interventions elsewhere (e.g., Taiwan or North Korea) and less for the defense of Korea. And Seoul is concerned about the long-term implications of a rearmed Japan. The North has similar concerns because it is more susceptible than ever to a crippling US surprise attack, and the prospect of the involvement of a rearmed Japan is unsettling. In contrast, Russia in Northeast Asia is not as concerned insofar as Russia has no militarized points of contention with the US or Japan in Northeast Asia, and the strengthened alliance seems to be focused on regions that have no Russian defense commitments. Russia views Japan more as an economic partner than as an enemy, notwithstanding an intractable territorial dispute and the actions of its ally the US, which seems intent on encroaching on Russia's "near abroad." Finally, the stronger military alliance role of Japan could complicate relations with Europe and exacerbate transatlantic estrangement by encouraging US military interventionism and a dismissive attitude toward multilateralism that Europeans find so objectionable.

Japan in search of hard and soft power

Japan's interest in hard power reflects the insecurity that it has felt in recent years stemming from terrorism after 9/11, US displeasure with Japan's past unwillingness to help in international security issues, and rising tension with China and North Korea. There also is a new generation of leaders that simply wants Japan to have greater international clout. The drive toward hard power is led by conservative nationalists, who want to return Japan to "normal" status, i.e., to give it military capacities, rights, and privileges commensurate with its economic capabilities and national interests. It is unsurprising that under the conservative governments of Koizumi Junichirō, Abe Shinzō, Fukuda Yasuo, and Asō Tarō since 9/11 that the greatest progress has been made.

Japan is also trying more to use its economic power to affect security affairs. In the past, Japan used mostly carrots in the form of official development assistance (ODA) to advance its interests. Japan gave ODA to developing countries to promote stability and a pro-West orientation during the Cold War. It also used ODA as a substitute for a military contribution to the western alliance. In recent years Japan has tried to use targeted economic sanctions to influence specific security issues. One example is the imposition of economic sanctions on Pyongyang as punishment for its development of weapons of mass destruction (WMD). At the same time, it is dangling the prospect of generous economic assistance to induce North Korea to give up its nuclear weapons and account for Japanese citizens it abducted in the 1970s and 1980s. Thus, it is not only through the military dimension that Japan seeks enhanced strategic clout.

Finally, as explained by Tsuneo Akaha in his chapter, there has been growing Japanese interest in soft power as a medium for strategic influence. The belief now current in Japan is that, to qualify as a major power, hard power is not enough. In this sense the criteria for becoming "normal" are widening to include soft power even among hawks.

The main focus of each chapter in this book is directed toward Japan's changing alliance relationship with the US, and the effect this has at the level of Japan's bilateral relations in the region. Strategic relations traditionally have been discussed in terms of a hard power model (i.e., a power politics model in which order is established through force by one or more great powers). But, in various ways hinted at in this book, soft power factors are becoming more relevant to the strategic future of Japan and East Asia. Because the strategic relevance of soft power is not always clear, and authors in this volume deal with different aspects of soft power, we will address some reasons for the confusion that can result when the idea of soft power is invoked.

The balance of hard and soft power in East Asia

Joseph Nye calls soft power "the ability to get what you want through attraction rather than coercion or payments."[5] Nye theorizes that this ability derives from a country's cultural appeal—its "personality" as it were. Soft power has not been an important concept in East Asia until recently because there has never been a serious challenge to US soft power until now. Another reason for the growing attention paid to soft power is that, in an international system that is increasingly norm driven, this kind of power becomes strategically relevant because it gives those who enjoy it a superior ability to exert influence in international security institutions and emerging norms.

Soft power and hard power issues

How could soft power make a difference in a predominantly hard power strategic environment? Soft power can substitute for hard power in some circumstances, and may even do a better job of creating lasting stability. Europe has immensely improved its security after the cold war by attracting and co-opting its former enemies, rather than resorting to force and intimidation to achieve security through military domination. Moreover, hard power alone is not sufficient to achieve political objectives. As can be seen in Iraq and Afghanistan today, hard power alone is insufficient to establish stability in the wake of interventions, and a lack of soft power can lead to political failure after even the most successful military campaign.

In East Asia, soft power could matter greatly if there were a standoff in hard power terms between the US and China. It might be worth considering whether declining US and Japanese soft power, and Korea's history of close cultural relations with China might in future tip Korea toward strategic partnership with China if forced by circumstances to choose. And China's growing soft power influence in Southeast Asia could give it a strategic advantage in a geopolitically important region. The US military bases in the region rest on the willingness of countries to host them and cooperate with the US. If China becomes politically influential, and culturally and economically favored within the region, there could be important strategic implications for the US.

Alternatively, East Asia might move away from hard power politics. Multilateral management of regional security relations is the professed aim of almost all countries in the region. Were a regional security regime to take shape, soft power will be more relevant in such questions as: should the US be included as a member (as it is presently not in the ASEAN + 3 or the East Asian Summit meetings), what legal and institutional norms will guide behavior, what goals will be set for the group, and how leadership is determined.

Who has soft power in East Asia?

On the soft power side of things the regional balance is less clear. Though the methodology of soft power measurement is not well developed, we at least have measures of how well countries are regarded by looking at global opinion polls, which should indicate, however imperfectly, the degree to which a country holds the power of attraction over others.

In East Asia the situation can be summarized as follows: US soft power in East Asia is in decline.[6] In contrast, China is making soft power advances, and it is working hard to develop it especially in Southeast Asia. Japan wants to find ways to capitalize on its surprising potential for soft power, but it has no clear strategy to do so yet.

The US and China

Joshua Kurzlantzick warns in his 2007 book, *Charm Offensive*, that China is displacing the US as the preeminent soft power in Southeast Asia. Kurlantzick's assessment is based on his expertise as a veteran journalist covering the region. Based on the China–ASEAN Comprehensive Economic Cooperation Agreement signed in 2002, China will have a free trade area with all ten ASEAN countries by 2020 that excludes the US and Japan. Meanwhile, China is quickly broadening relations in Southeast Asia in other ways, especially through the distribution of economic assistance, subregional economic programs, and active cooperation in non-traditional security areas. China is likely to displace US influence unless the US takes China's challenge seriously.[7] To support its initiatives, China has advantages that are only now being exploited. The region's economic fate is increasingly tied up with China's emergence as an economic superpower. China is a looming presence on the borders of both maritime Southeast Asia and Indochina, and local Chinese communities have wealth and influence throughout the region.[8]

Other experts dismiss Kurlantzick's concern as alarmist because he ignores the large advantage of the US in soft power resources. He also discounts the possibility that China's aims might be benign[9] and does not fully explore China's limitations.[10] Others point out that the countries of Southeast Asia can be resistant to China's soft power.[11] China's growing military and economic power has been causing some feelings of insecurity among neighbors and, at least in the democratic countries, China suffers a black eye with respect to its democracy and human rights practices.[12]

It could also be true that China's engagement with ASEAN through multi-lateralism and cooperative security will socialize China to the peaceful and open multilateralism of the Declaration on the Conduct of Parties in the South China Sea (DOC) that it signed with ASEAN (2002) and ASEAN's Treaty of Amity and Cooperation (TAC) that China signed in 2003.[13] China's socialization into the "ASEAN Way" that informs these documents would make it another member of a Southeast Asian security community.[14]

Polls suggest that Kurlantzick's concern regarding the decline of US influence compared to that of China is not entirely misplaced. The 2007 Global Survey by the Pew Research Center indicated that the US was rated unfavorably in the two Southeast Asian nations surveyed (66 percent of Indonesians and 69 percent of Malaysians). But these countries had very favorable views of China (65% and 83% respectively). Of the forty-six countries, the US was more liked in South Korea and Japan (42% of South Koreans and 67% of Japanese). Of the forty-six countries surveyed, only five had a net negative view of China. In contrast, eighteen of forty-five countries had net negative views of the US.[15]

A BBC World Service poll conducted in 2008 came to similar conclusions. Thirty-four countries were polled on the kind of influence that major countries had on the world. The US came out with a net negative assessment: 35 percent felt US influence was positive but 47 percent were negative. In contrast, China had a net positive rating—47 percent positive and 32 percent negative. As in the Pew poll, Koreans and Japanese were better disposed toward the US than to China, but this ranking of preference was reversed in Southeast Asia.[16]

A third global opinion poll on attitudes towards China's rise found that on balance it was welcomed, but it also showed that China was as distrusted as the US. In a sample of fifteen countries, ten did not trust the US "to act responsibly" and the same number did not trust China. In East Asia, four countries (South Korea, Thailand, the Philippines, and Indonesia) believed that China roughly equaled US influence in Asia, and Australia saw China exceeding the United States in Asian influence.[17]

However, a June 2008 poll on the question of soft power in East Asia by the Chicago Council on Global Affairs and the East Asia Institute of South Korea surveyed five East Asian countries and the United States. It found that in terms of soft power resources China was significantly weaker than the U.S. or Japan. Soft power ratings were constructed by measuring a target country's economic, cultural, human capital, diplomatic, and political strengths. The countries were then rated in each category and also were given an overall score.[18] However, it is not clear how the measured soft power inputs are related to actual outcomes, i.e., the overall balance and intensity of general attitudes toward the three powers.

Japan's soft power

Generally speaking, if the question is which country is viewed most favorably, Japan outperforms China and the US in a global sample of countries by a wide margin. If the sample is restricted to East Asia, the situation is mixed, but Japan has surprising strength. Though authors in this volume tend to focus on Japan's soft power problems, these problems should be viewed against a general backdrop.

In the 2007 Chicago Council poll cited above, Japan was "trusted to do the right thing" by majorities in 10 out of 16 countries, a large contrast to the 10 out of 15 countries that *distrusted* China and the US. Asian countries in the poll that trusted Japan more than China were Indonesia (79% vs. 59%) and the Philippines (67% vs. 59%). South Korea's distrust of Japan (81%) was high, but only slightly less than its distrust of China (79%).

The BBC poll gave Japan the number two global ranking, behind first place Germany and ahead of the EU. On average 56 per cent polled around the world said that Japan had a mostly positive influence and only 21 percent felt that Japan's influence was mostly negative, which included the negative assessments of Japan by China (55%) and South Korea (52%). However, South Korea was about equally negative toward China (50%). In Southeast Asia, Indonesia (74%) and the Philippines (70%) saw Japan as a positive influence, which were better ratings than what they gave to China (58% and 48% respectively).

The Chicago Council on Global Affairs soft power survey also had Japan ahead of China. Japan rated higher than China in all soft power components except culture, and the two developing countries in the poll, Indonesia and Vietnam, rated Japan's soft power highest of all. Sino-Japan mutual perceptions are on balance negative as might be expected. The BBC poll showed that 55% of Chinese had unfavorable views of Japan, and 59% of Japanese had unfavorable opinions of China.

What these polls suggest is that the US and China have image problems globally, whereas Japan has a very good global image. China is overtaking the US in Southeast Asia, but Japan seems to be ahead of both. In Northeast Asia, the US retains a soft power advantage because there is more distrust between neighbors than between members of the group and the US.

Soft power as a fuzzy concept?

Readers may notice variation in the way that authors in this volume use the term "soft power," but this is not by itself a shortcoming and is not unusual. Soft power is a term that has become ubiquitous but its meaning remains unclear despite Joseph Nye's efforts to nail down the concept. Nye states, "In international politics, the resources that produce soft power arise in large part from the values an organization or country expressed in its culture, in the examples it sets by its internal practices and policies, and in the way it handles its relations with others".[19] In other words, a nation derives its soft power from: (1) cultural values that are widely admired; (2) domestic and international behavior that is consistent with those values; and (3) the fairness and ethics with which it treats others.[20] Nye says elsewhere that soft power "arises from the attractiveness of a country's culture, political ideals, and policies."[21]

Nye insists that culture is the source of soft power. But this claim is open to debate. The Chicago Council on Global Affairs poll cited above makes culture only one of five (i.e., economic, cultural, human capital, diplomatic, and political) means to soft power. The Congressional Research Service in its study of China's soft power included "international trade, overseas investments, development assistance, diplomatic initiatives, cultural influence, humanitarian aid and disaster relief, education, and travel and tourism." One expert on China opines, "People often conflate soft power with investment and economic development, but I define it as culture, education, and diplomacy."[22] Joshua Kurlantzick notes that: "In the context of Asia today, both China and its neighbors enunciate a broader idea of soft power, the idea that soft power implies all elements outside of the security realm, including investment and aid."[23] In other words, there is no agreed formula for soft power. Why this is so is discussed later.

Nye believes that hard power and soft power are distinct from one another, and that one does not require the other. Nye states: "Sometimes countries enjoy political clout that is greater than their military and economic weight would suggest because they define their national interest to include attractive causes such as economic aid or peacekeeping."[24] Not everyone agrees. Samuel Huntington asserts that hard power is the prerequisite or foundation of soft power. For him, culture and ideology become attractive "when they are seen as rooted in material success and influence."[25]

It is too simple to say that soft and hard power are categorically different, or that causality only runs in one direction from soft to hard, or hard to soft power. Today, US soft power is related to its retention of strategically located military bases. Osama bin Laden uses a cultural legacy of Islam to create hard power. Hitler used a Nazi vision of German culture to create an incredibly powerful war machine. Though Huntington may be right that hard power can create soft power, it is also apparent that the soft power of ideas and values rooted in culture can create and sustain hard power. In other words, though the two are not interchangeable, there is a degree of fungibility between soft and hard power. The philosopher Bertrand Russell dealt with the complexity of power and its causes by conceiving of power as varied and transmutable in form, but of the same essence:

> Like energy, power has many forms, such as wealth, armaments, civil authority, and influence on opinion. No one of these can be regarded as subordinate to any other. ... Wealth may result from military power or from influence over opinion, just as either of these may result from wealth.[26]

The puzzle of soft power

Soft power is the ability to get another to do something without using threats or blandishments. But the realist and liberal models of international relations do not explain how such power can exist. There is nothing in the realist model to explain why one actor would obey another if there is no fear or selfish material desire in play. The liberal institutionalist model also cannot satisfactorily explain soft power because ultimately, actors engage only in utility maximizing behavior regardless of whether the behavior is governed by specific or diffuse reciprocity. Soft power is supposed to be rooted in irrational affective factors.

The constructivist approach is better able to explain the concept of soft power. The practical benefit of thinking of international relations in terms of social relationships rather than the interplay of egoist utility maximization by individuals is that it provides a more coherent way to explain the mechanics of how and why soft power works. Social theorists have long analyzed why people do others' bidding in the absence of coercion or bribes. To take one explanation of this "irrational" behavior, Max Weber constructed the concept of authority (*herrschaft*). Authority does not command obedience because it rests on contractual utilitarianism. It rests on a subjectively felt obligation or duty rooted in cultural values and institutions. According to Weber, the sources of authority are three: tradition, charisma, and legal institutions. The concept of charismatic authority is the most relevant to our discussion of soft power.

Charismatic authority attaches to an individual because of his or her unique personal qualities, just as soft power attaches to a nation because of its unique cultural attributes. It is non-transferable and according to Weber it arises out of "devotion to the exceptional sanctity, heroism or exemplary character of an individual person, and of the normative patterns or order revealed or ordained by him."[27] This is a close resemblance to the way Nye characterizes soft power.

It is ironic, given how international relations has been theorized in terms of the maximization of personal utility at the expense of others that, of all things, affection illustrates the logic of soft power. You are drawn to another simply for being who he or she is. You will sacrifice and give gifts that are unbidden merely to sustain or improve a relationship. In a social world, affection is an important motivator of behavior and a source of power.

Once the social basis of soft power is acknowledged, it is easy to see why so many different attributes are said to create soft power. Any quality or skill able to charm and gain the admiration of others can be a source of soft power. Even the hard power of a modern army is not excluded from generating soft power if others accept it as a standard of excellence and a mark of cultural superiority to be emulated. Nor is an economy excluded if it is a widely admired success.

Japan's soft power dilemmas

Postwar Japan has been handicapped from the start with respect to the types of power it commands. Early Occupation policy liquidated its hard power. The Tokyo War Crimes Tribunal stripped post-defeat Japan of soft power. And domination by the US sacrificed Japan's foreign policy independence. This left Japan with economic power as the most promising area to develop. Thus, it is little wonder that Japan has great economic power but less military and soft power than other nations of comparable size and wealth.

Since the 1991 Persian Gulf War the US has made it ever clearer that Japan must enhance its military contribution to the alliance even if this means amending the Constitution. Japan's response under the conservative LDP has been to incrementally reinterpret Article 9 in a way that has brought Japan to where it is today—acting in new alliance roles that make constitutional revision a post hoc necessity.

Interest in soft power has been emerging as Japan seeks to remedy its skewed profile of power and influence. As a veteran Japanese Trilateralist put it,

> proper balance is needed for a nation to be regarded as a power, whether hard or soft, in the international arena. At least a minimum necessary level should be maintained in each of the key fields: military, economic, cultural and foreign policy.[28]

Merely having these types of power is not enough, however. The elements of power must be mutually reinforcing if they are to constitute what Nye has called "smart power."[29]

Japan has growing cultural appeal due to the spread of its pop culture, ingenious and highly sought after consumer products, charming traditional arts and crafts, and exotic cuisine.[30] But Japan has failed to make proper amends for World War II and put the stigma of the Tokyo War Crimes Tribunal behind it.[31] Moreover, it lacks the "smart" kind of soft power that can leverage hard power. Japanese pop culture will not provide a justification for a stronger military or add clout to its diplomacy. Japan has to evince soft power in the area of political values to support the kind of foreign policy and security role that it wants. For example, the US has used democracy and human rights very effectively to convince others that its power is justified and will not be misused, and that its foreign policy is guided by a positive purpose.

Gaiko Forum, a journal that is a Ministry of Foreign Affairs (MOFA) mouthpiece, has been leading the discussion of soft power in Japan. There has been a steady stream of articles since 2002 arguing that Japan needs to find ways to further strengthen its soft power appeal.[32] Abe Shinzō[33] and his colleague Asō Tarō[34] published books when they were aspiring candidates for prime minister, and each discussed the importance of soft power, as Akaha explains in his chapter. Also, "The Council on Security and Defense Capabilities Report: Japan's Visions for Future Security and Defense Capabilities" released in October 2004 dealt explicitly with soft power, and it provided input to the National Defense Program Guidelines (NDPG) published two months later in which Japan aims for a "multi-functional" SDF that can be used for disaster relief and humanitarian assistance to enhance its soft power.[35] However, only in 2008 have there been signs (in the form of a university education exchange program modeled on the ERASMUS program in the EU, and a new mandate for the Japan Foundation to reach a more popular audience through its nineteen overseas offices) that Japan is implementing any kind of strategy beyond expanding the peaceful missions of the SDF.

Soft power pitfalls

There are a few final points to make regarding Japan's unique set of soft power issues. Right wing conservatives in the LDP, exemplified by Prime Minister Koizumi, have let their pride sacrifice the national interest as they themselves define it. To revive a military role in the world as conservatives wish to do, Japan must give assurances that it clearly recognizes the wrongs its army committed in the past. Koizumi's visits to Yasukuni Shrine hurt this cause. Only a *mea culpa* will allay fears that a rearmed Japan could repeat the mistakes of the past.

Next, Japan wants to build soft power through the use of the SDF in overseas humanitarian missions and ODA. The state can be useful in nurturing and amplifying a nation's soft power, but the more overtly political and contrived is the promotion, the less effective it will be. Giving the SDF an ancillary mission in disaster relief could appear to be a transparent attempt to make its controversial expanding hard power role more acceptable.

A third point is that what used to work for Japan may no longer work today. The Japanese Miracle was greatly admired in the 1980s. But it is irrelevant today because it cannot work in a borderless global economy. Thus, Japan must find new soft power assets to replace those that have become obsolescent.

Finally, Japan's cultural insularity limits the number and quality of its relationships with actors in the outside world. This is problematic because, as indicated earlier, soft power only works through social relationships. Japan's cultural insularity reduces its ties to the outside world, suggesting that Japan will have a handicap for years to come.³⁶ Samuel Huntington made this point in a different context some time ago in the following way:

> However strong the trade and investment links Japan may forge with other East Asian countries, its cultural differences from those countries and particularly from their largely Chinese economic elites, preclude it from creating a Japanese-led regional economic grouping comparable to NAFTA or the European Union. At the same time, its cultural differences with the West exacerbate misunderstanding and antagonism in its economic relations with the United States and Europe. If, as seems to be the case, economic integration depends on cultural commonality, Japan as a culturally lone country could have an economically lone future.³⁷

Organization of the book

Phillip Meeks (Chapter 1) looks at the peculiar nature of the US–Japan alliance from an unconventional perspective. The alliance is somewhat anomalous in that it contravenes classic realist theory. Despite the common rhetoric use in connection with the alliance, Meeks asserts that it does not exist to face a common enemy in the traditional sense, and so balance of power or balance of threat model of alliance does not fit so well. Instead, a balance of interest model seems to work better because it is positive shared interests that bind the two sides together. The US and Japan are economic rivals, but this is not a real threat to a continuing alliance. Meeks suggests that rivalry is muted by their shared interest in an open global economy and economic security, and the competitive strengths of each side are less often matched in head-to-head competition. The soft nature of their common goals therefore makes soft power more relevant to the achievement of alliance goals.

In Chapter 2 David Arase reviews Japan's turn toward hard power and the post 9/11 militarization of the US–Japan alliance. Arase suggests that regional tensions (fostered by US geostrategy to an extent), direct US pressure on the Japanese government, generational change, and right wing elements in the LDP have succeeded in bringing Japan to the edge of Constitutional revision. Fundamental change has become possible because systemic, institutional, and normative factors that previously precluded change have been rearranged after 9/11. Further militarization, including Constitutional revision, is possible if external tension and the power of the right wing in the LDP is sustained. A delicate balance in domestic politics introduced after the fall of Prime Minister Shinzō Abe has pushed the right wing aside and created an opportunity to de-escalate tensions with Japan neighbors, but there is no guarantee that things will not tip back to favor the right wing agenda again.

In the Chapter 3, Tsuneo Akaha reviews the steps Japan has taken to enhance both its hard power and soft power, and then discusses the dilemma Japan faces when it seeks to remedy both hard power and soft power deficits with neighbors. The difficult issue of North Korea is likely to make Japan choose to continue a hard power approach even if this detracts from its soft power efforts. The problem is that even if it dismantles its known nuclear facilities under international supervision, North Korea could still keep its secret facilities and weapons in hiding. Soft power can do little to resolve this issue and so Japan will continue to favor hard power and alliance with the United States.

Jing-dong Yuan (Chapter 4) examines China's changing perspectives on the evolving US–Japan alliance. He explains that the four factors that guide China's thinking on the US–Japan alliance are: (1) the alliance's changing scope and missions, (2) the alliance as cover for Japanese remilitarization, (3) the alliance as a factor that interferes with China's policy toward Taiwan issue, and (4) the effect that the tenor of China's separate bilateral relations with Japan and the US can have on the threat to China posed by the alliance. However, under China's "New Security Concept" there is less emphasis on hard power and more emphasis on regional multilateralism and cooperative security, especially in Southeast Asia, where soft power becomes more strategically relevant. China's aim is to stabilize its periphery and undermine US encirclement strategies, and China has made substantial gains in Southeast Asia through soft power strategies.

Pinkston (Chapter 5) points out that in North and South Korea, soft power has always been a crucial part of security strategy since the ancient kingdoms. As a relatively small nation the Koreans have always relied on it to support relations with neighboring big powers. Pinkston suggests that this remains the case today, especially with respect to North Korea in relations with the South. He also points out how Japan's soft power deficit with North and South Korea weakens the influence of the US–Japan alliance and impacts the outlook for hard power security relations in Northeast Asia.

Russia's role in Northeast Asia is sometimes hidden because it maintains a low posture, but in Chapter 6 Sergei Sevastyanov remedies this with a thorough review of Moscow's geopolitical and geo-economic interests in Northeast Asia. Russia's relations with Japan are hampered by their dispute over islands north of Hokkaido, but Japan's soft power appeal is positive nonetheless. Sevastyanov explains that the two countries have a potential partnership because they have parallel material interests, especially with regard to energy and the development of the Russian Far East, and he explains why Russia is not prepared to sacrifice territory to advance the relationship. With respect to the US–Japan alliance, the author notes a certain degree of ambivalence on the part of Russia but he offers an outline of a mutually acceptable accommodation.

Christopher Hughes (Chapter 7) looks at how the US–Japan alliance and the North Atlantic alliance are moving in opposite directions with respect to enabling an aggressive and militarized US unilateralism. It may be that, for Japan and Europe, US hard power is counterproductive and increasingly irrelevant as their interests are, more than ever, to build beneficial forms of cooperation within their respective regions and to establish a rule-governed global order. Both Japan and Europe also prefer to promote by example the benefits of liberal political and economic values, and to rely more on economic assistance to create stability. Hughes suggests that the militarization of the US–Japan alliance weakens not only the constraints put on the US, but also leaves Europe more exposed when it questions US policies. And to the extent that Japan becomes locked into US positions toward China, North Korea, Iraq, and elsewhere, European positions will diverge from those of Japan. Hughes leaves one to ponder the ramifications for global order of a Japan too willing to enable the US appetite for the use of hard power.

Notes

1 Japan Ministry of Defense, "Japan–U.S. Security Arrangements."
2 June Teufel Dreyer, "China's Power and Will: The PRC's Military Strength and Grand Strategy."
3 Office of the Secretary of Defense, *ANNUAL REPORT TO CONGRESS: Military Power of the People's Republic of China 2006.*
4 U.S. Department of Defense, *Quadrennial Defense Review Report – 2006*, vi–vii.
5 Nye, *Soft Power*, 10.
6 Nye, "The Decline of America's Soft Power: Why Washington Should Worry."
7 Kurlantzick, *Charm Offensive.*
8 Liu, "Beijing's Regional Strategy and China-ASEAN Economic Integration."
9 Sutter, *China's Rise in Asia*, 51.
10 Huang and Ding, "Dragon's Underbelly: An Analysis of China's Soft Power."
11 Congressional Research Service, "China's Foreign Policy and 'Soft Power' in South America, Asia, and Africa."
12 Ibid.
13 Yuan, *China–ASEAN Relations: Perspective, Prospects and Implications for US Interests.*
14 Acharya, *Constructing a Security Community in Southeast Asia.*
15 Pew Research Center, "Global Unease With Major World Powers."
16 BBC World Service, "Global Views of USA Improve – World Public Opinion."
17 The Chicago Council on Global Affairs, "World Publics Think China Will Catch Up With the US—and That's Okay – World Public Opinion."
18 The Chicago Council on Global Affairs, "Soft Power in Asia: Results of a 2008 Multinational Survey of Public Opinion."
19 Nye, *Soft Power*, 8.
20 Ibid., 11.
21 Ibid., 5.
22 Pan, "China's Soft Power Initiative – Council on Foreign Relations Backgrounder."
23 Kurlantzick, "China's Charm: Implications of Chinese Soft Power."
24 Nye, *Soft Power*, 26.
25 Huntington, *The Clash of Civilizations and the Remaking of World Order*, 92.
26 Russell, *Power*, 4.
27 Weber, *Economy and society: An Outline of Interpretive Sociology*, 215.
28 Gyohten, "Japan's Soft Power Reconsidered."
29 Nye, "Think Again."
30 McGray, "Japan's Gross National Cool."
31 Lam, "Japan's Quest for 'Soft Power'."
32 Aoki, "Toward Multilayered Strength in the 'Cool' Culture."

33 Abe, *Utsukushii kuni e (Toward a Beautiful Country)*.
34 Asō, *Totetsumonai Nihon (Exuberant Japan)*.
35 Akaha, "Soft Power in Japan's Security Policy: Implications for Alliance with the US."
36 Itoh, *Globalization of Japan: Japanese Sakoku Mentality and U.S. Efforts to Open Japan*.
37 Huntington, *The Clash of Civilizations and the Remaking of World Order*, 134–35.

Part I
Japan and the US–Japan alliance

1 "Soft" power, interests and identity
The future of the US–Japan alliance

Philip Meeks

Introduction: Machiavelli's soft power dilemmas

This chapter will analyze briefly several different elements of both soft power and security alliances in the case of the United States and Japan since World War II. The dilemma of Machiavelli's prince was about the power of fear versus the power of respect and affection, in other words, about the value of hard versus soft power. Machiavelli sided with future realists that fear was more important and hence the need for maximum hard power. But Machiavelli didn't expound on what it would take to be the world's greatest power, its hegemon. He also had little to say about alliances, their motivations and to what extent soft power can enhance the mutual loyalty and cohesion between two asymmetric partners. He might have concluded that the more power a kingdom desires, the more necessary it is to make its rivals fear it.

Soft power depends upon respect and admiration which is especially rare in a world of cultural diversity of values and action styles. Soft power assumes at least some minimal mutual peace and trust among most nations. It may only flourish when fear and threats are minimal. Realists believe in both the reality and preference of fear or economic compensation rather than respect and trust. For them, soft power is only a luxury except in a soft world, which the human one is clearly not. But soft power advocates also know that a softer world is a threat to those whose interests thrive under assumptions of fear and mistrust. In a softer world, alliances would thrive on mutual trust, not mutual fears of threat or needs to balance power. In this analytical context, "soft power" is defined as getting other nations or political actors to do things they otherwise wouldn't do because of the respect and/or admiration one has (regardless of military or economic strength). As will be discussed later, "soft" power is rarely achieved without considerable economic resources.

Twenty years ago, there was alarm about Japan's growing economic power coupled with the collapse of the Soviet military threat. Some American authors predicted that Japan would strive to replace Russia as the second most powerful global military power and challenge United States economic hegemony. Little was it realized that Japan would experience a decade of economic recession as the United States rebounded with its best decade of economic growth since the 1960s. Those who played up the Japanese challenge were too alarmist and those who played down the Japanese threat were more prophetic.[1]

Rarely have scholars had the occasion to coin a term that is almost exclusively associated with their writing. Elsewhere in this volume the origins and nuances of the concept of soft power are examined in great detail. Joseph Nye Jr. starts his seminal book, *Soft Power*, with an age-old definition of power.

> [P]ower is the ability to influence the behavior of others to get the outcomes one wants. But there are several ways to affect the behavior of others. You can coerce them with threats; you can induce them with payments; or you can attract and co-opt them to want what you want.[2]

The most commonly examined dimension is soft power's *broad multicultural appeal*. The influence of both American and Japanese popular culture, films, art, music, food and sports is well documented, and the success of its automobiles, computers, audio and video equipment is proven by sales figures. The appeal across diverse cultures for diverse and higher quality consumer goods has produced substantial soft power appeal for both the United States and Japan. China's growing soft power appeal seems to be based on substantially lower costs for acceptably lower quality goods. Their soft power is based on an economic formula for higher incomes and more consumer goods, which brought down Soviet socialism far more effectively than the threat of thousands of dangerous nuclear weapons.

Another dimension of economic soft power is *persuasion without external threats or incentives*. Japan's ability to build economic relations based on the neo-liberal model has dispelled charges of Japanese colonial and neo-colonial strategies of forced exploitation. The neo-liberal approach, and the environmental impact of Japanese trade and investment are not without vocal critics about severe local costs but these are probably more accepted by a more diverse world polity than ever before.

Nye identifies aid, bribes, payments and sanctions as the primary instruments of economic hard power.[3] They are different in his opinion because they are coercive or based on material inducements. Certainly the seizure of foreign bank accounts fits anyone's definition of "hard" economic power. However, economic boycotts are coercive but recent history shows that these sanctions take a very long time to work and usually are unable to achieve universal compliance. Some other country will openly or covertly evade a boycott to gain the enhanced benefit of trade in these circumstances. It may be that the threat is more effective than the actual use of economic sanctions.

So we confront a dilemma – is hard power "hard" if it can never be used except under the most extreme circumstances? Nothing could be seen as more "hard" than nuclear weapons, but are they most effective when used? Would the world ever "excuse" Iran or North Korea for using nuclear weapons if they were invaded by the United States or any other country? Without a general sense of legitimacy, a massive, unilateral use of hard power – military or economic – can create a diplomatic backlash that few countries can afford for very long. Ironically weak and poor countries may have a greater incentive to use hard power because they have very little to lose. The more hard power a country has, the more likely it is that it will have to resort to soft power tactics unless it is willing to pay a very high price both internationally and domestically.

Economic inducements violate strict interpretations of soft power and yet fall far short of the hard power of military coercion. The generosity of a lender to poor countries will substantially improve its image, other things being equal. Japan received great attention for its "yen diplomacy" in the 1980s by becoming the world's top aid donor. But some of the shine was tarnished by economic strings tied to this aid. This added to the general disillusionment with aid in the US experience. Token amounts of Japanese aid were given to the poorest countries, such as reforestation grants to Haiti and African countries. They were much appreciated but usually accomplished little more than slowing down the descent into misery in these areas.

Overall this seems to leave economic power in the middle ground of the continuum of power from hard to soft rather than clearly on the side of hard power. Inducements of various sorts may only help to tip the balance in negotiating differences rather than constitute real coercion. As many observers have remarked, soft power probably cannot exist without some hard power but economic power may be a more effective means of increasing soft power over time.[4]

Clearly, hard military power has become increasingly expensive in both economic and soft power terms. World military expenditure in 2006 was estimated at $1.2 trillion in current prices. This constitutes an increase of 3.5 per cent in real terms since 2005 and an increase of 39 per cent since its lowest total of $834 billion in 1998 (see Table 1.1)

In constant 2005 dollars, the United States spent $7.7 trillion from 1992 to 2006, which was 16.1 percent more than the next ten largest spenders combined and represented about 42 percent of the world's total military expenditures. For the same time period, this averages out at a little over 4 percent of US GDP, which intuitively seems quite modest but is almost a third greater than the percentage of GDP spent by Britain or France and 316 percent greater than Japan. Predictably, military spending by the United States has increased in the wake of the September 11, 2001 attacks, from $345 billion in 2001 to $529 billion in 2006, an increase of 53.3 percent. These expenditures have rapidly increased the national debt.

Table 1.2 shows US military aid before and after the 9/11 attacks. Not surprisingly, Israel leads the list with nearly $10 billion in military aid for the years 1999–2001 and a little over $9 billion for the years 2002–4, totaling $18.9 billion for the six-year period. Egypt came in second with 12.1 billion for 1999–2004 with roughly the same amounts before and after the terrorist bombings. By contrast, the amounts for third- and fourth-place Pakistan and Jordan

Table 1.1 Military expenditures and % GDP 1992–2006 (*2005 US $ mil)

Def Exp *	1992–2006
% of GDP	Avg Annual % GDP
Saudi Arabia	11.18
Russia	5.73
US	4.08
U.K.	3.10
S. Korea	2.97
France	2.96
India	2.94
China	2.04
Italy	2.00
Germany	1.82
Japan	0.98

Source: SIPRI Yearbooks, various years

Table 1.2 U.S. Military aid before and after 9/11 (US $mil)

Country	1999–2001	2002–2004	Total 99–04
1. Israel	9,823	9,094	18,918
2. Egypt	6,122	6,025	12,148
3. Pakistan	9	4,152	4,161
4. Jordan	981	2,670	3,651
5. Colombia	1,529	2,048	3,598
6. Afghanistan	8	2,663	2,671
7. Turkey	5	1,324	1,330
8. West Bank & Gaza	630	271	901
9. Peru	263	445	709
10. Bolivia	281	320	602

Source: "Collateral Damage," Center for Public Integrity, 2007. (www.publicintegrity.org/militaryaid/World.aspx).

respectively jumped dramatically. Pakistan received nearly all of its $4.1 billion after 9/11 because it had been cut off following its nuclear weapons testing in 1998. Jordan's military aid nearly tripled from $981 million to $2.67 billion. Afghanistan and Turkey also went from very little military aid to quite substantial sums of $2.6 billion and $1.3 billion respectively. Meanwhile, military aid authorized for Palestinian security forces was cut by more than half from $630 million to $271 million.

The twenty-two member countries of the OECD Development Assistance Committee, which represent the world's largest donors, contributed $103.9 billion but this was down 5.1 percent in real terms from 2005.[5] About 20 percent of this amount was in terms of debt relief, primarily to Iraq and Nigeria. This ODA (official development assistance) represents 0.3 percent of combined GDP. In 2006, net ODA by the United States fell in real terms by 20 percent, to $22.7 billion. That represents on 0.17 percent of GDP. Or, in other terms, in 2006, the United States spent twenty-three times as much on military expenditure as it did on development foreign aid. Japan's net ODA in 2006 was $11.6 billion or 0.25 percent of GDP. This represented a fall of 9.6 percent in real terms partly due to the nation's extraordinary generosity in 2005 because of the Indian Ocean tsunami. Japan's net ODA, in real terms, has been declining since 2000 except for an increase in 2005 due to debt relief to Iraq. Its military expenditure to ODA ratio, therefore, was only about 4 to 1.[6]

Soft power in terms of esteem, gratitude, admiration, of course, is often in the eyes of the beholder and translating that into favorable decisions on tough choices is another thing. For example, here (Table 1.3) is a list of the top ten recipients of ODA for 2005 for the United States and Japan (OECD, DAC).

It would be very interesting to find out how much soft power has been generated by this aid, and the impact of different kinds of ODA. Arase (2005) states that Japanese ODA policy comes from very different circumstances. In simple terms, Japan has focused on loans for developmental infrastructure whereas the United States has been more likely to give technical assistance and training.[7] Moreover, Arase explains that US ODA is required to serve other strategic foreign policy goals and respond to more challenging domestic political pressures.[8] "[T]he Japanese aid system, on the other hand, has been relatively insulated from interventions by elected politicians and interest groups in civil society."[9]

The United States has been the unquestioned leader in almost any imaginable major category of power. Yet in the wake of its increasing unpopularity, the recent lead editorial in the *Economist* made this assessment:

> Nearly six years after September 11th, nervousness about the state of America's "hard power" is growing. Iraq and Afghanistan have stretched the Pentagon's resources. An army designed to have 17 brigades on active deployment now has 25 in the field. ... There is the emergence of China as a rival embryonic superpower, with an economy that may soon be bigger than America's (at least in terms of purchasing power). ... Nor is

Table 1.3 Top ten recipients of ODA for 2005 For the United States and Japan

United States (US $mil)		Japan (US $mil)	
1. Iraq	6926	1. Iraq	2096
2. Afghanistan	1060	2. China	1662
3. Egypt	750	3. Indonesia	963
4. Sudan	575	4. Thailand	765
5. Ethiopia	552	5. Philippines	706
6. Jordan	368	6. Viet Nam	670
7. Colombia	366	7. India	651
8. Palestinian Authority	227	8. Ghana	532
9. Uganda	225	9. Zambia	385
10. Pakistan	224	10. Sri Lanka	317

Source: OECD, International Development Statistics, Paris: OECD, 2007.

it just a matter of geopolitics. American bankers are worried that other financial centres are gaining at Wall Street's expense. Nativists fret about America's inability to secure its own borders. As for soft power, Abu Ghraib, Guantanamo Bay, and America's slowness to tackle climate change and its neglect of the Palestinians have all, rightly or wrongly, cost it dearly. ... Yet America is being underestimated. Friends and enemies have mistaken the short-term failure of the Bush administration for deeper weakness. Neither American hard nor soft power is fading. Rather, they are not being used as well as they could be. ... From the perspective of relative rather than absolute supremacy, a superpower's strength lies as much in what it can prevent from happening as in what it can achieve. America's "negative power" is considerable. ... The surveys that show America's soft power to be less respected than it used to be also show the continuing universal appeal of its values – especially freedom and openness. ... win the battle for hearts and minds and you do not need as much hard power to get your way.[10]

The next section of this chapter will argue that the contemporary US–Japan alliance needs to be examined in the context of soft power dynamics with an emphasis on two dimensions: (1) changing international identities and (2) balancing domestic and foreign interests.

Alliances, identity and international relations theories

So-called "realist" theories of international relations have been more employed and criticized than any other set of explanations in the last sixty years. In general, these theories assume international conflict and competition as the "natural" or most likely relations between sovereign nation-states. Survival strategies of this perspective emphasize self-maximizing national interest actions with a heavy dose of military spending and preparedness. A strong economy is a prerequisite for a strong military capability but is mostly a means to an end. International economic alliances may be an appropriate intermediate tactic in some situations but should never be trusted for long-term security and prosperity. This "realism" is contrasted with naïve "idealism" or liberal/neo-liberal emphases on building multi-lateral and collective institutions or issue regimes that use compromise and consensus to maximize international order and stability.

Alliance theories, for the most part, have been developed as an offshoot of realist theories. A commonly accepted definition of an alliance could be a formal relationship of security cooperation between two or more nation states although some definitions include informal agreements as well. Alliances are one of the most important dynamics of international relations systems and have been the subject of hundreds of studies. Most realist theories of alliances focus on the question of how states respond to threats. Or as Walt puts it, "do states seek allies in order to balance a threatening power, or are they more likely to bandwagon with the most threatening state?"[11] A conventional interpretation of the Cold War is that it was a competition for allies between the "Free World" led by the United States against the "Communist World" headed by Soviet Russia. US policymakers repeatedly expressed the belief that allies were primarily attracted by displays of military superiority and unbreakable will regardless of the threats that they might face. Furthermore, the dominant assumptions of US foreign policy during the Cold War emphasized the ideological cohesion of the Communist World and unquestioned loyalty to Soviet Russia and its interests. Some current policy justifications of the US security actions have equally assumed a unified anti-American cohesion among the world's various terrorist organizations. Conversely, the fragility of alliance commitments to the United States is stressed in worst-case scenario policy formation. Most alliance theories forwarded since World War II fall within the large framework of realist "balance of power" hypotheses. Morgenthau and Waltz are the most cited examples of this approach.[12] Another well-received variation is Walt,[13] which emphasizes a "balance of threat" approach. Ultimately, Schweller's alternative is a "balance of interests" model rather than a balance of power or balance of threat model.[14] This allows him to account for two levels of alliance behavior. At the unit level, it refers to the price a state is willing to pay to defend its interests relative to the price it is willing to pay to expand its interests. At the system level, it refers to the relative positions of status quo and revisionist states.

Reiter's lengthy analysis also brings important attention to another variable that is sometimes recognized but often neglected.[15] That is, the distinction between the alliance choices of major versus minor powers. From an identity perspective,

> the greater simplicity of minor powers' foreign interests means that experiences can be more easily coded as successes or failures, as a minor power focuses mostly on the question of how its choice of alliance or neutrality affected the national security and territorial integrity of the homeland. A great power, on the other hand, must assess the effects of an experience—such as a major war or diplomatic crisis—along a number of dimensions because of its extended foreign policy interests.[16]

Although there is much attention in popular public debate about the appropriate responsibilities of major and minor partners in an alliance, quantitative evidence has precluded the ability to test theories that correspond to more sophisticated levels of military/economic/cultural capabilities. Intuitively, "super-powers" exceed "great powers" somehow in both global reach and unprecedented military and economic resources. But is it appropriate to use terms where these two dimensions are greatly unsymmetrical? Is Japan an economic superpower but a military minor power the way Russia was often portrayed as a military superpower but an economic minor power? As the dimension profiles of contemporary states grow to unprecedented levels and with greater differentials along the power spectrum, where are the measurable or perceived thresholds between weak/poor, middle level and strong/rich states?

"Compulsory" power is the most common understanding of power that emphasizes the futility of resistance to the superior partner. "Institutional" power, by contrast, is indirect control through institutions, rules and procedures that, in the context of alliances, guides and constrains all members of the alliance to some extent. Even in a bilateral alliance, there are passive/aggressive forms of behavior that the weaker partner can use to dilute control by appealing to limitations in formal treaties and agreements. "Structural" power is focused on the determination of social capacities and interests. Structural power distributes asymmetric benefits which affect the interests of actors in different ways. Thus, differing interest priorities may produce greater satisfaction for subservient partners or mutual satisfaction for both. The alliance between the United States and Japan has lasted for such a long time, in part, because it enhanced the military hegemony of the United States, which it desired, while providing substantial economic benefits to the Japanese, which was their top priority. Finally, "productive" power is demonstrated through discourse and dialogue that is socially productive for all subjects. Productive power "concerns the boundaries of all social identity, and the capacity and inclination for action for the socially advantaged and disadvantaged alike, as well as the myriad social subjects that are not constituted in binary hierarchical relationships."[17] In other words, in alliances, productive power transforms the understanding of the roles played by the partners as the alliance changes their own sense of identity through managing the responsibilities and challenges to their partnership. Both the United States and Japan gained unprecedented wealth in the pursuit of containment of the ideological and military power of communism, the Soviet Union and China. The wealth of Japan, in fact, financed the final phase of military superiority of the United States in the 1980s that brought an end to the world's fears about Russian aggression.

Ultimately, however, there is much credibility in the argument that the identities of governments will determine the nature of an alliance relationship. What does it mean for the United States to be a solitary superpower rather than a competing one in a bipolar world? Given the lack of sustained interests in international issues by Americans, as documented by imperial advocates, how much longer will they support current burdens in the absence of rival nationalistic threats? What is Japan's vision of its role in the world in the next decades of the twenty-first century? Does it want to become a great world power or only a regional one? Does that goal mandate the return to traditional hard power acquisitions that would substantially alter its current military restrictions? Would it ultimately require dissolving its current security alliance with the United States? Is it prepared to make new Asian alliances to contend with China's rapidly increasing power?

Tamamoto makes note of the claim that there is not a precise equivalent of the word "identity" in Japanese. The word *shutaisei* is translated more often as "subjectivity, independence, or the rule of individualism." He quotes Masao Miyoshi as stating, "The uncritical pursuit of *shutaisei* in Japan may be still one more example of Japan's gestures toward Westernization, and thus ironically proof of its lack of *shutaisei*."[18] World War II marked the end of Japanese *shutaisei* and the beginning of American *shutaisei*, Tamamoto claims. Thus, according to this cultural interpretation, Japanese conceptions of national identity are paralyzed between envy/resentment of American *shutaisei* and the unwillingness to resume the costs of pursuing Japanese *shutaisei*.

Apparently, many American commentators do not believe that Japan will be suspended forever in ambiguity about rising nationalism. Matthews agrees with Tamamoto that many younger Japanese are increasingly resentful that Japan's "yen diplomacy" and generosity in foreign aid in Asia have not resulted in greater respect or appreciation of their nation in that region or elsewhere.[19] What they have noticed is respect (and fear) of greater American military aggression. It is increasingly unacceptable that China and even North Korea, India and Pakistan have nuclear weapons but that they do not. These nationalistic attitudes will inhibit greater international or regional institution building preferred by neo-liberals in Asia. Greater corporate disloyalty may also bring greater national disloyalty.

In a recent article, US Secretary of State Condoleezza Rice boldly asserts that the "old dichotomy between realism and idealism has never really applied to the United States because we do not really accept that our national interest and our universal ideals are at odds."[20] Her somewhat lengthy overview of US foreign policy goals and achievements gives only brief attention to Asia. She asserts that

> although many assume that the rise of China will determine the future of Asia, so, too – and perhaps to an even greater degree – will the broader rise of an increasingly democratic community of Asian states. This is the defining geopolitical event of the twenty-first century, and the United States is right in the middle of it.[21]

Her only mention of the "strong democratic alliance" with Japan puts it after Australia and other "key states in Southeast Asia".[22] She characterizes Japan as "an economic giant that is emerging as a 'normal' state".[23]

A sense that Washington is both losing clout and interest in Asian issues in favor of the Middle East and the "War on Terrorism" is noted by Funabashi.[24] He worries that as Asian countries adapt to the new economic and military realities in the region, they need more, not less US engagement. Above all, China seems to better appreciate the appeal of soft power and instead of relying only on Cold War dynamics in the US–Japan security alliance,

> Washington must deepen its commitment to multilateral institution build in Asia, as well as make earnest strides toward boosting American "soft power" there through innovative approaches to pressing challenges such as climate change and the backlash against globalization.[25]

All of these questions point to the importance of identity of states in the international hierarchy and the consequences of these identities, real and/or imagined, internally and/or externally ascribed, to theories of alliances especially under conditions of rapid changes in global power and prestige. This brings us back again to the usefulness of the "balance of interests" model rather than a balance of power or balance of threat model. How well can the United States and Japan strengthen their alliance by adjusting their relationships at both the global and Asian regional levels?

US and Japanese interests since the end of the Cold War: terrorism, trade, MNCs, and energy

At the heart of realist theories about alliances is the common interest in greater security. But the end of the Cold War radically changed the dynamics of threats to security. The realist world of anarchy and nation-state sovereignty requires insecurity as a permanent condition and the natural consequence of all humans to want to expand and maximize their power relative to others'. Gorbachev, who oversaw the collapse of the old Soviet system, recently stated that the end of the Cold War could have ushered in a new era of cooperation that minimized nationalist power competition. "The Americans want so much to be the winners. The fact that they are sick with this illness, this winners' complex, is the main reason why everything in the world is so confused and so complicated."[26] With the old enemy gone, rogue states – Iraq, Iran, North Korea, Afghanistan, Libya, etc. were now the threats to the United States and by extension the whole world. These are authoritarian regimes that sponsor terrorism and seek to acquire weapons of mass destruction. What seems to be especially threatening is that, unlike past national rivals, these states are not likely to be deterred by the certainty of retaliation. Hence, a new policy of pre-emptive "defense" is required. Critics of the term point out that, after the US–Pakistani reconciliation after the 9/11 attacks, Pakistan was removed from this list. Hence the term rogue state seems to be applied to any state that is hostile to the United States without necessarily being a greater threat to anyone else.[27] It is not clear what effects rogue states (or others) have on terrorist groups that they "support". As Bynam observes:

> Although states can boost a terrorist group's overall capabilities, many state-supported groups remain weak or ineffective. Still others have collapsed despite state backing because of their own incompetence or lack of appeal. Most important, the effect of state support is not uniform. ... States also place limits on their proxies and can even set back the group's cause.[28]

According to the US Office of Counterterrorism, "terrorism is premeditated, politically motivated violence perpetrated against noncombatant targets by sub-national groups or clandestine agents."[29] Noncombatant targets include, however, "military personnel (whether or not armed or on duty) who are not deployed in a war zone or a war-like setting."[30] These definitions are contained in statutory acts but elsewhere in various places a terrorist group is any group whose activities "threaten the security of US nationals *or* the national security (national defense, foreign relations, *or* the economic interests) of the United States."

Some Japanese scholars have suggested that the Japanese government joined the "war on terror" proclaimed by Bush, Jr. without any definition of the enemy, in spite of the hot debate in Japanese media. It adopted the US understanding of 9/11 attacks as attacks against "freedom and democracy." Among the commonly cited reasons for Prime Minister Koizumi Junichirō's quick reaction to join the fight on terrorism even though it had not been the target of any recent international incidents are the lingering trauma of US criticism about too little financial support after the first Gulf War and fear of American withdrawal from the Security Alliance treaty.[31] Other analysts seem concerned not only that Japan lacks an official definition of terrorism and that the NPA (National Policy Agency) does not differentiate guerilla activities from terrorism but that there seems to be very little academic Japanese scholarship on modern terrorism.[32]

The following figures (Table 1.4) appear to be better than previously published studies by the US State Department. These figures compare the incidents, injuries, and fatalities before and after the 9/11 attacks for various regions of the world.

Japan has yet to suffer from any explicit terrorism allegedly linked to its security alliance with the United States as the UK and Spain have. However, if that should happen in the near future it will be a major test of the compatibility of the two countries' security interests. No two countries have more in their common interest in the stability and growth of the world economy than the United States and Japan. They are the two largest national economies in the world. Together they account for 36.5 percent of the world GDP.

Both the United States and Japan continue to "look over their shoulders" at the meteoric rise of the Chinese economy, which has moved up from sixth place in 2004 to a projected third place in 2008, an increase of $1.4 trillion dollars in four years (76.9%). Japan's economy, meanwhile, has fallen, by IMF projections, by $306 billion from 2004 to an estimated $4.30 trillion before rebounding to $4.45 trillion in 2008. Another fast riser is Russia,

Table 1.4 Global businesses as targets of terrorism

Year	Attacks	Percent
1996	235 of 367 attacks	(64.0%)
1997	329 of 454 attacks	(72.4%)
1998	282 of 398 attacks	(70.8%)
1999	278 of 477 attacks	(58.2%)
2000	383 of 559 attacks	(68.5%)
2001	397 of 531 attacks	(74.7%)
2002	122 of 237 attacks	(51.4%)
2003	93 of 207 attacks	(44.9%)

Source: MIPT Terrorism Knowledge Base (www.tkb.org).

moving from sixteenth place in 2004 to an estimated ninth rank by 2008, an increase of $753 billion (127.4%). It should be noted, however, that even the unlikely economic alliance of Japan, China, and Russia would only create a combined economic total of $9,213 billion – about 64 percent of the US or about 55 percent of the combined economic power of the European Union.

A frequent American complaint for more than thirty years has been Japan's free ride on defense financed by the United States through the costs of the alliance.[33] American critics have been complaining for decades that the "degree of effort" by Japan has been insufficient and somehow damaging to American economic competitiveness. Meanwhile those in the "no more Japan-bashing" camp have retorted that investment and fiscal factors have been vastly more important.[34]

Another thorny statistic over the years has been the trade deficit between the United States and Japan. According to IMF figures, trade between the two countries in 1999–2000 came to a total of $13.5 billion. For the United States, trade with Japan was a little over 9 percent. For Japan, trade US trade was a little over 22 percent of its total of total trade for 1999–2005. There has been a US trade deficit of $541 billion in the seven-year period; this is only about 14 percent of the total international trade deficit of $3.9 trillion for 1999–2005. However, the trade deficit with Japan represents only 3.7 percent of total US trade for those seven years. Various American administrations have repeatedly tried to get Japan to liberalize to rectify this deficit, with some success. Japan also has invested nearly one trillion dollars in US treasury bonds. Some might be surprised to see that for 1999–2005, the US had $1244 billion in total trade with China (mainland) resulting in a deficit of $894 billion. Adding in trade with Taiwan and Hong Kong, 12.4 percent of total US world trade was with the Chinese. By contrast, combined Chinese trade was 22.7 percent of Japan's total world trade. In summary, the United States has higher absolute dollar denominated trade with Chinese markets than Japan but only half as much of its world trade interests at stake.

A third set of competing interests is the rivalry between global corporations hosted by these two countries. In recent years General Electric has had the highest market value. In 2005, it was valued at $377 billion followed closely by Exxon Mobil at $361. US corporations made up eleven of the top fifteen. The largest Japanese multinational corporation by far was #14 Toyota Motor valued at $158 b. The next two largest Japanese corporations in terms of market value were #25 Mitsubishi UFJ Financial Group ($126 b) and #49 Mizuho Financial Group ($76 b). A set of 2007 rankings by *Fortune* magazine of the top Global 500 according to revenues counted 162 US companies compared to 67 for Japan.[35] But the US State Department reports that businesses are the most likely targets of international terrorism. So, these powerful global firms will share a concern regarding terrorist violence.

The final vital interest considered here in the context of the US-Japan security alliance is energy politics, specifically oil imports. The national sources of their oil imports are quite different. The United States imported 44.7 percent more oil than Japan but was dependent for only a little less than 20 percent on the Persian Gulf states. Japan, on the other hand, got almost three quarters of its oil from the Persian Gulf. In actual barrel terms for 1993–2005, Japan imported about twice as much. In terms of a specific country supplier, both the US and Japan for this period imported about 7 billion barrels of oil from Saudi Arabia. The big difference is the U.A.E. where Japan imported just slightly less than from Saudi Arabia, whereas the single biggest supplier for the United States was Canada followed by Venezuela. Another significant difference is that Japan got about 9 percent of its oil from Iran. Japan is Iran's biggest oil customer, which causes strain on its alliance with the United States.

In summary, contrary to most alliance theories, the US–Japan security alliance is more about common interests than mutual threats, at least since the end of the Cold War. Terrorism is a new kind of security threat to both countries but Japan has not yet suffered any serious attacks in apparent retaliation for its support of US military actions in the Middle East. International trade and global corporations are at the heart of two largest economies in the world. Competing interests are rooted in the different global regions that they care most about rather than between two sets of nationalistic firms. Two crucial focal points are the focal points in oil security of the two countries and the appropriate cost sharing to provide that security. Japan's economic difficulties of the past fifteen years and its almost complete dependence on Persian Gulf oil imports leave it particularly vulnerable to American foreign policy decisions.

Conclusion

Richard Samuels' recent book *Securing Japan* provides some excellent insights into the future complexity of US–Japanese security alliance.[36] He divides Japanese foreign policy into four important factions. The most dominant one, at least under the Koizumi and Abe Shinzo administrations, was the "normal nationalists" – they openly seek to bulk up the most modern military in East Asia and seek to equalize the alliance to build an even stronger military defense. A second group he calls the "neo-autonomists" whose goal is also greater military strength but with a credible nuclear deterrent independent of the United States. In their view, only this would achieve truly "normal" status as a great power and require the elimination of US bases in Japan. A third faction, he identifies as the "middle power internationalists" who would hope to maintain and even increase Japan's world prestige by stressing economic prosperity and lowering its military posture. In Samuels' words, they would "bulk up Japan's considerable soft power in a concerted effort to knit East Asia together without generating new threats or becoming vulnerable."[37] The least powerful but not insignificant group is the "pacifists". "They would eschew hard power for soft power and campaign to establish Northeast Asia as a nuclear free zone, expand the 'defensive defense' concept and negotiate a regional missile control regime ... "[38] They hope to achieve autonomy through prosperity but, as Samuels documents, they have lost most of their popularity with the Japanese public and are not linked to the traditional political parties.

Many observers have commented on the remarkably amiable relationship between President George Bush Jr. and former Japanese Prime Minister Koizumi Junichirō.[39] Much of it was based on their mutual perceptions of security threats and uneasiness about China's rapid increases in economic development. There is not much public sentiment in the United States for a wholesale retreat into global isolation but the weariness of conflicts in the Middle East and declining economic conditions have taken their toll. The security alliance with the United States remains popular in Japan unlike in Western Europe. Indeed, as even a neo-realist like Menon concludes:

> The right and the left in America [and in Japan] both agree that advancing democracy abroad is a worthy aim, and there are many ways to act on that consensus without recourse to war. All of them involve "soft power" which has many facets and must be applied with patience and without expectation of dramatic, quick results. The war in Iraq is instructive about the perils of an alternative approach based on hard power. ... Soft power often elicits scoffs – by those who think that it is, well, too soft – but those doing the scoffing are often the very ones who are most dedicated to spreading American [and Japanese] democratic values, which themselves are a form of soft power.[40]

It remains to be seen what the new US administration in 2009 will set as its foreign policy priorities and the importance of the US–Japan security alliance in the next decade. It will be interesting to see exactly how it copes with the rapid decline of US soft power. In May of 2008, Prime Minister Fukuda Yasuo gave a speech in Manila on Japan's Asian diplomacy. He claimed that he was resurrecting the "Fukuda doctrine" of his father, Prime Minister Fukuda Takeo, from the late 1970s. He called for a greater emphasis on Asian diplomacy and soft power consistent with the strengthening of the Japan–US alliance. That would appear to place him in the "Asianist" side of Samuel's "middle power internationalists" and not in the preceding administrations' "normal-nationalist" faction.

Some Japanese commentators welcomed this change from Koizumi's "lopsided" emphasis on ties with the United States or Abe's China "encirclement" foreign policy.[41] Fukuda's popularity in Japan, however, continued to plummet and his attempts to establish a statesman-like image for himself have received little help from the Bush administration or members of his own political party. His promise to double Japanese foreign aid to Africa by 2012 was skeptically viewed as a mere ploy to gain African support for a permanent Japanese seat on the UN Security Council.[42]

"Soft" power, interests and identity 33

As noted several times in this chapter, the sixty-year history of the post-World War II US–Japan security alliance has been quite unique in the experience of major power alliances over the past two centuries. The soft power legacies of both countries were greatly enhanced by their remarkable economic achievements. The radical asymmetry of their military hard power has been a double edged *katana* for the Japanese. It minimized Asian fears of Japanese military revival but hampers Japanese ambitions to have a permanent seat on the U.N. Security Council. The rapidly growing power of China has tempted some Japanese political elites to risk eroding its soft power prestige in exchange for more hard power leverage. Its alliance partner, the United States, has sacrificed soft power good will in its ambition to reshape the Middle East to its advantage. It will continue to be difficult to precisely measure the hard power realities and soft power subtleties at the heart of these two vital countries. Some observers believe that the alliance can be energized by tapping into the soft power resources of these two great countries.

Notes

1 George Friedman and Meredith Lebard, *The Coming War with Japan*, New York: St. Martin's Press, 1990; E. Fingleton, *Blindside: Why Japan is Still on Track to Overtake the US by the Year 2000*, London: Simon & Schuster, 1995; and Bill Emmot, *The Sun Also Sets: The Limits to Japan's Economic Power*, New York: Random House, 1989.
2 Joseph Nye, Jr., *Soft Power: the Means to Success in World Politics*, New York: PublicAffairs/Perseus Books, 2004.
3 Ibid., p. 31.
4 See, for example, Cooper, "Hard Power, Soft Power, and the Goals of Diplomacy," in David Held and Mathias Koeing-Archibugi (eds.), *American Power in the 21st Century*, Maiden, MA: Blackwell, 2004, pp. 167–80.
5 OECD, *International Development Statistics*, Paris: OECD, 2007.
6 Ibid.
7 David Arase, "Japan's and the United States' Bilateral ODA Programs," in Arase, *Japan's Foreign Aid*, New York: Routledge, 2005, pp. 117–32.
8 Ibid., p. 123.
9 Ibid., p. 126.
10 *Economist*, June 30, 2007.
11 Stephen Walt, *The Origins of Alliances*, Ithaca, NY: Cornell University Press, 1987, p. 3.
12 See, respectively, Hans Morgenthau, *Politics Among Nations*, 3rd edition, New York: Alfred Knopf, 1963; and Kenneth Waltz, *Theory of International Politics*, New York: Random House, 1979.
13 Stephen Walt, *The Origins of Alliances*, Ithaca, NY: Cornell University Press, 1987.
14 Ibid., p. 99.
15 For examples of the former, see Robert Rothstein, *Alliances and Small Powers*, New York: Columbia University Press, 1968; Efrain Karsh, *Neutrality and Small States*, London: Routledge, 1988; and Christen and Snyder (note 14).
16 Reiter, p,. 496.
17 Ibid., p. 56.
18 Masaharu Tamamoto, "Ambiguous Japan: Japanese National Identity at Century's End," in J. Ikenberry and M. Mastanduro (eds.), *International Relations Theory*

and the Asia-Pacific, New York: Columbia University Press, 2003, p. 205. Tamamoto's quote is in reference to Masao Miyoshi, *Off Center: Power and Culture Relations between Japan and the United States*, Cambridge: Harvard University Press, 1991, p. 97.
19 Eugene Matthews, "Japan's New Nationalism," *Foreign Affairs*, vol. 82, no. 6 (November/December 2003), pp. 74–90.
20 Ibid., p. 25.
21 Ibid., p. 7.
22 Ibid., pp. 7–8.
23 Ibid., pp. 7–8.
24 Yoichi Funabashi, "America and the New Balance of Power," *Foreign Affairs*, vol. 87, no. 5 (Sept./Oct. 2008).
25 Ibid., p. 111.
26 AP, July 28, 2007.
27 William Blum, *Rogue State: A Guide to the World's Only Superpower*, reprinted in paperback in 2005 – Monroe, ME: Common Courage Press, 2000.
28 Daniel Bynam, *Deadly Connections*, New York: Cambridge University Press, 2005, p, 53.
29 Department of State, *Patterns of Global Terrorism*, Washington, DC, 2006, p. 322.
30 Ibid., p. 318.
31 Tomohito Shinoda, "Koizumi's Top-Down Leadership in the Anti-Terrorism Legislation: The Impact of Political Institutional Changes," *SAIS Review*, vol. 23, no. 1 (Winter/Spring 2003): 19–29.
32 Naofumi Miyasaka, "Combating Arms Proliferation," in Masashi Nishihara, ed., *The Japan–U.S. Alliance: New Challenges for the 21st Century*, New York: Japan Center for International Exchange, 2000, pp. 161–81.
33 Rajan Menon, *The End of Alliances*, New York: Oxford University Press, 2007, p. 103.
34 Fred C. Bergsten, et al., *No More Bashing: Building a New Japan–United States Economic Relationship*, Washington, D.C.: Petersen Institute, 2001.
35 *Fortune*, July 23, 2007.
36 Richard Samuels, *Securing Japan*, Ithaca, NY: Cornell University Press, 2007.
37 Ibid., p. 194.
38 Ibid., p. 194.
39 Tomohito Shinoda, *Koizumi Diplomacy*, Seattle: University of Washington Press.
40 Menon, p. 193.
41 *Japan Times*, May 30, 2008.
42 Bruce Gale, *The Straits Times*, June 5, 2008.

2 Japanese security policy
From soft to hard power

David Arase

Introduction

It would have been outlandish just ten years ago to believe that Japan today would be laying the groundwork for revision of its Peace Constitution, militarizing its role in the alliance with the US, and having top Liberal Democratic Party (LDP) leaders call for a national debate on the need for nuclear weapons.[1] How does a nation that had been pacifist for two generations since the end of World War II change directions so radically? How much further can we expect Japan to pursue hard power? This chapter attempts to answer these questions in the context of Japan's regional relations.

It is difficult to capture the complex arrangement of Japan's foreign policy determinants using one of the highly abstract mainstream theoretical approaches in international relations that reduce explanation to a single factor. Instead, theoretical modesty and an eclectic approach will be used here. It sacrifices the simplicity and universality of a single theoretical framework, but gains a fuller and more nuanced appreciation of the contingent nature of Japanese security policy.[2] This approach points to constraints at different levels to explain policy. The three levels of analysis are: international structure; national institutions; and normative factors. Each level imposes a distinct kind of constraint. The supposition is that when constraints are factored out, the net result should explain the direction and stability of policy in any given period. Post-World War II Japanese security policy is characterized using this approach in order to create a means to indicate the direction of Japan today.

Resistance to rearming: 1951–89

Structure

At the level of international structure, US policy was to use postwar Japan to contain the Soviet Union. This made it necessary for the US to keep bases in Japan. Occupied Japan had little choice but to acquiesce to US demands when negotiating the end of the Occupation. Japan agreed to host bases and sacrifice a degree of its sovereignty, but it was unwilling to offer up soldiers or pay cash out of pocket to support general US containment strategy. This was not too troubling to the US because at that time it was so dominant that it did not need what little Japan could offer at that time to maintain the strategic balance. Circumstances permitted Japan to negotiate a "free ride" on defense as the postwar period took shape.

Institutions

Institutions created during the Occupation of Japan (1945–51) set the long-term domestic framework for postwar policy. The institutional cornerstones of Japan's security policy laid down in this period were the postwar Japanese Constitution (1946), conservative rule (eventually consolidated with the formation of the Liberal Democratic Party in 1955), and the US–Japan Security Pact (1951).The irony is that the US took a hand in creating structures that later limited its ability to make Japan into an active military ally.

The US originally intended to leave Japan democratized and demilitarized after World War II.[3] The Constitution that General Douglas MacArthur imposed on Japan reflected this aim. Article Nine read as follows:

> Aspiring sincerely to an international peace based on justice and order, the Japanese people forever renounce war as a sovereign right of the nation and the threat or use of force as a means of settling international disputes.
>
> *In order to accomplish the aim of the preceding paragraph, land, sea, and air forces, as well as other war potential, will never be maintained. The right of belligerency of the state will not be recognized.*

The US quickly came to regret Article 9 when China's ruling Nationalist Party (KMT) lost a post-World War II civil war with the Chinese Communist Party in 1949. This meant that the US lost a KMT-ruled China as its strategic partner in Asia. Having now to rely primarily on Japan to maintain a strategic containment perimeter in Asia, the US reversed its Occupation policy and began to encourage Japan to rearm.[4] To keep military bases in Japan, the US negotiated the Mutual Security Assistance Pact signed in 1951. The treaty institutionalized the status quo of that time, i.e., the presence of US military bases in Japan, but with very little, if any, military role for Japan itself.

Government decision is the mechanism that defines policy, and that is why the continuity in power of Japanese conservatives, who eventually constituted the Liberal Democratic Party, is important. The LDP's foreign policy line, which remained constant until recently, has been called the Yoshida Doctrine after Yoshida Shigeru, the prime minister responsible for negotiating the Security Pact and the San Francisco Peace Treaty (1951). Yoshida and his followers in the Jiyūtō (Liberal Party) wanted to put Japan's full energy toward the recovery of its economic strength, while leaving the defense of

Japan to the US.[5] This policy was supported by the institutional framework provided by the Constitution (no army – no war) and the Security Pact (no active external military obligation or commitment).

The Yoshida Doctrine came under attack from right-wing conservatives who, after being purged from public life in the early years of the Occupation, later returned to politics with US Occupation support. They viewed the emasculatory Constitution imposed on Japan as a humiliation, if not a sacrilege to the Emperor. In short, they wanted Constitutional revision and military rearmament.[6] Their failure to change Japan's direction, despite US encouragement, helps to illustrate the constraints that kept the Yoshida doctrine in place for so long. Figures such as Ichirō Hatoyama (a convicted and paroled war criminal) and Kishi Nobusuke (an unindicted Class A war criminal and a member of General Hideki Tōjō's war cabinet) dominated the Democratic Party (Minshutō).[7] Hatoyama Ichiro succeeded Yoshida as Prime Minister in 1954 whereupon he released a number of Class A war criminals from jail, and had one, Mamoru Shigemitsu, in his Cabinet. After a brief interval, Kishi succeeded Hatoyama as Prime Minister (1957–60). Both men tried to steer Japan back toward prewar political morality, constitutional revision, and military rearmament and, in this sense, were reactionary right wing conservatives.[8]

Postwar norms

The Liberal Party merged with the Democratic Party (Minshutō) in 1955 to form the Liberal Democratic Party (Jiyūminshutō). It was a marriage of convenience created by the business community and the US to keep leftists out of power. At the moment of its creation the right wing led by Kishi had the upper hand in the new LDP, but Yoshida's vision was supported by his followers in the LDP and business community, and their coolness toward rearmament was reinforced at the normative level by popular pacifism. Kishi's attempt to revive prewar norms and institutions, and they way he forced the renewal of the US–Japan Security Treaty in 1960, ended up threatening political stability and discrediting the right wing agenda. This left the Yoshida Doctrine as the only viable conservative foreign policy basis for LDP rule.[9] It fitted the institutions, national priorities, and the mood of the people, and could be tolerated by the US at that time.

The political reforms of the early Occupation were an opportunity for the democratic majority to wrest power from the militarists and rebuild Japanese institutions and culture on a more liberal basis. The Emperor was desanctified, public values supported democracy and limited government power, and Article 9 gained totemic status as the symbolic rejection of militarism and hard power in international politics. In short, most of Japan embraced the opportunity for greater liberty.[10] As the Tokyo Riots sparked by the forced renewal of the US–Japan security treaty in 1960 showed, the new political culture would not accept a revision of Article 9, the return to international military involvements, and right wing rule.

38　David Arase

Thus, structural, institutional, and normative factors cradled the Yoshida Doctrine which, together, made it exceedingly difficult to change. The hegemonic international structure allowed Japan to "free ride" on the US commitment to defend the free world. The Constitution and the Security Treaty institutionalized a demilitarized order, and the path-dependent nature of institutional change meant that subsequent normal, incremental change would be limited in scope. Finally, postwar Japanese identity embraced democracy and erased, or at least dispersed and drove underground, prewar militarism and Emperor Worship. The new postwar democracy permitted free elections, leftist political parties, and intellectual discourse to shape a national identity that would not accept a government effort to re-imagine Japan as a military power.

Crisis, change, and the role of the US

US pressure on Japan to rearm made common cause with conservative hawks in Japan, but by and large their shared agenda made progress only in times of tension or crisis that required an urgent response. The first case of success grew out of the Korean War (1950–53). General Douglas MacArthur ordered the formation of a 75,000 Japanese National Police Reserve.[11] This force evolved into the Self-Defense Forces (SDF) when the Self Defense Forces Law was passed in 1954. It only passed the Diet because the Korean War had created a situation that the US and conservative elements in Japan could use as leverage. Under heavy US pressure, the government argued that the Constitution permitted a force that was exclusively for self-defense and pledged many guarantees to this effect.

The Cabinet Legislative Bureau determined that the Constitution permitted an exclusively defensive force constrained by these principles: no SDF role except in the defense of Japan (taken to mean its territory); no collective defense (i.e., no defense of another state or its interests); no possession of offensive weaponry; and no overseas dispatch of troops. Civilian control over the SDF was assured by making the Self Defense Agency subordinate to the civilian Cabinet ministries. Later in May 1957, the Cabinet issued the Basic Policy for National Defense to confirm this exclusive defense doctrine. It also cited the US alliance as the foundation of Japan's security policy. Exclusive defense (*senshūbōei*) continues to be the basis of defense policy today, but only as a tattered fig leaf as will be seen.

The next crisis was the US loss in the Vietnam War. In 1969 President Richard Nixon asked US allies to be more self-sufficient in defense (the Nixon doctrine) as the US pulled back. Prime Minister Satō Eisaku called for an "autonomous defense" (*jishūbōei*), which could be taken to mean the development of a stand-alone defensive capability, as opposed to the limited defense doctrine then enshrined in the Basic Policy. Then-Defense Agency Director Nakasone Yasuhiro took the lead in promoting this change, but in the end changed very little. The 4th Five Year Defense Plan (1972–77) contemplated an independent ability to defend against an invasion.[12] However, the scale of the buildup was questionable on fiscal and policy grounds. The dispute between autonomous and exclusive defense advocates led to the 1976 National Defense Program Outline (NDPO). This stopped SDF growth short of what hawks wanted, Prime Minister Miki Takeo capped defense spending at 1 percent of GDP, and the hawks gained only a vague commitment to consider the external environment when making plans in future.

The next opportunity to press for change was the Soviet invasion of Afghanistan in 1979 and the pronounced buildup of the Soviet Pacific fleet. Under US pressure Prime Minister Suzuki Zenkō committed Japan to patrol sea lanes in international waters as far as 1,000 nautical miles from Japan, an important symbolic SDF role beyond territorial limits. But it gave no commitment to assist US forces in anything but the defense of Japan. When Suzuki allegedly used the word "alliance" to describe Japan's security relationship with the US during a trip to Washington, D.C., a domestic controversy erupted. That word as it is commonly understood suggested that Japan would support the US in war, which implicitly violated the exclusive defense doctrine and the potential entanglement with US war plans stirred public controversy. This ultimately led to the resignation of the foreign minister, Itō Masayoshi.

To sooth an offended and angry US, the LDP replaced Suzuki with the hawkish Nakasone Yasuhiro, who said all the right things. He called Japan an "aircraft carrier" for the US and called the Soviet Union its major foreign threat.[13] Nevertheless, Nakasone did not deliver more than small, symbolic departures from the Yoshida Doctrine. Prime Minister Nakasone appeased the US by promising to help develop Strategic Defense Initiative (SDI) technology despite the possible violation of a no arms export rule. Nakasone also broke the 1 percent of GDP defense spending limit by a small fraction in 1987, and he freely called the bilateral security relationship an alliance, despite the connotation of collective defense that made many Japanese uneasy. Thus, Nakasone made small, symbolic gestures to stabilize the bilateral relationship. Japan's real concessions were financial. Japan called its official development assistance (ODA) doubling plans a western alliance contribution.[14] Nakasone also gave the shaky Chun Doo Hwan regime in South Korea a 4 billion dollar loan in 1983 to stabilize his regime at the behest of the US. Japan also increased its financial support for US bases to $1.5 billion. These financial measures ("checkbook diplomacy") allowed Japan to avoid substantive concessions in defense policy.

By the end of the cold war, the alliance was still a one-sided arrangement. The structure of international politics was dominated by the US. The LDP was unwilling to move away from the Yoshida Doctrine and, aside from the creation of the SDF, formal institutions had not changed. Pacifism and the ideological left political parties were still intact.

Reluctant accommodation to new realities: 1989–99

With the fall of the Berlin Wall in 1989, the US and Japan became economic rivals with no common enemy to unite them. A realist would have expected the US–Japan alliance to end as each side no longer needed to rely on or trust the other side for security.[15] Indeed, there was tension and bitter quarreling arising from this structural development in the form of trade and defense friction. However, this change in international structure did not cause a break. The economic rivalry involving an unarmed Japan did not have the impact that it would have had with an armed Japan and thus, deep bilateral economic interdependence became a primary consideration in the calculus of the relationship.[16]

Nevertheless, the change in international structure had subtle and profound corrosive effects. Under a unipolar structure that no longer required the geographical containment of a rival, the US could credibly threaten to abandon Japan because it no longer had an absolute strategic need for bases there. Without US protection, Japan would lack guaranteed access to Persian Gulf oil, western markets, and protection against a wider and more unpredictable range of threats, including those next door. In this subtle structural shift, the US and its right wing collaborators in the LDP gained leverage. However, factors at the other levels still supported the status quo. The Constitution and the Security Treaty remained unchanged. The LDP had no strategic vision to replace the Yoshida Doctrine. And Japan was still strongly pacifist and committed to Article Nine. But in the 1990s, the new paradigm in international structure gave Japan incentives to change, spurred by external crises in the same pattern as in the past.

The 1990–91 Persian Gulf War hit Japan hard at the institutional and normative levels. Japan's alliance contribution to the war was $13 billion, but this checkbook diplomacy earned Japan little credit. The US, not to mention other western allies, disdained Japan and Congress angrily demanded future Japanese participation in the collective defense of western interests. Moreover, the war had been authorized by the UN. This made it awkward for pacifists and neutralists to refuse participation in it because they believed in the authority of the UN to manage international security. To meet international expectations in future contingencies would require Japan to get around Article 9 restrictions and put "boots on the ground" in the next go around.

Japan's response was the International Peace Cooperation Law (1992), which allowed the SDF to go overseas, but only for UN peacekeeping in a strictly non-military role. Pacifists had a hard time resisting this because the purpose was to protect peace under UN auspices. This law broke important institutional and normative barriers against direct involvement in international security matters. It set a legal procedure ("Special Measures") to authorize sending the SDF abroad. It seemingly broke the exclusive defense principle of keeping troops at home. Above all, it required a questionable reinterpretation of Article 9 that the generally pacifist public feared would create a slippery slope toward constitutional revision.

North Korea provided the next crisis. In 1993, North Korea successfully tested a Nodong missile that brought most of Japan in firing range. A few years earlier, North Korea had begun to refine nuclear weapons material at a reactor in Yongbyon. The combination of North Korean missiles and nuclear bombs gave a fright to Japan. As the US prepared to attack North Korea, the US found that Article 9 prohibitions were impediments to action in Japan, causing a new round of recriminations.

A new *modus vivendi* was signaled in the 1995 Nye Report that announced no change in US troop levels in Asia. This meant that a deal had been worked out in which US bases were to stay in Japan indefinitely. Only this time, the new structural paradigm compelled Japan to concede to US demands for it to do more. Japan responded with the 1995 National Defense Program Outline (NDPO). This gave the SDF a new alliance mission, vague though it was, to address "situations in the areas around Japan that have a direct effect on Japan's security."[17] This was another breach in the exclusive defense doctrine, this time in the areas of geographical limits and collective defense.

This departure was consolidated at a summit meeting of Prime Minister Hashimoto Ryutarō and President Bill Clinton in April 1996 that announced a new interpretation of the security treaty that gave emphasis to Article VI (peace and stability in the "Far East"). In May, China made its fourth nuclear test in three years. Japan made vigorous protests but China ignored them and did a fifth test in August. Also in 1995 and, on a larger scale in 1996, China fired missiles around Taiwan to intimidate pro-independence elements there. The 1996 event was serious enough for the US to send two aircraft carriers to show its commitment to preserve stability. If anything this gave the US and domestic right wingers even more leverage to push remilitarization.

The US–Japan Defense Guidelines signed in September 1997 fleshed out Japan's new regional role.[18] Article 9 was reinterpreted to allow the SDF to support US forces responding to security "contingencies" in areas surrounding Japan, albeit in non-combat roles such as rear area naval patrols, logistics, search and rescue, medical services, and information sharing. Regional contingencies were situations "which, if they remained unchecked, may bring about direct armed attack against Japan." This could not exclude Korea and Taiwan insofar as US action there could easily bring US military bases in Japan under attack. This broadening of Japan's defense role was given timely justification by the launch of the North Korean Taepodong missile in August 1998. The panic this caused led Japan to revise its notions regarding what Japan could and should do to preserve itself. Norms were changed enough to permit Diet passage of the Law Ensuring Peace and Security in Situations in Areas Surrounding Japan in August 1999.

By the end of the 1990s, the factors underlying security policy had undergone subtle but significant adjustments. In a unipolar world, the US had greater leverage over Japan, and a refusal to do more to defend itself would have had clear consequences for Japan's security. International crises reinforced this structural factor, forcing decisions to change the status quo. Unlike the cold war, China and North Korea were now potential threats next door to Japan, and the protection of the US could no longer be taken for granted. New laws changing the role of the SDF, declarations that expanded the scope of the alliance to cover the Far East, greater operational integration with US forces, and reinterpretations of Article 9 began to change the architecture of Japan's security institutions. The Japanese public began to redefine what was proper for Japan to defend itself. The changing situation led the US to reassess its Japan policy. The so-called Armitage Report of 2000 called on the new Bush administration to turn Japan into an ally comparable to the UK.[19]

A new role after 9/11

The terrorist attack on 9/11 provided an opportunity to expand Japan's alliance role by consolidating the change in security norms and justifying further institutional change to improve Japan's security. Conditions in Japanese politics also favored change. Koizumi Junichirō had become Prime Minister in 2001, and his assertive nationalism reflected the continuing influence of the right wing in the LDP. When the US requested Japan's assistance to fight terrorism, Prime Minister Koizumi quickly agreed to join the US-led coalition that invaded Afghanistan. Determined not to repeat the mistake of the first Persian Gulf War, Koizumi introduced the Anti-Terrorism Special Measures Law in the Diet on October 5. It authorized the SDF to give logistical support to the US-led invasion of Afghanistan. The law was quickly signed before the end of the month. The Anti-Terrorism Law passed the Diet in less than six weeks after 9/11, a remarkable acceleration of change compared to the four years it took to get the 1999 Special Situations Law passed (measured from the 1995 NDPO).

Koizumi again expanded the role of the SDF after the US invasion of Iraq in March 2003. Koizumi pushed the Special Measures Law on Humanitarian and Reconstruction Assistance through the Diet by July. This broke precedent by putting SDF ground troops in Samara, Iraq. The novelty was that the ground mission was neither requested by the host country nor was it UN-sanctioned (as required by the PKO Law). It also dispatched the SDF far outside the geographical limit seemingly set in the 1999 Situations Law. Despite all this, it took only three weeks for the law to pass the Diet.[20]

Equally indicative of the new mood was the passage of three War Contingencies Laws in June 2003. These authorized the rapid deployment of the SDF, in some cases without civilian oversight, to defend Japan against foreign attack, the first such legislation enacted since World War II. This kind of law was demanded by the right wing in earlier years, which had always elicited strong resistance from the opposition. The difference now was that there seemed to be a plausible rationale for action, which made the opposition parties more compliant. The LDP held discussions with the main opposition party, the Democratic Party of Japan (DPJ), and subsequently the laws passed with bipartisan support. This was the first time since World War II that such radical changes to Japan's defense posture passed with this kind of solid Diet support. This feat was repeated in 2004 when a complementary set of War Contingencies Laws was passed in the same way. This was followed by a general election in 2005 that was a landslide victory for the LDP led by the hawkish Koizumi, with the party winning 296 Lower House seats. This gave the LDP, with the smaller New Kōmeitō Party as a junior coalition partner, over a two-thirds majority in the Lower House, allowing it to pass legislation over Upper House vetoes, and it put amendment of the Constitution within reach in that chamber. Something indeed was changing in Japan's political culture and identity.[21]

The 2005 National Defense Program Guideline (NDPG) released in late 2004 laid out a military program for the coming decade. The NDPG aimed for a multi-functional SDF, able to perform defense missions, disaster relief and recovery, and UN collective security missions. However, what was eye-catching was the goal of acquiring flexible, high-tech fighting forces equipped for rapid deployment as far away as the Middle East. And coordination with US forces in such situations was emphasized.[22]

The five-year Mid-Term Defense Plan issued concurrently with the NDPG outlined procurement objectives, among which were the acquisition of helicopter carriers, spy satellites, and a system of missile defense.[23] Japan also asked the US to sell its F-22 stealth fighters, and in another first, the Air Self Defense Forces (ASDF) began long distance practice bombing runs over distant islands in the Pacific used for this purpose by the US military. Taken together, these changes were remarkable when compared to the earlier periods of resistance (1951–89) and reluctance (1989–2000). It would seem that overseas deployment of the SDF in support of US war aims is now legal, with certain provisos. For the time being, all that seems to be required are special laws to authorize overseas actions that one could say would not have had a Constitutional basis in previous eras of Japanese politics and foreign policy.

Domestic politics

The strong leadership of the conservative nationalist Prime Minister Koizumi Junichirō helps to explain the speed and scope of change, but election reform in 1994 and administrative reform in 1999 explain in legal and procedural terms how policy was able to change so quickly.

In the old bureaucratically dominated policymaking process a ministry or agency would develop a policy in consultation with other interests and then give it to the ruling party (the LDP) to turn into law. The nature of the process made policy change slow, incremental, bureaucratically self-serving, and myopically preoccupied with procedural issues ("turf"), losing sight of the larger national need that should be served. One of the key aims of administrative reform was to raise the power of politicians relative to the bureaucrats in decision-making in order to address this issue.[24] This produced the Amendment of the Cabinet Law and the Law to Establish the Cabinet Office in 1999. The former law established the authority of the Prime Minister to submit proposed laws to the Diet without first clearing them with the bureaucracy. The Cabinet Office Law gave the Prime Minister, acting through his Chief Cabinet Secretary, the power to impose mandates on the bureaucracy and to oversee its activities. The result has been to give the Prime Minister more power to initiate policy.

Another obstacle to creative policymaking was the dominance of factions in LDP affairs. Cabinet posts, including the Prime Minister, tended to be allocated to factions according to their strength in numbers of Diet members. A related obstacle was the use of seniority as a criterion for choosing people for high office. This made it possible to put older, undistinguished men qualified only by seniority into Cabinet posts. More able peers or younger, more ambitious politicians had to await their turn.[25]

The election reform of 1994 (implemented in 1996 election) began to change the type of person elected to the Diet. This reform introduced 300 single seat-plurality districts and 200 proportional seats (which were later reduced to 180) in the Lower House. With a party nominating only one candidate in a district, factional backing would become less important.[26] And the public's desire for reform and honest government made fresh ideas and voter appeal important considerations in candidate nominations. After the 2003 election there were 48 Lower House Diet Members in their twenties and thirties, which reflected the new opportunities for younger politicians, especially in the Democratic Party of Japan that had roughly equaled the LDP in electoral success that year.[27] With this turnover in the Diet came new attitudes toward Japan's international role and obligations.

Koizumi should be credited with strong leadership,[28] but other factors were in play as well. Structural, institutional, and normative factors that had previously resisted change were more than ever conducive to a change in Japan's security role. The shock of 9/11 provided the US and nationalists in Japan a perfect justification for more institutional change.

The US alliance factor

The US is more than ever going public with its pressure on Japan to enlarge its military mission. This helps give legitimacy to right wing conservatives who are the only ones eager for the task. On a 2004 visit to Japan, Secretary of State Colin Powell said:

> If Japan is going to play a full role on the world stage and become a full active participating member of the Security Council, and have the kind of obligations that it would pick up as a permanent member of the Security Council, Article 9 would have to be examined in that light.[29]

A second and updated Armitage Report released in 2006 stated that, "Although ... how Japan chooses to organize itself, resolve Constitutional questions, and expend resources are decisions that Japan must make for itself, the United States ... has a strong interest in how Japan approaches such matters."[30]

In another reinterpretation of the alliance, the US–Japan Joint Security Consultative Committee (JSC), composed of the foreign and defense ministers of both sides, announced a list of "common strategic objectives" in February 2005.[31] The inclusion of "the peaceful resolution of issues concerning the Taiwan Strait" attracted attention because it was the first time Japan made an explicit reference of this kind. What attracted less attention were other goals such as: "promote the reduction and non-proliferation of ... WMDs," "prevent and eradicate terrorism," and "maintain and enhance the stability of the global energy supply." The global scope is suggested by the SDF deployments in Iraq and Afghanistan, which have no other mandate but to help its US ally. The response of the Democratic Party of Japan to this development was to yawn and thus, the public hardly noticed.[32]

This was followed by the "US–Japan Alliance: Transformation and Realignment for the Future," that the JSC approved on October 29, 2005.[33] Defense Minister Ōno Yoshinori described the change in the alliance as follows:

> The Japan-US alliance to date, if anything, was for the purpose really of defending Japan through the use of Japanese bases and US forces whereas we're now talking about joint activities in various areas between Japan and the United States in order to improve the peace and security around the world.

Secretary State Condoleezza Rice commented: "a relationship that was once only about the defense of Japan or perhaps about the stability in the region, has truly become a global alliance."[34]

The new alliance aims for a seamless partnership between SDF and US combat forces from the command level down to the unit level. The agreement states:

> close and continuous policy and operational coordination at every level of government, from unit tactical level through strategic consultations, is essential to dissuade destabilizing military buildups, to deter aggression, and to respond to diverse security challenges. Development of a common operational picture shared between US forces and the SDF will strengthen operational coordination.

The "common operational picture" suggests a combined command of forces.

The JSC issued a document on May 1, 2006 entitled, "The United States–Japan Roadmap for Realignment Implementation." When the realignment of bases is done, the Ground Self Defense Force Central Readiness Command Headquarters will join the US command at Zama.[35] Together, the co-located army headquarters will coordinate their respective rapidly deployable forces. Similarly, the US Air Force and the Japan Air Self Defense Force will co-locate their air and missile defense commands at Yokota airbase outside Tokyo.

Within the new global alliance framework the expansion of SDF capabilities can be accommodated for some time to come. For this reason there is some concern that, looking into the future, Japan could develop beyond what is strictly needed for the alliance or its own local defense,[36] and this could generate tensions with neighbors.[37]

The regional outlook

China

The deterioration of Japanese perceptions of China since the mid-1990s has been striking. In newspaper polls taken in 1995, only 1 percent in Japan felt relations with China were poor, and 89 percent felt relations were fair, good, or very good.[38] Another 1995 poll found that 71 percent believed China would be an ally in twenty years.[39] However, in March 2006 the Foreign Ministry released poll numbers that showed only 6.9 percent thought relations with China were good. In contrast, 66.7 percent thought they were not good. The leaders of the major political parties have called China a potential threat.[40] The largest opposition party, the Democratic Party of Japan, adopted a resolution on February 23, 2006 describing China as a threat, a sentiment already widespread in the LDP. The government's official position is milder—China is not a threat, but a security concern.

China's GDP has already surpassed that of Japan in purchasing power terms. At official exchange rates, China's GDP is on track to overtake Japan by 2015, and it will surpass the US GDP by mid-century. China's military spending has been growing in double digits for the past twenty years and this has procured land, sea, air, ballistic missile, and anti-satellite weapons of increasing sophistication This military growth, along with no demonstrated willingness to negotiate arms limits, and a stated intention to use force to take Taiwan if necessary, give both Japan and the US a shared concern and a stronger alliance. It does not help that China has denounced the US–Japan alliance as cover for Japan's remilitarization and the containment of China.[41] This could push Japan even more in the direction of hard power.[42]

China and Japan have a burgeoning economic relationship that both sides are eager to develop, but after Koizumi took office in 2001, they developed an openly antagonistic political relationship. Chinese fury was touched off by Koizumi's annual visits to Yasukuni Shrine, a symbol of war and militarism rooted in prewar Japan's state Shinto. Japanese annoyance turned into anger at the way the Chinese government used history to stir up anti-Japanese demonstrations in China and to blacken Japan's international image. There are other points of contention, e.g., the Chunxiao gas field dispute in the East China Sea; China's obstruction of Japan's bid for a permanent seat on the UN Security Council; rivalry for leadership in East Asia; military competition; wariness of the other's military intentions, and so on. Many of these issues could be managed if there was a degree of trust and political will on both sides to negotiate differences. The year 2008 marked a change in tone at least. There was an exchange of warship visits that was held with great fanfare, an exchange of state visits—the first since the visit of President Jiang Zemin to Japan in 1998—and a three way summit meeting (China, Japan, and South Korea) in Fukuoka in December. There has been a marked change of Chinese emphasis toward conciliation and potential partnership but Japan harbors concerns about China's sincerity.

Taiwan

The US–Japan alliance is the key to Taiwan's survival. China considers Taiwan to be a renegade province that it will claim by force if necessary. Only the US Navy deters China. China does not have the ability to deter US intervention, but a rapid military buildup across from Taiwan could give it to China if no countermeasures are made. The tense situation strengthens the alliance and makes Japan's rearmament more likely because if China took Taiwan the US position in East Asia would be compromised and Japan's oil lifeline connecting it to the Middle East would be indefensible against Chinese interdiction. When Japan declared that it had a stake in preserving stability in the Taiwan Strait, Taiwan was reassured but this could also suggest to China that Japan would actively help the US militarily contain China, and that Japan was on the road to remilitarization. When tensions rise in the Taiwan Strait, the situation provides another justification for Japan to move toward collective defense with the US.

There is a surprising degree of mutual good feeling between Taiwan and Japan, despite Japan's colonial rule there from 1895 to 1945. The Taiwanese were forced to learn Japanese, but Japan's rule was not as harsh as elsewhere and living standards greatly improved. It was a profound disappointment to Taiwan that when the KMT took it over in 1947, it acted like an alien occupying force and excluded the population from government. In addition, the "native" Taiwanese had developed apart from China for generations. The "mainlanders" under Chiang Kai Shek used iron authoritarian rule under martial law to govern Taiwan, which ended only in 1987. In other words, the native Taiwanese suffered greatly after the Japanese left. Given all this, in retrospect, many Taiwanese view Japanese rule as having been relatively benign, and Japanese conservatives take great satisfaction from this. This Taiwan–Japan cultural tie may seem odd, but the former Taiwan President Lee Teng-hui, who presided over Taiwan's democratization after 1987, demonstrates this point. He is a native Taiwanese educated in Japanese colonial schools and then at Kyoto Imperial University. He speaks fluent Japanese and his brother served and died in the Japanese army. Although he spent most of his political life climbing the ranks within the KMT, which had dedicated itself to perpetuating mainlander rule, after the party entrusted him with the presidency he led Taiwan toward native Taiwanese majority rule. He now does not hide his desire for separation from China nor his friendly feelings toward Japan. When he visits there, he draws public attention and evokes memories in Japan of its deep ties to Taiwan. In May 2007, for example, he visited Yasukuni Shrine to pay respects to his brother whose spirit resides there. The nostalgic link between Japan and Taiwan makes a Japanese effort to "save" Taiwan more heartfelt and obligatory for powerful Japanese conservatives. But it should be noted that after the anti-independence KMT replaced the pro-independence Democratic People's Party (DPP) in power in the spring of 2008, tensions between China and Taiwan have eased considerably, reducing the salience of the Taiwan question for Japan at least for the time being.

North Korea

The test launch of a Taepodong II missile by North Korea on July 5, 2006 was unsuccessful but the missile is designed to reach the continental US. This raised the issue of extended deterrence for Japan: Would the US defend Japan against North Korea if it meant sacrificing Seattle? The same question has already been posed by China, but the rationality of the Chinese leadership has never been in question. This new North Korean threat likely prompted former Prime Minister Nakasone Yasuhiro on September 5 to suggest that Japan should reconsider a decision made back in the 1960s not to develop a nuclear deterrent. After a provocative nuclear test by North Korea on October 15, Nakagawa Shōichi, chairman of the LDP's Policy Research Council, said on television that, without favoring any outcome, Japan should debate the nuclear option.[43] Foreign Minister Asō Tarō also said that Japan needed to debate the nuclear issue, but stressed that the government was still committed to the Three Non-Nuclear Principles.[44] Prime Minister Abe tried to calm the ensuing criticism by pledging that he would not deviate from the non-nuclear principles, but he kept discussion alive by later saying: "if we cannot discuss nuclear issues at all we will not be able to manage non-proliferation with the US."[45] And in mid-November, the Cabinet Office quietly indicated that: "Even with nuclear weapons, we've understood that possessing them would not necessarily violate the constitution as long as it is kept within limits," but also it reiterated that the Three Non-Nuclear Principles would be observed.[46]

The escalating North Korean threat also underlined the need for a missile defense system, which the US and Japan are jointly developing and will jointly operate. The US Ambassador in Japan, Thomas Schieffer, publicly called on Japan to shoot down missiles even if they might be headed for the

US. However, under the collective defense taboo, Japan cannot protect another nation from attack. Ambassador Schieffer warned: "[Japan's] answer will be absolutely critical to the function and future of our alliance."[47] Thus has tension on the Korean peninsula driven Constitutional revision.

In a surprising diplomatic turn in September 2007, North Korea pledged to report all its nuclear bomb and proliferation activities by the end of the year in exchange for normalization with the US and economic assistance from the international community. Though it did not meet the deadline, North Korea handed over the list in June 2008 and, in a symbolic gesture, blew up the cooling tower at its Yongbyon reactor site.

South Korea

Japan's unresolved issues with South Korea are the interpretation of history, Yasukuni Shrine visits, and an ownership dispute over the island called Takeshima in Japanese and Dokdo in Korean. And there have been differences with the policies of South Korean president Roh Moo-hyun, who favors appeasing North Korea. Roh was not happy with Japan's hard attitude toward North Korea. Another issue is hypersensitivity toward Japan's growing interest in hard power. These frictions fuel South Korean suspicions regarding Japanese intentions. South Korea has asked the US to sell it F-22 fighters. The reason given was a need to offset Japan's growing capabilities.[48] The indirect South Korea–Japan security relationship created by their separate bilateral security treaties with the US—a kind of South Korea–Japan virtual alliance—has always been weak.

The more fundamental issue behind the squabbling has to do with South Korea's changing strategic role in Northeast Asia. After normalization of relations between the US and North Korea, South Korea will have less need for US protection, making a more strategically autonomous South Korea a question of concern to Japan. The new Lee Myung-bak presidency begun in late 2007 is more conservative and pro-US, with views close to that of Japan with respect to North Korea, i.e., it takes a hard line. Lee is also willing to give greater weight to trade than history in bilateral ties. But the Dokdo issue is still a raw sore in relations that does not appear ready to heal and the question of South Korea's future strategic role has only been deferred.

ASEAN

In contrast to Northeast Asia, Japan's relations with Southeast Asia have a strong soft power and multilateral component.[49] With the exception of Singapore, Japan's World War II activities in Southeast Asia were not as searing as they had been in Northeast Asia. Postwar Japan's diplomacy began to focus on the Association of Southeast Asian Nations (ASEAN) in 1978 when Prime Minister Takeo Fukuda cultivated ASEAN as a dialog partner during his tour of the region. ASEAN was founded in 1967 to strengthen relations among the western-oriented Southeast Asian nations (Malaysia, Singapore, Indonesia, the Philippines, and Thailand). By 1978 ASEAN was developing a common diplomatic and trade agenda that Japan wished to support. The so-called Fukuda Doctrine symbolized Japan's desire for active friendly engagement with Southeast Asia. The new Fukuda Doctrine included a 1 billion dollar fund provided by Japan to be used by ASEAN members in cooperative economic development projects. This initiative helped steer ASEAN toward its present role as a sub-regional economic cooperation organization.

Japan's soft power strategy has been to promote educational exchange, give official development assistance (ODA), and support ASEAN's consolidation through active trade and investment in the region. In the 1980s Japan offered massive amounts of ODA, trade, and investment to link Southeast Asia to Japan's prosperity. However, the "flying geese" pattern of growth that Japan proposed to lead did not inspire enthusiasm and never got off the ground. In the late 1980s to early 1990s Japan supported the track-two group meetings of ASEAN strategic studies think tanks, and this helped to spawn the ASEAN Regional Forum (ARF) in 1994. Japan also strongly supported regional economic cooperation first through the Pacific Economic Cooperation Conference (PECC), a non-official conference process that was dedicated to trade facilitation through informal consultations on specific issues of shared concern. The success of the PECC led to the start of the official Asia Pacific Economic Cooperation (APEC) forum in 1989, which Japan strongly supported up to the 1997 Asian Financial Crisis. Thus, Japan has played a helpful background role in the strengthening of ASEAN.

Japan's initial response to the Asian Financial Crisis (AFC) was to volunteer to create a $100 billion Asian Monetary Fund (AMF) to stabilize Asian currencies. The idea was shot down by the US and China, but Japan continued in a low key way to promote financial regionalism. The crisis led the ASEAN + 3 (ASEAN plus Japan, China, and South Korea) group in 1998 to begin the Chiang Mai Initiative. This led to a growing bilateral currency swap arrangement to stave off future currency crises. The East Asian Vision Group commissioned by ASEAN + 3 in 1998 explored the feasibility of East Asian cooperation, and the subsequent official East Asian Study Group (EASG) has developed agreed principles to begin building a regional community. Japan has strongly supported these initiatives and has earned good will as a result.

As a would-be leader Japan has a soft power challenge to meet China's coordinated regional diplomacy that is wooing ASEAN. If China achieves political predominance in Southeast Asia, it can leverage this to prevail over the rest of the region.[50] China has a distinct advantage due to the cultural legacy its empires left there, and the overseas Chinese living in the region have grown rich and influential. China is taking the initiative in forming regional functional cooperation, and has become a substantial aid donor in Indochina to rival Japan. In addition, geography gives it a natural advantage, e.g., it is the northern coast of the South China Sea, and the Mekong River originates in Qinghai and passes through Burma, Laos, Thailand, Cambodia, and Vietnam.

Japan's approach to Southeast Asia has involved peacekeeping and peace-building missions in Cambodia, East Timor, Aceh, and Mindanao. It gave neighbors help during the SARS epidemic and recovery assistance after the Indian Ocean tsunami of 2004. Thus, Japan has an ongoing regional engagement strategy that, in addition to ODA and trade, supports ASEAN's institutional development and encompasses peacemaking, post-conflict recovery, peace building, and humanitarian relief.[51] However, when all is said and done, Japan is having less of a soft power impact than China.

ASEAN is keen to partner with China in multilateralism and cooperative security, but it does not want to become a mere appendage to China and so it has been working to keep other major powers involved in the region. Assuming that ASEAN succeeds and furthermore realizes its desire to be the first building block in East Asian regionalism, the two most likely outcomes are the ASEAN + 3 formula (plus China, Japan, and South Korea), or the East Asian Summit (EAS) formula (i.e. a group consisting of ASEAN + 3 plus another 3 (i.e., Australia, New Zealand, and India). Japan is competing with China to influence the ultimate outcome. China favors ASEAN + 3 because China would naturally be predominant. Japan favors the EAS formula because it will reduce China's size advantage, dilute its vote, and give Japan more potential allies. This is an interesting case of soft power competition because the resolution of this question requires powers of persuasion.

Political developments

A number of younger politicians in both the LDP and the DPJ agree on Japan's need for improved defensive capabilities, helped by tensions with neighbors. For example, in 2003, after North Korea kicked out international inspectors and restarted plutonium production, eighty-eight LDP and seventy-nine DPJ Diet Members formed an ad hoc group called the Association of Junior Lawmakers to Create a Security System for the New Century. It called for economic sanctions against North Korea, the exercise of collective defense, and a warning about China as a growing threat. The general sentiment favored constitutional revision.[52] In Japan at large, pacifism is still a key value but events have made Article 9 seem anachronistic.[53] The Socialists and Communists who categorically reject revision only won 16 of the 480 seats in the 2005 Lower House election. The LDP and the Democratic Party of Japan (DPJ) together hold 409 seats, and the DPJ has had hawkish leaders like Maehara Seiji.

Koizumi handed the Prime Minister's office to Abe Shinzō in September 2006. The youthful Abe was the first Prime Minister born after World War II and he symbolized a generational change of leadership. Abe was also the grandson of Kishi Nobusuke and was raised to power by LDP right wingers who may have wished to see Kishi's ambitions of revision and rearmament finally realized by his grandson. In his September 2006 inaugural speech in the Diet, Abe set course in this direction: collective defense, revision of the Constitution, greater defense preparedness, and a more assertive diplomacy. Abe appointed a commission of defense experts (chaired by himself) to design an office to coordinate diplomatic, defense, and intelligence activity analogous to the role played by the US National Security Council. Abe also indicated an intention to explore ways to expand collective defense without amending Article 9.[54] With Abe in charge of a ruling coalition that had a two-thirds majority in the Lower House and the majority in the Upper House, the obstacles to revision and rearmament no longer seemed so insurmountable.

However, the hawkish leader of the DPJ, Seiji Maehara, was forced to resign in April 2006 to take responsibility for misbehavior by a DPJ member. The veteran of many political wars, Ichirō Ozawa, took over DPJ leadership. Ozawa had risen to the top in the LDP before he turned his back on the party and, by causing the LDP to lose a vote of confidence, forced the LDP from power in 1993, if only briefly. As the new DPJ leader, Ozawa steered the party away from LDP positions in defense and economy to build a distinctive brand image that appeals to the public and is making headway at the expense of the LDP. Ozawa sees the purpose of revision only in terms of improving Japan's ability to participate in UN authorized actions, and does not give alliance obligations precedence.

After taking power in September 2006, Abe did manage to upgrade the rank of the Defense Agency to Defense Ministry with DPJ support,[55] pass a law that established a procedure to amend the Constitution, and pass two education reform laws that greatly weakened the leftist national teachers union and succeeded in reintroduced the teaching of patriotism in schools. These were respectable accomplishments for the right wing but he overestimated the credit this earned him with the public, especially when he rammed through the Constitutional amendment referendum law in an extended session of the Diet. Abe also failed to show enough concern about political corruption in his Cabinet, the loss of 50 million pension records that threatened the retirement security of millions, and the pain caused by economic liberalization.

Abe's mistakes gave Ozawa an opportunity. Abe's approval rating was down to the 20 percent range when in July 2007 he led the LDP into a disastrous Upper House election defeat. It lost the LDP its majority to the DPJ, ending any prospect of constitutional revision for at least three years (until the next Upper House election). Ozawa continued to sharpen his party's brand image after the election by stonewalling the renewal of the Anti-Terrorism Law in the next session of the Diet.

Abe further bungled matters when he refused to resign after the election. He waited to resign until two days after he had given the Prime Minister's opening speech to the new Diet session in September, leaving the LDP in disarray at a critical moment. This mystifying behavior also tainted Abe's close associate Tarō Asō, who had been complicit in Abe's disastrous decisions. The young and hawkish Asō was next in line to lead a government for the LDP, but his role in Abe's debacle made the plan untenable.

The only candidate in a position to replace Abe was 71-year-old Yasuo Fukuda. As the new Prime Minister from the fall of 2007, Fukuda devoted himself to the issues Abe had ignored, and replaced Abe's sharp lean toward the US and defense issues with a theme of global welfare and a more Asia-oriented diplomacy. He eased tensions with China and South Korea, and North Korean unexpectedly agreed to end its nuclear program under international supervision. With improving prospects for stability the balance of public opinion in Japan shifted back in favor of keeping Article 9.

Will Japan continue to seek hard power?

The LDP defeat in the July 2007 Upper House election and the reduction of tensions in Northeast Asia could stall further change at least for the time being. It takes political leadership and the stimuli of external events to further the expansion of hard power. For the moment it is not clear that these factors exist. The LDP has lost control of the Upper House, and the DPJ under Ozawa's leadership has gained enough strength to threaten the LDP majority in the next Lower House election due by September 2009. The soft power appeal of the US has declined as a result of the George W. Bush administration's brutal war on terror. Externally, Japan's relations with China and South Korea are warming, and the North Korean threat seems to be receding. Tensions in the Taiwan Strait have also eased after the victory of the KMT in the 2008 election. It is suggestive that the Nagoya High Court ruled in April 2008 that the Air Self Defense Force mission transporting troops into Baghdad was unconstitutional.[56] And public support for leaving Article 9 alone rose to two thirds according to a May 2008 poll by the Asahi Shimbun, accompanied by a new grass roots movement to preserve Article 9.

This does not mean, however, that domestic political pressure to revise the Constitution is ending. In May 2008, 239 present and former Diet Members joined the Diet Members Alliance to Establish a New Constitution, and it includes prominent members of the DPJ.[57] Nor does today's sunny weather in Northeast Asia mean that the climate has changed. Most experts on North Korea believe it will hold back on full disclosure of its nuclear program and will not give up the weapons it already has. Thus, the situation is still a tinderbox, and could give pro-revision elements and the US enough traction to push Japan toward further increases in hard power.

The role of soft power

Japan has been so preoccupied with hard power issues that it does not yet coordinate soft and hard power within an overall foreign policy strategy.

Within the government only the Ministry of Foreign Affairs (MOFA) seems to give soft power serious thought. However, no matter how hard MOFA may try to brand Japan using widely admired aspects of its culture, the unwillingness of Japan's conservatives to admit Japan's responsibility for the atrocities committed by Imperial Japan besmirches its image. Thus, Japan's soft power does not do as well as it could in supporting Japan's hard power.

This leads to a second point, i.e., neither is Japan's pursuit of hard power enhancing its soft power. One might expect a rich and strong nation to command more respect and admiration, other things being equal. But in Japan's case, a hard power buildup undermines Japan's positive image as a peace-loving nation that abhors the use of force. Moreover, Japan's military buildup can have a sinister aspect. If Japan will not recognize its army's past mistakes, what will stop it from repeating them in future? Japan's ultimate national purpose is unclear. Power attached to a positive, moral purpose commands respect and acceptance, and can generate more soft power. However, power that has no clear moral purpose, and does the bidding of another country that has demonstrated faulty judgment, undermines soft power.

Conclusion

Starting first with international structure, followed by institutional and normative change, Japan changed course in the 1990s and ended the decade with the precedent-setting Special Situations Law that opened the door to circumventing Article 9 strictures. The shock of 9/11 when Japan was under the leadership of prime minister Koizumi led to substantial institutional and normative progress toward rearmament and an enhanced security partnership with the US. Consequently, Article 9 revision and a rearmed Japan is no longer out of the question.

However, the public's continuing reluctance to become entangled in US global security strategy, and its growing intolerance of LDP corruption and mismanagement mean that the LDP's grip on power is tenuous. Continued progress toward revision and rearmament depends on LDP rule. Recent exogenous changes work to make the case for revision less compelling. China has improved relations with Japan since Koizumi left office, and the situation on the Korean peninsula seems to be moving in fits and starts in a positive direction. The new Democratic Party administration of President Barak Obama is less fixated on building military power and, at any rate, the entire world is focused on overcoming the deepening global recession that began in 2008.

But the future is less clear. Institutional and normative obstacles to change have been so compromised that all that is needed is a big enough exogenous security crisis to tip the scales toward revision. On the international front, the underlying disputes, tensions, and rivalry between China and Japan have not been replaced by a common purpose, and North Korean nuclear weapons will keep Japan feeling insecure and thinking about the need for more hard power options. In other words, structural issues like China's expanding power and North Korea's new nuclear threat, institutional changes such as legislation and policy interpretation that undermines Article 9, and a new wariness and sense of vulnerability felt by the Japanese public mean that there is no guarantee that Japan will remain where it is for the next decade.

Notes

1 "LDP policy chief calls for debate on Japan's nuke arm option," *Japan Economic Newswire*, October 15, 2006; "Aso calls for policy debate to renew non-nuclear commitment," *Mainichi Daily News*, October 24, 2006; "Abe says no to nukes but allows discussion," *The Japan Times*, November 19, 2006.
2 Peter J. Katzenstein, "Japan, Asian-Pacific security, and the case for analytical eclecticism," *International Security*, vol. 26, no. 3, pp. 153–85.
3 Theodore McNelly, "The Renunciation of War in the Japanese Constitution," *Political Science Quarterly*, vol. 77, no. 3. (Sept. 1962), pp. 350–78, 353.
4 George Kennan, "Review of Current Trends, U.S. Foreign Policy, Policy Planning Staff, PPS no. 23. Top Secret. *Foreign Relations of the United States*, 1948, Volume 1, Part 2, February 28, 1948, Declassified June 17, 1974. (Washington DC Government Printing Office, 1976) 524–25.
5 Dower, *Empire and Aftermath, 1878–1964*, Cambridge, MA: Council on East Asian Studies, Harvard University Press, 1979, pp. 429–34. Kenneth B. Pyle, *Japan Rising: The Resurgence of Japanese Power and Purpose*, Cambridge, MA: The Century Foundation, 2007, pp. 31–32.
6 Dower, pp. 444–49.
7 Michael Schaller, "America's Favorite War Criminal: Kishi Nobusuke and the Transformation of U.S.–Japan Relations," *JPRI Working Paper* no. 11: July 1995 http://www.jpri.org/publications/workingpapers/wp11.html.
8 Richard Samuels draws a distinction within this group between neoautonomists who want independence from the US (e.g., Hatoyama) and normal nationalists who wanted a continuing alliance with the US (e.g., Kishi). Richard J. Samuels, *Securing Japan*, Ithaca, NY: Cornell Studies in Security Affairs, Cornell University Press, 2007, p. 112.
9 Theodore McNelly "American influence and Japan's no-war Constitution," *Political Science Quarterly*, vol. 67, no. 4 (December, 1952), pp. 589–98.
10 Mari Yamamoto, "Japan's Grassroots Pacifism," *Japan Focus* (February 2005). <http://japanfocus.org/products/details/2102>; *Grassroots Pacifism in Post-War Japan: The Rebirth of a Nation*, Sheffield Centre for Japanese Studies, Routledge Curzon, 2004.
11 Kobun Ito, "Japan's Security in the 1970s," *Asian Survey*, vol. 10, no. 12 (December 1970), pp. 1031–36.
12 George Magnuson, "Selling the U.S., by George!," *Time*, February 14, 1983, p. 1.
13 Memorandum of Conversation, March 23, 1981, Secretary Alexander Haig and Foreign Minister Masayoshi Ito, archived at *National Security Archive*, The George Washington University, Washington, DC <http://www.gwu.edu/~nsarchiv/japan/hoshuyamaohinterview.htm>.
14 Kenneth Waltz, "The Emerging Structure of International Politics," *International Security*, vol. 18, no. 2 (Fall 1993), pp. 44–79.
15 Joseph S. Nye, Jr., "America's Asian Agenda: Coping with Japan," *Foreign Policy*, no. 89 (Winter, 1992–93), pp. 96–115; Robert Gilpin, *The Political Economy of International Relations*, Princeton, NJ: Princeton: Princeton University Press, 1987.

16 Michael Green, "The Challenges of Managing U.S.–Japan Security Relations," ed. Gerald L. Curtis, *New Perspectives on U.S.–Japan Relations after the Cold War*, Tokyo: Japan Center for International Exchange, 2000, pp. 241–64.
17 Lucian W. Pye, "The United States and Asia in 1997: Nothing Dramatic, Just Incremental Progress," *Asian Survey*, vol. 38, no. 1, A Survey of Asia in 1997: Part I. (January, 1998), pp. 99–106.
18 Richard Armitage and Joseph Nye, *Special Report: The United States and Japan: Advancing Toward A Mature Partnership* (Washington, DC: National Defense University Press, October 2000).
19 Tomohito Shinoda, "Koizumi's Top-Down Leadership in the Anti-Terrorism Legislation: The Impact of Political Institutional Changes," *SAIS Review*, vol. 23, no. 1 (Winter-Spring 2003), pp. 19–34.
20 Junko Hirose, "The Legislative Record: The Japan National Diet in 2003," *Japanese Journal of Political Science*, 4 (2003), pp. 361–63.
21 *National Defense Program Guideline 2005*, Cabinet Office, Government of Japan, <http://www.jda.go.jp/e/index_.htm>.
22 "Overview of Japan's Defense Policy," in *The Defense of Japan 2005*, The Japan Defense Ministry, Government of Japan <http://www.jda.go.jp/e/publications/overview/english.pdf>.
23 Lesley Connors, "Next steps for Japan: Administrative Reform and the Changing Polity," *Asia-Pacific Review*, vol. 7, no. 1 (May 2000), pp. 109, 122.
24 Nathaniel Thayer, *How the Conservatives Rule Japan*, Princeton, NJ: Princeton University Press, 1969.
25 Gary Cox, Frances Rosenbluth, and Michael Thies, "Electoral Reform and the Fate of Factions: The Case of Japan's Liberal Democratic Party," *British Journal of Political Science*, 29 (1999), pp. 33–56.
26 "60% of Young Lawmakers for Revising Constitution's Article 9" *Japan Economic Newswire, Lexis-Nexis*, World News/Asia Pacific, June 9, 2003.
27 Nobuhiro Hiwatari, "Japan in 2004: 'Courageous' Koizumi Carries On," *Asian Survey*, vol. 45, no. 1 (February 2005), pp. 41–53.
28 "U.S. Questions Japan's Pacifism" *BBC News*, August 13, 2004, <http://news.bbc.co.uk/1/hi/world/asia-pacific/3561378.stm>.
29 Richard L. Armitage and Joseph R. Nye, *The U.S.–Japan Alliance: Getting Asia Right Through 2020*, Washington, D.C., The Center for Strategic and International Studies, February 2007, p. 21.
30 "Joint Statement of the U.S.–Japan Security Consultative Committee," Office of Press Relations, U.S. Department of State <http://www.state.gov/r/pa/prs/ps/2005/42490.htm>.
31 "DPJ Considers Japan–U.S. Accord Reasonable, SDP Objects," *Japan Economic Newswire*, February 20, 2005.
32 "U.S.–Japan Alliance: Transformation and Realignment for the Future," Security Consultative Committee Document, Ministry of Foreign Affairs of Japan, October 27, 2005. < http://www.mofa.go.jp/region/n-america/us/security/scc/doc0510.html>.
33 "Remarks With Defense Secretary Donald Rumsfeld, Japanese Minister of State for Defense Yoshinori Ōno, and Japanese Foreign Minister Nobutaka Machimura," U.S. Department of Defense, October 29, 2005 <http://www.state.gov/secretary/rm/2005/55775.htm>.
34 "U.S., Japan Move to Bolster Alliance," *The Korea Herald*, September 15, 2006.
35 "Japan May Develop Fighters after US Rebuff," *Reuters*, August 29, 2007.
36 Thomas J. Christensen, "China, the U.S.–Japan Alliance, and the Security Dilemma in Asia," *International Security*, vol. 23, no. 4 (Spring 1999), pp. 49–80.
37 Opinion poll taken on 1/28/95 by *Yomiuri Shimbun*, released on February 1, 1995 available at JPOLL <http://www.ropercenter.uconn.edu/jpoll/JPOLL.html>.

38 Opinion poll taken on 3/10/95 by Nihon Keizai Shimbun, released on April 23, 1995 available at JPOLL <http://www.ropercenter.uconn.edu/jpoll/JPOLL.html>.
39 On December 8, 2005, DPJ President Seiji Maehara called China a "threat" during a visit to Washington, DC. Koizumi voiced agreement with Maehara soon afterward. "Maehara Speech Splits DPJ," *The Daily Yomiuri*, December 11, 2005, p. 3.
40 Wu Xinbo, "The End of the Silver Lining: A Chinese View of the U.S.–Japanese Alliance," *The Washington Quarterly*, vol. 29, no. 1 (2005), pp. 119–30.
41 Thomas J. Christensen, "Fostering Stability or Creating a Monster? The Rise of China and U.S. Policy toward East Asia," *International Security*, vol. 31, no. 1 (Summer 2006), pp. 81–126.
42 "LDP Policy Chief Calls for Debate on Japan's Nuke Arm Option," *Japan Economic Newswire*, October 15, 2006.
43 "Aso Calls for Policy Debate to Renew Non-Nuclear Commitment," *Mainichi Daily News*, October 24, 2006.
44 "Tōshu Tōron: Kakuyū Rongi de Shushō ga Hatsugen Yōgo" [In Parliamentary Debate: Prime Minister Defends Using Word in Discussing Nuclear Power], *Mainichi Shimbun* (Mainichi News), November 8, 2006. "Abe Watched Over Nuclear Debate," *BBC News/Asia-Pacific*, November 10, 2006.
45 "Japan Can Be Allowed to Possess "Necessary Minimum" Nuclear Arms-Government," *BBC Monitoring Asia Pacific-Political*, November 14, 2006. "Report: Japanese Government Says It Can Hold Nuclear Arms for Self-Defense," *Associated Press*, November 14, 2006.
46 "Schieffer's Call for Missile Defense Help Raises Constitution Issue," *The Japan Times Online*, October 28, 2005, <http://www.japantimes.co.jp/>.
47 "South Korea Seeks to Introduce F-22 Class Fighters," *People's Daily Online*, April 28, 2007.
48 Yeo Hay Hwee, "Japan, ASEAN, and the Construction of an East Asian Community," *Contemporary Southeast Asia: A Journal of International and Strategic Affairs*, vol. 28, no. 2 (2006), pp. 259–75.
49 Joshua Kurlantzick, *Charm Offensive: How China's Soft Power Is Transforming the World*, New Haven, CT: Yale University Press, 2007.
50 Lam Peng Er, "Japan's Human Security Role in Southeast Asia," *Contemporary Southeast Asia: A Journal of International and Strategic Affairs*, vol. 28, no. 1 (2006), pp. 141–59.
51 "New Generation Driving Political Realignment," *The Daily Yomiuri*, March 5, 2004.
52 Richard J. Samuels, *Securing Japan*, pp. 117–19.
53 "Tokuhō: Nihon-ban NSC Kyūkyoku no Nerai wa" [Special Report: Is the Ultimate Aim a Japanese Version of the NSC?], *Chunichi Web Press*, November 24, 2006, <http://www.chunichi.co.jp/>.
54 "Bōeichō no Shōshōkaku Kanren Hōan, Minshu ga Jōken Tsuki de Sansei" [Bill to Promote Defense Agency to Ministry Status—DPJ Gives Conditional Agreement], *Yomiuri Online*, November 25, 2006, <http://www.yomiuri.co.jp>. "Bōeishō Hōan, Konkokkai de Seiritsu e ... Ichigatsu ni mo Shō ni Shōkaku" [Defense Ministry Bill, Passage This Diet Session ... Promotion to Ministry Status by January], *Yomiuri Online*, November 25, 2005, <http://www.yomiuri.co.jp>.
55 "High court: ASDF mission to Iraq illegal," *The Japan Times Online*, April 18, 2008 <http://search.japantimes.co.jp/cgi-bin/nn20080418a1.html>.
56 Gavan McCormack, "Japan: Through the Looking Glass," *Asia Times Online*, June 26, 2008 <http://www.atimes.com/atimes/Japan/JF26Dh01.html>.
57 "Constitutional debates shouldn't be put on hold". *The Daily Yomiuri*, May 3, 2008, p. 4.

3 Japan's soft power–hard power balancing act

Tsuneo Akaha

Soft power in Japanese security policy

As noted in the introductory chapter, a nation can draw its soft power from the values it expresses in its culture, in the examples it sets by its internal practices and policies, and in the way it handles its relations with other nations. In the security realm, what values does Japan express in its culture, what examples does it set, and how does it handle its international relations?

Simply put, postwar Japanese culture has nurtured a strong popular yearning for peace and aversion to war. The "peace constitution" both supported and was supported by the popular pacifism.[1]

The domestic and international conditions at the turn of the century seemed to support Japan's long-established policy of limiting its defense spending. At $46,895 million, the nation's defense spending in 2003 was slightly less than 1 percent of its GNP. Another long-established element of Japan's soft power was the system of civilian control over the military. Based on Japan's lesson from its disastrous militarist past, civilian control was supported by strong national consensus, and the public support of the system showed no sign of eroding.

In 1996, the Council on Defense Affairs issued a report entitled "The Direction of Japan's Security and Defense." In the so-called "Higuchi Report," the prime minister's advisory group assessed the post-Cold War security environment in Asia-Pacific, discussed basic issues facing Japan's security policy and defense capabilities, and recommended a shift from a Cold War-oriented defense strategy to a multilateral security strategy. Virtually all key elements of national defense and national security discussed in the report had to do with the hard power requirements for Japan's own national defense and its contribution to the maintenance of international security. They included the need to redirect the nation's growing military capabilities toward the needs of multilateral security cooperation, ways to strengthen security cooperation with the United States, and the qualitative improvement of Japan's defense capabilities.[2]

In contrast, the 2004 successor to the 1996 report stepped into the realm of soft power in Japanese security policy. In the new report, Chairman of the

Council on Security and Defense Capabilities, an advisory group for Prime Minister Koizumi Junichirō, specifically called on the nation to "make the best use of Japan's hard and soft power as a means to preserve peace and security."³ Recognizing the increasingly multi-faceted nature of security threats in the post-9/11 world—ranging from conventional military threats to terrorism, the proliferation of weapons of mass destruction, environmental threats, and HIV/AIDS and other types of human security problems—the Council's report called for the development of an Integrated Security Strategy encompassing measures to prevent direct threats from reaching Japan and minimize the damage should such threats reach Japan. The document also discussed the need to undertake efforts to "reduce the chances of threats arising in various parts of the world with the aim of preventing such threats from reaching Japan or affecting the interests of Japanese expatriates or corporations overseas."⁴ According to the report, the Integrated Security Strategy would be based on a three-fold approach: (1) Japan's own efforts, (2) alliance with the United States, and (3) "cooperation with the international community to defend the homeland and, at the same time, to strive for improving the international security environment."⁵

The 2004 report stated, "Efforts to eliminate potential sources of threats in various parts of the world, based on cooperative arrangements with the international community, will become increasingly important to Japan's security strategy."⁶ The report was critical of Japan's past failure to recognize the importance of cooperation with the international community beyond self-help efforts and alliance with the United States. The report noted, "[T]here is no doubt that diplomatic activities and interaction with other countries at the grass-roots level in various fields have improved other countries' understanding of Japan and have played a role in the country's defense, albeit indirectly."⁷ It is self-evident that if Japan is to expand its international cooperation to prevent the emergence of threats around the world, it will need to utilize its soft power more effectively and to invest in its further development.

Among the efforts the report advocated for international cooperation was the "contribution of personnel and various types of human resources acting in close collaboration with each other, including the SDF, the police, Official Development Assistance (ODA)-related organizations, private enterprises, non-governmental organizations (NGOs) and others." The report went on to say,

> Initiatives undertaken via ODA and other financial-assistance programs to counter infectious diseases, such as HIV/AIDS, or efforts to achieve "human security," including help in raising education standards and training human resources as well as projects to eliminate poverty, are also important activities for preventing conflicts and bringing stability to various parts of the world.⁸

It stands to reason that these activities will require not only a commitment of financial and material resources but also an effective use of soft power, including a demonstration of principled and disciplined behavior and application of ideas with broad appeal.

The recent record of Japanese foreign policy shows evidence of Japan's desire to establish its soft-power presence in various parts of the world. Here we can discuss only the most prominent examples, illustrating both Japanese efforts and challenges facing them.

Perhaps the most visible and successful use of Japanese soft power as a national policy instrument can be found in the field of official development assistance (ODA). Japan's ODA policy has been given a prominent role in its effort to promote international peace and security. Japan is one of the world's leading providers of official development assistance. Between 1994 and 2004, Japan shouldered almost one-fifth of the world's total volume of development assistance.[9] Tokyo's ODA policy has been guided by some basic principles that represent the nation's own experience in postwar economic development and its understanding of the international community's expectations for Japan. Until recently, for example, Japanese ODA policy was guided by "*yoseishugi*", or request-based ODA programs. This principle reflected Japan's preference for self-directed and disciplined management of developmental projects. As well, Tokyo's long-established focus on Asian aid recipients was both a reflection of Japan's commercial interests in the region and a product of its Asia-oriented knowledge and expertise, not to mention its historical ties to the region. For a long time Tokyo was reluctant to link ODA decisions to the human rights condition in recipient countries and this reflected its reluctance to preach democracy and human rights abroad.[10] Moreover, Japan's pacifism and anti-nuclear sentiment informed Tokyo's ODA policy with respect to the military and nuclear policies of aid recipients. For example, Japan demanded a more transparent defense policy and cessation of nuclear weapons tests in China. Even though these demands had gone largely unheeded, Japan continued to consider recipients' military and nuclear policies in its ODA programs. More recently, the growing environmental thrust in Japan's ODA policy reflected the nation's lessons from its own experience with the hazardous environmental and health effects of postwar industrialization and urbanization.

The role of ODA in Japan's security policy was explicitly mentioned in the ODA Charter that the government approved in August 2003. The charter stated that the purpose of ODA was "to contribute to the peace and development of the international community, and thereby help ensure Japan's security and prosperity."[11] The document spelled out Japan's commitment to address wide-ranging issues related to development – from poverty, famine, and refugee displacement, to natural disasters, the environment, and infectious diseases, to gender, democracy, human rights, ethnic and religious conflict, and terrorism. The Japanese government adopted a medium-term ODA policy in February 2005, in which a significant amount of space was devoted to the discussion of the human security perspective on development and development aid. The document outlined priority issues: poverty reduction; sustainable growth; global issues, including environmental problems and natural disasters; and peace-building. It described Japan's approach to peace-building as comprising efforts to prevent the occurrence and recurrence of conflicts, emergency humanitarian assistance in the immediate aftermath of conflicts, post-conflict reconstruction assistance, and medium- to long-term development assistance.[12] Throughout these phases, the document's emphasis was on the alleviation of human suffering from the human security perspective.

In a speech on Japanese ODA in 2006, Foreign Minister Asō Tarō stated, "ODA is essentially about having other countries first use the precious money of the Japanese people for the benefit of the Japanese people later on. When you think about it, there are not many other endeavors which require such a long-term strategy as ODA."[13] In the same speech, Asō referred to ODA as a "diplomatic tool," called for the establishment of an ODA Council to highlight the strategic importance of ODA policy, and compared the proposed structure to the nation's Security Council, the cabinet-level organ responsible for adopting Japan's security policy and priorities, both long-term and short-term.[14]

In summary, the above ODA policy principles have represented Japan's soft power and been supported by broad public understanding of the importance of ODA as an instrument of foreign policy.[15]

In the context of Japanese soft power, its economic assistance to China deserves particular attention both because of its large scale and for its potential impact on Japan's foreign and security policy interests in the region. With $965 million in total bilateral ODA from Japan in 2004, China was by far the largest recipient of Japanese economic assistance in the world and Japan was the largest donor of official economic aid to China as well.[16] Since its beginning in 1979, Japanese ODA in China emphasized large infrastructure development for economic growth. In recent years, however, Japanese aid targeted several priority areas, including environmental protection and public health, education and human resources development, Japanese language and culture study, and poverty alleviation.[17]

The importance of Japanese economic assistance to China went beyond economic and environmental dimensions. It also had a political significance. Steady economic growth in China was seen to contribute to social and political stability in the country; it was also hoped that Japanese assistance would improve Japan's image in China. Despite the significant size of Japanese ODA to China, however, there is a general sense among the Japanese today that their assistance is not appreciated by the Chinese.[18] Moreover, there is little evidence that Japan's ODA policy has had any significant political impact on China, particularly with respect to the latter's human rights record, defense policy, or nuclear and ballistic missile development.

"Cultural diplomacy" is clearly another area in which Japan can advance its soft power. In discussing Japan's current security agenda, a high-ranking Japanese diplomat wrote, "Diplomacy plays an important role in promoting [international] understanding toward Japan by conveying Japan's policy, culture, value system, and appeal."[19] Another senior Japanese diplomat stated that cultural diplomacy had been an important part of Japanese efforts to create a favorable international image and understanding of Japan. He reminded us that Japan had pursued these efforts for a long time and with considerable success. Japan's cultural diplomacy had been used to change the nation's image from "a militaristic nation to a pacifist one, from a deprived country to an advanced country."[20] Yet another Japanese diplomat wrote,

> In Japanese foreign policy, cultural exchange and cooperation are seen not only as tools for helping other peoples understand Japan and the Japanese as well as enhancing the [sic] Japan's image. It is also viewed as means for contributing to the efforts of other countries that face the kind of difficulties we ourselves experienced in achieving development.[21]

The official asserted that the healthy development of a nation required the preservation of its own culture and mentioned the Japanese government's support of UNESCO's adoption of the Convention on the Safeguarding of Immaterial Cultural Heritage in 2004 and its support of a symposium on "Modernization and Traditional Values" in the Middle East in 2003.[22]

These statements clearly show that "soft power" had become a part of the way of thinking among Japanese diplomats by the beginning of the twenty-first century. Moreover, this understanding had made its way into the discussion of official policy.

However, there are signs that Japan's soft power faces serious challenges. The most important challenge is the growing domestic call for enhancing the nation's military capabilities. The "reluctant realism" of the political leadership in the country is preparing the public for an eventual revision of Article 9 of the constitution.[23] This shift is a result of several factors. First, the political leaders have recognized the changing nature of the US–Japan alliance—from a system designed to deter direct threats against Japan to one that not only serves that purpose but also provides for regional and global peace and stability as a public good. Second, the Japanese political leadership has recognized the need to transform their nation into a "normal state" – a state that can more fully exercise the universally recognized right of self-defense and also play an international security role commensurate with its national power.[24] Third, the unpredictable security environment has added to their anxiety about national security and strengthened their determination to harness the nation's resources for a more active security policy. Prominent among security concerns in Japan are the proliferation of weapons of mass destruction, particularly in North Korea, the growing power of China, international terrorism, and international instability, particularly in the Middle East, which could threaten Japan's energy security.

Another formidable challenge to Japan's soft power is found in the nation's relations with its neighboring countries, particularly China and Korea. The problem can be called a "deficit of soft power" resulting from the legacy of history and lack of trust in those relations. We will discuss this problem at length in the next section.

The other security issue for which Japan's soft power is of little effect – at least to date – is the Middle East peace. As a Japanese diplomat observes, Japan has no negative legacy of history with this region of the world and has been holding dialogues with both the Israelis and the Palestinians. Japan has also extended $690 million in assistance to the Palestinians.[25] As laudable as these efforts may be, they have had no observable effect to date.

Japan's soft power deficit vis-à-vis China and Korea

The most serious international constraint on Japan's potential soft power is that its neighbors do not necessarily see the behavior of Japanese leaders in a positive light. Japanese diplomats clearly recognize this problem.[26]

China and South Korea have become more vociferous in their criticism of some of the expressions of Japanese nationalism in recent years. The most notable example is the chorus of Chinese and South Korean criticisms against former Prime Minister Koizumi's repeated visits to the Yasukuni Shrine, which commemorates the Japanese war dead, including Tōjō Hideki and other Class-A war criminals. The issue prevented a summit between Tokyo and Beijing during Koizumi's entire term as prime minister, a major setback in Japanese diplomacy. The controversy over Japanese history textbooks is another reminder of Japan's imperialist past that casts a dark shadow over its contemporary image in the eyes of its neighbors. Critical comments by Chinese and South Korean leaders have echoed the growing anxiety among their public about the ongoing Japanese debate on constitutional revision. In the Chinese case, anti-Japanese sentiments erupted in mass demonstrations in 2005, perhaps with government encouragement.[27] As discussed below, the ever-closer US–Japan defense cooperation is yet another target of criticism among some Asian neighbors regarding Japan's real intent behind its defense buildup. Reflecting the growing Chinese anxiety about the state of Sino-Japanese relations, the Chairman of the China Reform Forum, Zheng Bijian, states that Japan should maintain the peaceful development it has followed in the last sixty years and expresses concern about the growing call in Japan for constitutional revision.[28] Former South Korean President Kim Dae-jung echoed the same sentiment when he stated that not only was Japan distrusted by its neighboring countries, but that the shift of political balance to the right in Japan was accelerating. He added that without the trends to the right, it would be inconceivable for Prime Minister Koizumi to visit the Yasukuni Shrine repeatedly.[29] A seven-country survey in Asia in July 2006 revealed that about 85 percent of South Korean respondents thought Japanese prime ministers should not visit the shrine. Even in Japan, there was substantial (35.4 percent) opposition to such visits. Over 80 percent of South Korean respondents to the survey stated they had bad impressions of Japan.[30]

Japan's territorial disputes with the neighboring countries also continue to tarnish Japan's image as a cooperative partner in the formation of a post-Cold War regional security architecture. The jockeying for control of resource development around Senkaku (Diaoyu) and Takeshima (Tokdo) islands has become a high-tension drama affecting Japan's image in the region, with limited bilateral talks to resolve the issues showing little or no progress. Furthermore, as other chapters in this volume mention, the Japan–US joint statement regarding the future of Taiwan as an issue of concern to the bilateral alliance was seen by Beijing as Tokyo's effort to frustrate Chinese reunification by siding with Washington.

China has actively campaigned against Japan's bid to gain a permanent seat on the UN Security Council. Japan's diplomatic setback on this issue is in large measure due to its inability to reach reconciliation with China and other countries over its history of war and aggression. There is also substantial public opposition in South Korea to Japan's permanent seat on the Security Council.[31] This does not mean that there is no international support for Japan's application for a permanent Security Council seat. In fact, some Asian nations have expressed strong support for Japan's application, including Cambodia, India, Indonesia, Malaysia, Singapore, the Philippines, and Vietnam. The United States, Australia, Brazil, France, Germany, and the United Kingdom also support Japan's bid. Japan faces a formidable obstacle in China, a permanent member of the Security Council with growing international influence.

Koizumi's successor, Abe Shinzō, decided to repair Japan's damaged relations with China and South Korea by holding summit talks with President Hu Jintao and Premier Wen Jiabao of China and President Roh Moo-hyun in October 2006. Even though much of their meeting time was devoted to the discussion of the North Korean nuclear test, the leaders agreed that their bilateral relations should be improved. On the Yasukuni Shrine issue, Abe told the Chinese leaders that he would not publicly state whether or not he planned to visit the war memorial. With Abe playing up his nationalist credentials to maintain public support for his position on domestic and foreign policy issues, Japan's neighbors are not likely to "bury the hatchet" over history issues and Japan's assertive foreign and security policy. As we will see below, North Korea became an "easy target" of Abe's nationalist rhetoric. Asian neighbors – and some US politicians – have become alarmed by Abe's revisionist views of Japanese history and his public statements downplaying Japan's war responsibility, as evidenced in his statements denying Japanese wartime military's involvement in the forced prostitution of "comfort women"—Korean, Chinese, Dutch, and Japanese women—to provide sex service to Japanese soldiers. In his book "Utsukushii kuni e," Abe presented the Japanese revisionists' claim that the Tokyo war tribunal violated the international legal principle banning retroactive application of law when it judged Japanese wartime leaders as war criminals because, in their view, there was no established international law regarding "crime against humanity" or "crime against peace."³² In another book, which he co-authored with a former Japanese diplomat, Abe argued that Tōjō and other Japanese wartime leaders were never tried by domestic law and therefore as far as Japanese law was concerned, Japan did not consider them "war criminals."³³ Domestic critics were also concerned about Abe's nationalist political agenda, including education reform (designed to instill patriotism among the nation's schools children), constitutional revision, and the specter of a nuclear Japan.

Abe believed that the restoration of national pride, promotion of patriotism and the role of the state in public education, and pursuit of assertive foreign policy will enhance the nation's soft power. However, in this author's view, his nationalist agenda is bound to run into serious domestic and foreign challenges.

Abe's immediate successor in the Prime Minister's office, Fukuda Yasuo, took steps to mend fences with China and South Korea. Japan's neighbors showed willingness to restore a more cordial relationship with Japan. President Hu Jintao visited Tokyo in a "smile diplomacy" effort in May 2008, marking the first time the Chinese president visited Japan since Jiang Zemin's disastrous visit in 1998. Shortly after the summit, Tokyo and Beijing announced that Japan would participate in the "joint development" of oil and gas fields in a disputed area of the East China Sea. However, no sooner was the announcement made than the Chinese government quickly issued a statement that the agreement did not represent a change in Chinese sovereignty claims to the area. Clearly, then, the sovereignty issue remained unresolved.

Fukuda's successor, Asō Tarō, also believed in Japan's soft power. Calling Japan a "thought leader," Asō advocated a value-oriented foreign policy toward the "Arc of Freedom and Prosperity," running from Southeast Asia to Central Asia. He believed that Japan was in a position to play an important role in nation-building and the promotion of democracy, peace, freedom, human rights, the rule of law, and market economy throughout the region. His vision was based on his conviction that Japan, through its wartime and postwar experience, had learned how to overcome the dangers of parochial nationalism and how to build a liberal democracy and a prosperous market economy.³⁴

If Japan is to exercise its soft power in improving its relations with the neighboring countries, it will be helpful to have public support within Japan. Such support is not assured, however. Particularly problematic is the generally negative attitudes among the Japanese people toward China. According to public opinion polls conducted by the Japanese Cabinet Office, the proportion of Japanese who feel affinity toward China has steadily declined over the last two decades. Reaching the peak of 78.6 percent in 1979, it dropped to 51.6 percent in 1989 and 47.9 percent in 2003. Conversely, the proportion of Japanese who felt no affinity toward China rose from 14.7 percent in 1979 to 43.1 percent in 1989, and continued to rise and reached 48.0 percent in 2003. By 2005, the favorable proportion had dropped to an all-time low of

32.4 percent, while the unfavorable proportion had risen to record high of 63.4 percent.[35] These disturbing trends reflected the worsening state of bilateral relations between Tokyo and Beijing. Moreover, there was a growing concern among the Japanese public about the Chinese threat to Japanese security. In a public opinion survey conducted by the Japanese foreign ministry in March 2002, 18.2 percent of the subjects said China was already a security threat and another 38.7 percent said China would become a security threat in the future.[36] A more recent opinion survey by a Japanese newspaper revealed that over 65 percent of respondents said they could not trust China and 44 percent thought China was becoming a military threat to Japan. Only North Korea received a higher threat rating (77.7 percent) in the poll. Equally disturbing was the fact that about half of the respondents did not expect the nature of bilateral relations to change.[37] Echoing the growing unease among the public, then Foreign Minister Asō pointed to the two-digit increases in Chinese defense spending for eighteen years in a row and expressed concern about a "lack of transparency" in Chinese defense policy.[38]

Implications for alliance with the United States

As noted earlier, the 2004 report of the Council on Security and Defense Capabilities states that the Integrated Security Strategy would be based on a threefold approach: (1) Japan's own efforts, (2) alliance with the United States, and (3) cooperation with the international community to defend the homeland and, at the same time, to strive for improving the international security environment. In this author's view, the development and application of soft power as an instrument of security policy runs into difficulties at the intersection between the second and third elements. In the US–Japan alliance, future demands on Japan will lead more toward the expansion of hard power, particularly military capabilities and coordination of military planning and operation between the two countries.

Simply put, the very alliance with the United States may frustrate Japan's desire to be viewed as a supporter of international consensus on global issues, multilateralism, and peaceful resolution of international conflicts. If gaining broad international support for Japan's policy on major international security issues and convincing others to forge a common approach to those issues are the two overall goals of Japanese diplomacy, and if Japan is to utilize its soft power to achieve those objectives, it must be recognized that on some issues the alliance with the United States may undercut Japan's soft-power attraction.

The Iraqi case demonstrates this problem. A high-ranking Japanese diplomat acknowledged the dilemma. After observing, "As is obvious from the case of the Iraq War, the United States is prepared to act in its capacity as sole world superpower,"[39] the diplomat wrote,

> Unlike the days when coordination among Western powers aligned behind the United States was absolutely essential ... today broad international

coordination is not always compatible with the Japan–US alliance, no matter how fundamental both of them may be in shaping Japan's foreign policy. This incompatibility was inherent in the question of whether or not Japan should support the US- and UK-led military action against Iraq, because that action did not enjoy the full consent of the international community.[40]

He observed further, "In the context of their [US–Japan] bilateral alliance, it is difficult to imagine Japan and the United States taking divergent approaches in their basic security policies in situations such as the conflict in Iraq."[41] It should be noted that the Japanese government's decision to support the US military action in the absence of international consensus was met with strong disapproval among the Japanese public, who remained unconvinced that all peaceful means had been exhausted before the military action was taken. Japan's popular pacifism, the geographical distance between Iraq and Japan, and Japanese unfamiliarity with the Iraqi situation were behind the public's reluctance to endorse the US-led military attack on Iraq. The Japanese government's alliance realism vis-à-vis the United States had trumped the wisdom of the Japanese people. Realism had priority over soft power.

The passage of the Law Concerning Special Measure on Humanitarian and Reconstruction Assistance in Iraq in July 2003 enabled Japan to dispatch SDF teams to Iraq. In this action Japan wanted to establish a visible SDF personnel presence as part of its humanitarian assistance and post-conflict reconstruction aid. Although legal constraints limited what the SDF could do in Iraq, it did allow Japan to demonstrate a very important part of its soft power. The self-imposed limitations were a product of Japan's pacifism, which had been and continues to be an important part of the Japanese people's postwar identity. A key question was whether the local populations in Iraq saw the Japanese presence in that light. Or, did they view it as part of the US-led occupation of Iraq? Another important question was whether SDF personnel in Samawa could stay out of harm's way, for the death or serious injury of a Japanese soldier would have seriously undercut domestic support for Japan's current policy in Iraq. For all intents and purposes the Japanese SDF mission in Iraq was successful. By the spring of 2007, Japan had withdrawn all but an Air SDF mission stationed in Kuwait to provide transportation support for the US troops in Iraq. However, with the Iraq war spiraling out of control and mounting domestic calls in the United States for American withdrawal from what had become a civil war, the impact of the Japanese mission in Iraq remains uncertain at best.[42]

How will Japan's struggle to balance its hard power and soft power approaches to national security affect its alliance with the United States? The bilateral alliance is likely to be able to withstand the complications noted above, but Japan will not be able to fully employ its soft power if the alliance constrains Japan's ability to cooperate with its Asian neighbors.

The leaders in Tokyo and Washington are agreed on the mutuality of political and strategic interests that the alliance represents. Furthermore, there is strong public support in both countries for maintaining their alliance. In Japan, for example, over 75 percent of the public today believe that the bilateral security treaty is contributing to their peace and security, and this favorable assessment has been steadily growing over the last decade.[43] On the US side as well, there is overwhelming support for maintaining the bilateral alliance.[44] A 2006 public opinion survey in Japan and the United States revealed that over 65 percent of Japanese and 75 percent of American respondents believed the US–Japan security treaty served to maintain the stability of the Asia-Pacific region. Also, over 70 percent of respondents in both countries believed the United States would militarily aid Japan should Japan come under a military attack by another country.[45]

Japan's alliance with the United States has long complicated its relations with China. The United States views China increasingly as a challenger to its dominant position in Asia-Pacific and as a possible threat to US interests in the region. To the extent that Japan shares this view, Japan will continue to restructure and modernize its military capabilities to complement the anticipated changes in the US force structure in the region. Some observers in Japan believe that indeed China is the most important source of change in the balance of power in Northeast Asia and may be the most serious source of instability. A former Japanese diplomat asserted that a strengthened US–Japan alliance is essential to contain the destabilizing effect of China's growing power and deter its possible military action against Taiwan, which he considered to be the most serious conflict scenario in the region.[46] He advocated a constitutional revision, establishment of security and crisis management systems, and a re-redefinition of the alliance with the United States.[47] On the last point, he proposed that the bilateral security treaty should be revised so that each country may undertake action against a threat to the peace and stability of Asia-Pacific.[48] If followed, these steps would dramatically alter the nature of Japanese security policy, seriously straining Japan's relations with China.

Indeed, in early 2005, Japan took a step closer to the US position on the Taiwan issue by openly acknowledging the issue as a security concern. On February 19, US Secretary of State Condoleezza Rice and Secretary of Defense Donald Rumsfeld met with their Japanese counterparts, Minister of Foreign Affairs Machimura Nobutaka and Minister of State for Defense and Director-General of the Defense Agency Ono Yoshinori in Washington, D.C. and issued a joint statement. It observed that the ministers agreed that "persistent challenges continue to create unpredictability and uncertainty" and that "modernization of military capabilities in the region also requires attention,"[49] a thinly veiled reference to China's growing power. The ministers listed a series of "common strategic objectives." Although they referred to the "development of a cooperative relationship with China" as one of the objectives, they also included the "peaceful resolution of the Taiwan issue through dialogue and encouragement of China to improve transparency of its military affairs." China's response was immediate and firm. On February 21, the official New China News Agency quoted China's Foreign Ministry as saying China "resolutely opposes the United States and Japan in issuing any bilateral document concerning China's Taiwan, which meddles in the internal affairs of China, and hurts China's sovereignty."[50]

A month earlier the Japanese government had approved a new National Defense Program Outline (NDPO), which identified North Korea and China as security threats. On North Korea, the document stated, "[M]ilitary moves, such as the deployment and the proliferation of weapons of mass destruction and ballistic missiles, are a serious destabilizing factor in the security of the region." It also noted that China was "promoting nuclear and missile capabilities and the modernization of its navy and air forces, as well as expanding the scope of its activities in the ocean" and stated that "it will be necessary to keep an eye on developments from now on."[51]

North Korean threat and Japan's tilt toward hard power

The August 1998 North Korean launch of a Taepodong missile over Japan exposed Japan's vulnerability to its menacing neighbor. Immediately following the North Korean action, Tokyo imposed a package of sanctions against Pyongyang. The Japanese people began to have serious concerns about their nation's security, which they had believed was more or less guaranteed by the United States through the security alliance between the two countries. Even though the Japanese had been disturbed by the 1993–94 nuclear crisis in North Korea, they did not see it as an immediate threat to their security. When that crisis was resolved by the Agreed Framework between Pyongyang and Washington, the Japanese people felt reassured that the United States, their trustworthy ally, was able to find a diplomatic solution to the nuclear problem. However, the Japanese government viewed North Korea's missile threat serious enough to warrant a decision to proceed with its cooperation with the United States in the research, development, and eventual deployment of ballistic missile defenses (BMD), despite the enormous cost it would entail and the uncertainty about its technological feasibility.

The Japanese were further alarmed in 2002 when the international community learned that North Korea had been cheating on its pledge not to proceed with their nuclear weapons program. Pyongyang then declared it was withdrawing from the Nuclear Nonproliferation Treaty (NPT) and kicked out the International Atomic Energy Agency (IAEA) inspectors, who had been monitoring the Yongbyon nuclear facilities under the NPT inspections regime. The Japanese concern deepened as it became public knowledge that their entire country was now within range of North Korea's medium-range ballistic missiles. As if to vindicate the Japanese fears, North Korea in July 2006 test-fired a series of ballistic missiles, including an unsuccessful launch of a long-range missile that, if successfully developed, could reach US homelands.

In the wake of the missile launches, the Japanese public's concern about the North Korean threat intensified.[52]

Then came the North Korean nuclear test on October 9, 2006. Japan immediately turned to hard power. Japan actively campaigned for international sanctions against North Korea and the international community responded, with the United Nations Security Council passing a resolution condemning the North Korean action, calling on member states to impose economic sanctions against North Korea, and demanding North Korea to return to the NPT. Just a few days earlier, when North Korea announced it would conduct a nuclear test "in the future," Japan swiftly prepared a draft statement for the President of the UN Security Council for consideration among the Council members. With the cooperation of the United States and, somewhat surprisingly, that of China, the President of the Security Council, who happened to be a Japanese diplomat, was able to issue a statement on October 7 urging North Korea to refrain from a nuclear test and warning of serious consequences if Pyongyang did not heed the international call. Additionally, Tokyo threatened it would expand its sanctions against Pyongyang and urged other countries to join Tokyo in imposing sanctions against Pyongyang if North Korea went ahead with a nuclear test.

In February 2007, the Six-Party Talks, involving North and South Korea, China, Russia, the United States, and Japan, produced an agreement that North Korea would suspend its nuclear weapons program and eventually dismantle its nuclear facilities in exchange for international economic aid and diplomatic normalization with the United States and Japan. To implement the series of actions pledged in the agreement, the six parties set up five working groups: (1) on the denuclearization of the Korean Peninsula; (2) on US–North Korea diplomatic normalization; (3) on Japan–North Korea diplomatic normalization; (4) on economic and energy cooperation; and (5) on the establishment of a mechanism for Northeast Asian peace and security. During the first phase, the United States is to commence talks with North Korea for diplomatic normalization and remove Pyongyang from its list of state sponsors of terrorism and lift economic sanctions, but these actions require Congressional approval, which is far from being assured. Strong skepticism remained in Japan about the impact of the agreement on the denuclearization of North Korea.[53] Japan also is to resume diplomatic normalization talks with North Korea, but, as I will discuss later, some formidable obstacles stand in the way.

The six parties were scheduled to meet and discuss the implementation of the second phase of the February commitments, which was much more difficult than the first phase. During this still ongoing phase, North Korea is supposed to declare its entire nuclear program and disable all existing nuclear facilities in exchange for 950,000 tons of heavy oil.

Until the February agreement is completely implemented, we are in effect living with a nuclear North Korea, and there is no guarantee that the agreement will be fully implemented. For the reasons I will outline later, there is little incentive for North Korea to totally and irreversibly abandon its nuclear weapons development program, and it will use every excuse and tactic to postpone dismantlement of its nuclear program, including the uranium enrichment program, which it once said it had but has since denied.

There was a long delay in the implementation of the first phase of the agreement, to freeze the North Korean nuclear facilities at Yongbyon in exchange for 50,000 tons of heavy oil – due to a delay in the resolution of the North Korean money-laundering issue involving the Banco Delta Asia in Macao. After the $25 million that had been frozen under a US demand was released to North Korea via a Russian bank and the first South Korean shipment of heavy fuel oil reached North Korea, Pyongyang announced on July 14 that it had shut down its nuclear reactor at Yongbyon and also accepted a team of IAEA inspectors to inspect Yongbyon nuclear facilities.

In the meantime, the Japanese government announced a series of sanctions: a ban on the entry of North Korean ships into Japanese ports, a ban on imports from North Korea, and a prohibition of North Korean nationals' entry into Japan.[54] North Korean exports to Japan amounted to about 14 billion yen (nearly $123 million) in 2005.[55] Thus, a total ban on this trade was not insignificant for the struggling economy of North Korea, particularly in combination with the sanctions the United States had instituted against the North Korean money laundering through Banco Delta Asia in Macao. Doubts remained, however, on the effectiveness of these sanctions, particularly if China and South Korea remained reluctant to punish North Korea.[56]

Against this background, many people inside Japan and outside have raised a question which, for most Japanese people, had been unthinkable until very recently. The question is: would Japan go nuclear?

Several prominent figures, including former Prime Minister Nakasone Yasuhiro, have called for a debate about a nuclear option for Japan. Ichirō Ozawa, leader of the opposition Democratic Party of Japan (DPJ), advocated Japanese nuclear armament in 2002.[57] In a speech at Waseda University in 2002, Abe Shinzō stated that the possession of a nuclear weapon in and of itself is not necessarily against the Japanese constitution.[58] It is far from certain, however, that the Japanese leadership is ready to push for nuclear armament. In fact, in the wake of the North Korean nuclear test, Prime Minister Abe stated that Japan would continue with its policy, known as the "three non-nuclear principles," not to possess, not to develop, and not to introduce nuclear weapons in Japan.

There is no doubt that North Korea's nuclear test will give plenty of ammunition to the pro-defense and nationalist advocates in Japan to push for a nuclear option. Their cause would gather momentum if North Korea should proceed to conduct another nuclear test or if evidence emerged suggesting that the North Koreans were close to being able to mount nuclear warheads on their ballistic missiles. North Korea is suspected of having several more nuclear weapons.[59] North Korea's stock of separated plutonium is enough for about 4 to 13 nuclear weapons.[60]

The Japanese public's anti-North Korean sentiment reached an all-time high due to the issue of the North Korean abduction of Japanese citizens in the 1970s and 1980s. The nuclear test added fuel to the fire, with 62 percent of those polled in an October 2006 *Asahi Shimbun* survey favoring sanctions over dialogue with North Korea as the preferable approach to be taken by the international community.[61] The cities of Hiroshima, Nagasaki, and numerous other provincial and municipal assemblies all over the country have passed resolutions condemning the North Korean nuclear test.[62] The anti-North Korean sentiment does not readily translate into support for a nuclear option for Japan. A *Yomiuri Shimbun* opinion poll in November 2006 showed that nearly 80 percent of the respondents supported the non-nuclear principles. The same survey indicated that a substantial portion of the public (slightly over 50 percent) was opposed to even discussing a nuclear option for Japan.[63]

To go nuclear or not to go nuclear? That is essentially a political question, not a technological question. It is widely known that Japan has the technical capability and enough plutonium to manufacture a number of nuclear weapons. Speculations abound as to how long it would take for Japan to develop nuclear weapons if it made the political decision to go ahead. Some observers suggest it would take several months, while others say it would take just several weeks.[64]

Would the development of nuclear weapons violate Article 9 of the Japanese constitution? The so-called peace clause has served as the foundation of the nation's policy of limiting its military capabilities to only those required for "strictly defensive" purposes. Accordingly, Japan has eschewed development or possession of offensive weapons, such as aircraft carriers, strategic bombers, and nuclear weapons. Although, as I noted earlier, Abe believed it would be within Japan's right to self-defense to possess nuclear weapons, most Japanese would be opposed to the nuclear option for Japan.

If Japan were to develop nuclear weapons, it would have to withdraw from the NPT. Since joining the NPT regime in 1976, Japan has been a faithful participant in and an active advocate of the treaty.[65] Despite the less-than-ideal record of the international regime in preventing the proliferation of nuclear weapons, the NPT has been one of the most important pillars of Japan's policy. If Japan were to quit the regime, it would mean a complete turn-around in its policy. It would likely spell the collapse of the international regime and, as well, a political fallout for which Japan would be ill prepared to take responsibility.

Another formidable obstacle to Japan's nuclear armament relates to the nation's alliance with the United States. The nuclear option for Japan would indicate that Japan no longer considered the US nuclear umbrella adequate to meet its security needs. This would undermine the very foundation of trust between the allies and send a disturbing signal to Japan's neighbors, particularly China, that the US–Japan security treaty no longer served as "a cork in the bottle", i.e., as a cap on Japan's independent armament.

Another important question is at what point the Japanese government will scrap its current interpretation of Article 9 as prohibiting the exercise of "collective self-defense", that is the right to militarily defend an ally of Japan. This right is sanctioned by the international community, as expressly stated in the UN Charter. Therefore, if the Japanese government decided to change its interpretation of Article 9, Japan would be able to exercise its right to collective self-defense, and do so not only in combined military action with the United States, but also under a UN-sanctioned peacekeeping or military operation against a country or countries threatening the international peace and security, under Chapter VII of the UN Charter. What would constitute such a threat? In this author's view, another nuclear test by North Korea would be a prime candidate, as would the development of nuclear-tipped ballistic missiles in North Korea.

Short of going nuclear or reinterpreting the constitution, Japan is moving aggressively to strengthen its defense capabilities and its alliance cooperation with the United States. It is proceeding with the missile defense cooperation with the United States.[66] Patriot missiles have arrived in Okinawa. The United States has begun partial operation of the PAC-3 system at the US Kadena Air Base and the Kadena Ammunition Storage Area, deploying twenty-four missiles in the system. The Japanese government has also decided to move up the plan to deploy SM3 missiles as part of its missile defense system, originally slated for deployment toward the end of 2007 to mid-2007.[67] More recently, Tokyo has expressed an interest in purchasing F22A's, the most advanced fighter aircraft in the US arsenal.

As Pyongyang, Seoul, Beijing, Moscow, Washington, and Tokyo resumed their six-way talks to discuss the second phase of the February 2007 agreement, Japan's policy toward North Korea emerged as a possible obstacle. At the heart of the problem is Tokyo's linking of the abduction issue to diplomatic normalization with Pyongyang. Without a resolution to the kidnapping issue Japan would not normalize relations with the North, and without normalization, there would be no direct economic aid from Tokyo that Pyongyang badly needs and on which the other parties to the Six-Party Talks are counting. Additionally, as we noted earlier, Japan–North Korea normalization is a part of the Six-Party agreement and if this element does not move forward, it could delay nuclear disarmament in North Korea.

Some observers in Japan are concerned that Japan may become isolated if it continues to insist on linking normalization, economic aid, and abduction issues. There is also concern among some Japanese that the recent softening of US policy toward North Korea, evident in the start of direct bilateral talks between Washington and Pyongyang, might compromise Japan's interest in resolving the abduction issue and preventing North Korea's nuclear armament. Some Japanese are hinting that the United States might be able to live with a nuclear North Korea, whereas for Japan a nuclear North Korea would be a matter of national survival. Apparently to allay these fears and prevent a breakdown of the Six-Party process, the United States, South Korea, and

China have all emphasized to North Korea the importance of responding to Japan's demand on the abduction issue.[68]

Conclusion

The preceding analysis has shown that before the North Korean nuclear and missile development began to raise serious national concerns in Japan, the Japanese intellectual community, including diplomats and foreign-security policy analysts, had embraced soft power as a useful concept and a feasible instrument of national policy. Japanese foreign and security policy communities believed that their nation was favorably endowed with some elements of soft power. Their interest in soft power reflected their pride in their nation's economic achievements and their favorable assessment of Japan's postwar policy of avoiding entanglement in foreign conflicts and rejection of the use of military force for settling international disputes. However, even before the North Korean nuclear test, there appeared some serious complications and constraints on the use of soft power as an instrument of national security policy in Japan. Also, the growing uncertainty in Japan's security environment and the dramatic change in US strategic policy post-9/11 had prompted the Japanese security policy establishment to seek further expansion of their nation's hard power, including defense capabilities.

North Korea's missile and nuclear weapons development has tipped the balance clearly toward greater reliance on hard power. The quick pace at which the Japanese government marshaled international support for the anti-North Korean statement of the UN Security Council President following the North Korean announcement of a planned nuclear test and for the sanctions resolution of the Security Council in the wake of the actual nuclear text on October 9, 2006 marked the beginning of a more aggressive Japanese security policy based on the exercise of hard power. Japan's willingness to go beyond the scope of the Security Council resolution by instituting its own sanctions on North Korea is further evidence of this trend.

Beyond the North Korean situation, Japan's relations with its Asian neighbors, particularly China, will be of profound importance to where Japan's hard power and soft power will meet. Japan's relations with China will be affected in important ways by the state of Sino-US relations. Simply put, stable and predictable relations between China and the United States will help Japan shore up its soft power. On the contrary, strained Sino-US relations and strategic saber rattling between the Asian powers will encourage the advocates of hard power in Japanese national security policy.

It is ironic that the North Korean nuclear test came in the middle of Japan's effort to improve its relations with China and South Korea. By holding the bilateral summits with Prime Minister Abe and Fukuda, both the Chinese and the South Korean leaders appeared willing to give Japan time to demonstrate that it was serious about improving the bilateral relations. The nationalist political agenda in Japan will be closely watched by the leadership in Beijing. For China, the Yasukuni Shrine issue is a litmus test of Japan's seriousness. South Korea will also remain focused on how genuine Japan is in its effort to overcome the legacy of history and forge a future-oriented relation with them.

"Soft power" as an instrument of national policy has its limitations and in the post-9/11 world, Japan is being pressed to shore up its hard power, particularly in the context of its alliance with the United States. This presents the nation with a difficult task of finding an optimum balance between hard power and soft power in its security policy. How to translate its substantial and growing soft power potential into international influence while expanding its hard power-based cooperation with the United States remains a formidable task facing Japan in the early years of the twenty-first century.

Notes

1 For an insightful discussion of the postwar pacifism and its role in the development of Japan's security policy, see Thomas U. Berger, "Norms, Identity, and National Security in Germany and Japan," in Peter J. Katzenstein, ed., *The Culture of National Security: Norms and Identity in World Politics,* New York: Columbia University Press, 1996, pp. 317–56.
2 Bōei Mondai Kondankai, "Nihon no anzenhoshō to bōeiryoku no arikata: 21-seiki e mukete no tenbō" (The Desirable Direction of Japan's Security and Defense Capabilities: A Vision for the 21st Century), August 12, 1996.
3 The Council on Security and Defense Capabilities, "The Council on Security and Defense Capabilities Report: Japan's Visions for Future Security and Defense Capabilities," October 2004, p. 1.
4 Ibid., p. 5.
5 Ibid.
6 Ibid., p. 9.
7 Ibid., p. 7.
8 Ibid., pp. 9–10.
9 "Statement by H.E. Mr. Oshima Kenzo, Permanent Representative of Japan at the Meeting of the General Assembly on Informal Consultations on the Report of the High-Level Panel on Threats, Challenges, and Change and on the United Nations Millennium Project 2005 Report," February 22, 2004, accessed at the Japanese Ministry of Foreign Affairs website, http://www.mofa.go.jp/announce/speech/un2005/un0502-4.html (February 24, 2005), p. 3.
10 Tsuneo Akaha, "Japan: A Passive Partner in the Promotion of Democracy," in Peter J. Schraeder, ed., *Exporting Democracy: Rhetoric vs. Reality,* Boulder, CO: Lynne Rienner, 2002, pp. 89–107.
11 "Japan's Medium-Term Policy on Official Development Assistance" (Provisional Translation), Government of Japan, February 4, 2005, p. 1.
12 Ibid., pp. 4–18.
13 "Speech by Minister for Foreign Affairs Taro Aso—ODA: Sympathy Is Not Merely for Others' Sake," January 19, 2006, <http://www.mofa.go.jp/announce/fm/aso/speech0601-2.html> (accessed May 9, 2005).
14 Ibid.
15 For a succinct review of Japan's ODA performance since the 1970s, see Katada Saori, "Toward A Mature Aid Donor: Fifty Years of Japanese ODA and the Challenges Ahead," *Asia Program Special Report,* No. 128, Woodrow Wilson International Center for Scholars, Washington, D.C., February 2005, pp. 6–12.

16 The amount represented 16.20 percent of Japan's total bilateral ODA. Iraq was the second largest recipient of Japanese bilateral ODA, with $662 million (11.1% of total). Japanese Foreign Ministry, *Japan's Official Development Assistance Whitepaper, 2005, Statistical Appendix*. <http://www.mofa.go.jp/policy/oda/white/2005/ODA2005/html/siryo/index.htm> (accessed May 9, 2005).
17 Japanese Foreign Ministry, "Overview of Official Development Assistance (ODA) to China," June 2005, <http://www.mofa.go.jp/policy/oda/region/e_asia/china/index.html> (accessed May 9, 2005).
18 A Chinese participant in the New Japan–China 21st Century Committee complained that there were many Japanese media reports that the Chinese did not appreciate Japanese ODA even though China had repeatedly expressed its gratitude to Japan for its economic assistance. Japanese Ministry of Foreign Affairs, "Shin Nitchū yūkō nijuisseiki iinkan dai-nikai kaigō, gaiyō" (The New Japan–China 21st Century Committee, 2nd Meeting, Summary) http://www.mofa.go.jp/mofaj/area/china/jc_yuko21/gaiyo_0409.html (accessed May 9, 2005).
19 Nishida Tsuneo, "Ima Nihon ga chokumensuru anzenhoshōjō no kadai to gaikō no yakuwari" (The Security Issues Facing Japan Today and the Role of Diplomacy), *Gaikō Forum* (Japanese), No. 198 (January 2005), p. 22.
20 Ogura Kazuo, "Japan's New Cultural Diplomacy: A Personal View with a Historical Perspective," *International House of Japan Bulletin*, Vol. 24, No. 2 (Autumn 2004), p. 16.
21 Kawada, p. 23.
22 Ibid.
23 "Reluctant realism" is an apt expression used by Michael Green to capture the essence of Japanese gradual shift from postwar idealism and pacifism toward political realism accompanied by acceptance of a greater share of the burden for the nation's own defense and responsibility for international peace and security. See Michael Green, *Japan's Reluctant Realism*, New York: Palgrave, 2001. A nationwide opinion survey by the Asahi Shimbun in the spring of 2006 indicated that a majority of respondents recognized the need to revise the Japanese constitution. *Asahi Shimbun*, May 4, 2006, http://www.asahi.com/english/Herald-asahi/TKY200605040088.html (accessed May 8, 2006).
24 For the concept of "normal state," see Ichirō Ozawa, Louisa Rubinfein (trans.), *Blueprint for a New Japan: The Rethinking of a Nation*, Tokyo: Kodansha, 1994.
25 Kawada Tsukasa, "A New Internationalism," *Gaikō Forum*, Vol. 4, No. 2 (Summer 2004), p. 21.
26 For example, see Kuriyama Shoichi, "Wakai – Nihon gaikō no kadai (jo)" (Reconciliation – An Issue in Japanese Diplomacy), *Gaikō Forum*, January 2006, pp. 8–15.
27 See, for example, Qi Jing Ying, "Bridging The Gap: Riots Were About More Than Nationalism," *Asahi Shimbun*, April 24, 2006.
28 Zhen is also Chairman of the Academic Committee of the Central Party School of the Chinese Communist Party. *Asahi Shimbun*, April 26, 2006, http://www.asahi.com/strategy/0426b1.html (accessed May 5, 2006).
29 *Asahi Shimbun*, April 25, 2006, http://www.asahi.com/strategy/0425b1.html (accessed May 5, 2006).
30 *Yomiuri Online*, September 10, 2007, http://www.yomiuri.co.jp/feature/fe6100/koumoku/20060910.htm (accessed April 24, 2007).
31 Over 70 percent of South Korean respondents to a July 2006 public opinion poll believed that Japan did not deserve the coveted position. *Yomiuri Online*, September 10, 2006, http://www.yomiuri.co.jp/feature/fe6100/koumoku/20060910.htm (accessed April 24, 2007).
32 Abe Shinzo, *Utsukushii kuni e* (For a Beautiful Country [Japan]), Tokyo: Bungei Shunjū, 2006, pp. 69–70.

33 Abe Shinzō and Okazaki Hisahiko, *Kono kuni wo mamoru ketsui* (Determination to Defend This Country [Japan]), Tokyo: Fusōsha, 2006, pp. 70–71; also Abe, p. 70–71.
34 Asō Tarō, *Totetsumonai Nihon* (An Exuberant Japan), Tokyo: Shinchosha, 2007.
35 Cabinet Office, "Gaikō ni kansuru seron chōsa" (Public Opinion Survey on Diplomacy), October 2005, http://www8.cao.go.jp/survey/h17/h17-gaikou/images/z05.gif (accessed May 9, 2006).
36 Japanese Ministry of Foreign Affairs, "Nitchu kankei ni kansuru seron chōsa" (Public Opinion Survey on Japanese–Chinese Relations), March 2002, <http://www.mofa.go.jp/mofaj/area/china/yoron.html> (accessed May 9, 2006).
37 *Yomiuri Online*, August 11, 2006, http://www.yomiuri.co.jp/feature/fe6100/koumoku/20060811.htm (accessed April 24, 2007).
38 *Asahi Shimbun*, May 5, 2006, http://www.asahi.com/politics/update/0505/001.html (accessed May 8, 2006).
39 Tanaka Hitoshi, "Toward Active Diplomacy for the Japan-US Alliance and International Coordination," *Gaikō Forum*, Vol. 4, No. 1 (Spring 2004), p. 6.
40 Ibid., p. 7.
41 Ibid.
42 A public opinion survey in seven Asian nations in July 2006 showed that over 55 percent of South Korean respondents disapproved the dispatch of Japanese SDF overseas for humanitarian purposes, while a little over 40 percent approved it. Even among the Japanese respondents the opinion was deeply divided, with a 50-percent support and a 45-percent disapproval. *Yomiuri Online*, September 10, 2006, http://www.yomiuri.co.jp/feature/fe6100/koumoku/20060910.htm (accessed April 24, 2007).
43 Japanese Cabinet Office, "Jieitai-bōeimondai ni kansuru seron chōsa" (Opinion Survey on the Self-Defense Forces and Defense Issues), February 2006, http://www8.cao.go.jp/survey/h17/h17-bouei/index.html (accessed May 9, 2006).
44 A 2004 public opinion poll conducted by the Japanese Foreign Ministry indicated that well over 80 percent of American respondents thought the bilateral security pact should be maintained. Japanese Ministry of Foreign Affairs, "Beikoku ni okeru tainichi seron chōsa" (Public Opinion Survey in the United States on Japan," August 2005, <http://www.mofa.go.jp/mofaj/area/usa/yoron05/gaiyo.html> (accessed May 10, 2006).
45 *Yomiuri Online*, August 11, 2006, http://www.yomiuri.co.jp/feature/fe6100/koumoku/20060811.htm (accessed April 24, 2007).
46 Morimoto Satoshi, "Nichibei dōmei no shōrai to Nihon no sentaku: dōmei sai-saiteigi to sono yoken" (The Future of the Japan–US Alliance and Japan's Choice: Re-redefinition of the Alliance and Its Requirements), *Gaikō Forum* (Japanese), No. 198 (January 2005), pp. 45–46.
47 The first post-Cold War redefinition of the alliance took place in 1996; hence Morimoto's call for "re-redefinition".
48 Morimoto, p. 46. The existing treaty calls on the parties to take action when an armed attack takes place against either party within the area under Japanese jurisdiction and the sides consider it as a threat against their peace and security. So, Morimoto's proposal would change the justification for military action under the bilateral treaty from a direct attack on either party to a threat against the peace and security of the entire Asia-Pacific region.
49 "Joint Statement: US-Japan Security Consultative Committee," Washington, D.C., February 19, 2003, accessed at the Japanese Foreign Ministry website, http://www.mofa.go.jp/region/n-america/us/security/scc/joint0502.html (February 21, 2005).
50 Jim Yardley and Keith Bradsher, "China Accuses US and Japan of Interfering on Taiwan," *New York Times*, February 21, 2005, http://query.nytimes.com/mem/tnt.html?tntget = 2005/02/21/international/asia/21china.html (February 21, 2005).
51 Quoted in "Cabinet Approves New National Defense Program Outline and Mid-term Defense Program," Foreign Press Center, Japan website, December 13, 2004, http://www.fpcj.jp/e/shiryo/jb/0458.html (February 21, 2005).

52 A *Yomiuri Shimbun* public opinion survey in July revealed that over 75 percent of respondents strengthened their view that North Korea was a threat and over 90 percent supported the sanctions the Japanese government announced in retaliation against the missile launches. *Yomiuri Online*, July 11, 2006, http://www.yomiuri.co.jp/feature/fe6100/koumoku/2006071101.htm (accessed April 24, 2007).

53 For example, a *Yomiuri Shimbun* opinion survey on February 17–18, 2007 revealed that slightly less than 80 percent of the respondents had little or no expectation that the Six-Party agreement would lead to the resolution of the North Korean nuclear issue. *Yomiuri Online*, February 21, 2007, http://www.yomiuri.co.jp/feature/fe6100/koumoku/20070221.htm (accessed April 24, 2007).

54 North Korean residents of Japan are exempted from the ban on North Korean nationals' entry into Japan. (*Asahi Shimbun*, October 12, 2006, http://www.asahi.com/politics/update/1011/011.html (accessed October 13, 2006); Nakata Hiroko, "Japan makes it official: more punitive steps kick in," *Japan Times*, October 14, 2006, http://search.japantimes.co.jp/mail/nn20061014a1.html (accessed October 14, 2006); *Yomiuri Online*, October 11, 2006, http://www.yomiuri.co.jp/politics/news/20061011it14.htm (accessed October 12, 2006).

55 Nakata, "Japan makes it official."

56 It was believed that China supplied more than 70 percent of North Korea's fuel and 40 percent of its food. *Los Angeles Times*, October 10, 2006, http://www.latimes.com/news/nationworld/world/la-10106unnorkor.0.6277974.story?coll=la-home-headlines (accessed October 11, 2006).

57 Eric Johnston, "North's Gambit May Weaken Japanese Taboo on Nuke Talk," *Japan Times*, October 12, 2006, http://search.japantimes.co.jp/mail/nn20061012a4.html (accessed October 12, 2006).

58 The *Asahi Shimbun* ("Abe Shinzo: Japan's Policy Remains: No Nuclear Weapons" [06/12/02]) reported that the Deputy Chief Cabinet Secretary Abe Shinzō denied in an interview with the *Asahi Shimbun* a report carried by a weekly magazine that he is an advocate of Japan's nuclear armament. A lecture that Abe gave at Waseda University was believed to have led to the controversial remarks by Chief Cabinet Secretary Fukuda Yasuo that the Constitution does not ban Japan from possessing nuclear weapons. Asked if it is true that Abe said the possession of nuclear weapons and intercontinental ballistic missiles (ICBMs) does not violate the Constitution, he said,

> I presented the government view and explanations given by Prime Minister Kishi Nobusuke in 1959 and 1960 to the effect that the Constitution does not necessarily ban the possession of nuclear weapons as long as they are kept to a minimum and are tactical. As a matter of course, I said, "Japan stands by the three non-nuclear principles and possession of nuclear weapons is impossible." Just to make sure, I also later affirmed once again that policy debate and interpretation of the Constitution are not the same.

He also said,

> I never said the possession of ICBM does not violate the Constitution. In answer to the question, 'What about ICBMs?' I tried to explain that it is OK to shoot down ICBMs above Japan but it is unacceptable for Japan to fire ICBMs to attack others. But my answer was cut off halfway. Later, I clearly said that ICBMs that attack cities are unacceptable.
> (http://www.nautilus.org/archives/napsnet/dr/0206/JUN19.html [accessed October 12, 2006])

59 *Asahi Shimbun*, October 9, 2006, http://www.asahi.com/international/update/1009/009.html (accessed October 11, 2006).

60 David Albright and Paul Brannan, "The North Korean Plutonium Stock Mid-2006," Institute for Science and International Security (ISIS) June 26, 2006, http://www.isis-online.org/publications/dprk/dprkplutonium.pdf (accessed November 4, 2006).
61 *Asahi Shimbun*, October 10, 2006, http://www.asahi.com/politics/update/1010/011.html (accessed October 10, 2006).
62 *Yomiuri Online*, October 11, 2006, http://www.yomiuri.co.jp/politics/news/20061011a02.htm (accessed October 11, 2006).
63 *Yomiuri Online*, November 21, 2006, http://www.yomiuri.co.jp/feature/fe6100/koumoku/20061121.htm (accessed April 24, 2007).
64 Eric Prideaux and Akemi Nakamura, "Japan May Not Want to Go Nuclear but It's No Technical Hurdle: Analysts," *Japan Times*, October 11, 2006, http://search.japantimes.co.jp/cqi-bin/nn20061011a4.html (accessed October 12, 2006).
65 The latest expression of Japan's support of the NPT is its draft resolution on nuclear disarmament the nation submitted to the UN General Assembly in October. The draft specifically expressed deep concern over North Korea's announcement that it planned to conduct a nuclear test. U.N. General Assembly First Committee, October 10, 2006 (GA/DIS/3324), http://www.un.org/News/Press/docs/2006/gadis3324.doc.htm (accessed October 13, 2006).
66 There is now substantial, if not overwhelming support for the deployment of missile defenses. For example, over 60 percent of the respondents to an August 2006 *Yomiuri Shimbun* poll stated they thought Japan and the United States should cooperate to hasten the deployment of a missile defense system that could destroy enemy missiles. *Yomiuri Online*, August 13, 2006, http://www.yomiuri.co.jp/feature/fe6100/koumoku/20060813.htm (accessed April 24, 2007).
67 *Asahi Shimbun*, October 12, 2006, http://www.asahi.com/politics/update/1012/007.html (accessed October 12, 2006).
68 *Asahi Shimbun*, July 12, 2007, http://www.asahi.com/international/update/0711/TKY200707110539.html (accessed July 11, 2007).

Part II
Major powers' views of Japan and the US–Japan alliance

4 Chinese perspectives on the US–Japan alliance

Jing-dong Yuan

Introduction

This chapter examines China's changing perspectives on the evolving US–Japan alliance. Four considerations inform and influence how Beijing views the alliance and how its continued consolidation and expansion affects Chinese threat perceptions and national security interests. The first relates to the alliance's scope and missions. While Beijing tacitly acknowledges the alliance's role in restraining Japanese remilitarization and its narrow *Cold War* mission of defending Japan, it now sees the alliance as an instrument for sustaining US hegemony in the region. Second, China is increasingly worried that Tokyo is using the US–Japan alliance as a convenient cover for it to pursue a "normal state" status, including constitutional reform, the strengthening of the Japanese Self-Defense Forces (JSDF), and the dispatch of JSDF personnel overseas. A politically ambitious, militarily assertive, and economically revitalized Japan poses a serious challenge to China, given the historical past and the territorial disputes between the two countries.

Third, Beijing has serious concerns about the alliance's stated interest in interfering in what China considers its domestic affairs, namely, the Taiwan issue. The February 2005 US–Japan 2+2 statement and the bilateral action plans toward closer military integration, together with US military redeployment in Japan and the region, reinforce such concerns. Finally, Chinese perspectives on the US–Japan alliance must also be put in the broader contexts of the evolving and complex Sino-US and Sino-Japanese relations. Stable and better relationships could mitigate the potentially negative impact of the alliance on China while tension and deterioration of ties heighten Beijing's concerns and worse case assessments.

The next section describes the changing relationships between China and the United States, and between China and Japan. This is followed by a discussion of Chinese perspectives on the US–Japan alliance. Beijing sees a number of worrying trends that pose potential and real threats to Chinese security interests. These include the changing scope and missions of the alliance, as it now becomes a vehicle for sustaining and strengthening US primacy in the region; US–Japan cooperation in missile defense development and deployment; and the alliance's more explicit intent to interfere in the Taiwan issue. The chapter then looks at how, from Beijing's perspectives, the US–Japan alliance provides the convenient justification for Japan to modify its postwar security policy and embraces hard power as the path to a normal-state status, with serious consequences for China's security interests. The chapter then looks at how Beijing assesses the impacts of the US–Japan alliance and the growing Taipei–Tokyo ties on its fundamental interest in preventing Taiwanese independence and achieving the long-term goal of national unification. Finally, the chapter examines Beijing's responses to the challenges posed by the strengthening US–Japan alliance through the use of soft power, especially as it is applied to its relationships with Southeast Asian countries, in what analysts have described as a "charm offensive" to enhance its influence and promote its interests in the region.

Power shift: the changing China–Japan–US relations

Sino-US relations have lately been described as at their best since President Richard Nixon's historic 1972 visit to China. Not only are the two countries in close cooperation on issues ranging from the global war on terrorism to North Korea's nuclear weapons programs, Beijing and Washington have also sought with varying degrees of success to manage disputes that used to irritate bilateral relations. There are regular bilateral security, arms control, and defense consultations, enabling the two sides to discuss their differences through dialogue. At least three parallel channels have been developed. In August 2005, a semi-annual Strategic Dialogue (or what Washington prefers to call Senior Dialogue) was launched in Beijing. In December 2006, a Strategic Economic Dialogue, which would be held twice a year, was also initiated. The two dialogues cover a broad range of bilateral, regional, and global security and economic issues. In July 2009, the two dialogues merged into a high-profile Strategic and Economic Dialogue (S&ED), with its first held in Washington on July 27–28. And since the late 1990s, bilateral Defense Consultative Talks have been held annually.[1]

Such an amicable atmosphere is due in no small measure to Washington's post-9-11 efforts to seek major power cooperation in its campaign against international terrorism and to Beijing's desire to maintain a stable relationship with the United States.[2] However, there remain fundamental differences between the two countries over military alliances, the role of nuclear deterrence, missile defenses, use of force, and the resolution of the Taiwan issue. Indeed, both countries continue to view each other's objectives and policies with caution and even suspicion, and neither has let down its guard against future contingencies.[3]

Sino-US relations did not begin well with the incoming Bush administration. During the 2000 presidential campaigns, candidate George W. Bush described China as a potential strategic competitor for the United States. The new administration vowed to strengthen its alliance relationships and downplayed the importance of China in its Asia policy. Then came the April

2001 EP-3 incident and the largest US arms sales to Taiwan in a decade were proposed by the administration. The bilateral relationship dropped to the lowest point. The September 11 terrorist attacks on the United States provided a "strategic window of opportunity" for rebuilding the tattered Sino-US relationship. The Bush administration's international focus shifted to the war against terrorism, not to the possibility of a future challenge from China, at least not for now.[4] Chinese analysts recognize that the challenge for Beijing would be to maximize the benefits and minimize other negative impacts such as growing US global military presence and preemptive use of force.[5] For the time being at least, common interests in fighting global terrorism and defusing the North Korean nuclear crisis have seen Beijing and Washington enjoying a stable relationship.

At the same time, China and the US have different objectives and priorities for post-Cold War Asia. For Beijing, the end of the Cold War has removed a major threat (from the Soviet Union) to its territorial security and a peaceful environment is conducive to its goals of economic development and building the country into a stable, prosperous regional power. Economic prosperity, political stability, and national unity have become major goals for Chinese foreign policy. The United States, on the other hand, seeks to maintain its primacy in the region through its alliance systems and by strengthening its military presence. Washington is determined to prevent any power from rising to challenge its interests and looks to emerging democratization and continued marketization as the pillars to ensure regional stability.[6]

Sino-Japanese relations have also undergone significant changes since the end of the Cold War. While over the last three decades since the diplomatic normalization between the two Asian powers in 1972, extensive ties have been developed in the areas of trade, investment, and cultural exchanges, deep-rooted suspicions and distrust continue to hamper a full-fledged development of bilateral relations on a solid foundation.[7] There are many reasons behind the ambivalence of the bilateral relationship, including the legacy of the past, territorial disputes, the two countries' divergent views of the role of military alliances and suspicions in both capitals concerning each other's intentions and military buildup. Indeed, a serious challenge to the leadership in both capitals is the fact that never in history have both countries been powerful at the same time and this raises the question of how this potential competition for regional primacy is to be managed. This particular problem is vividly captured by Funabashi Yōichi, Japan's most widely read foreign affairs commentator: "A rising China will induce critical, painful, and psychologically difficult strategic adjustments in Japan's foreign policy. Japan has not known a wealthy, powerful, confident, internationalist China since its modernization in the Meiji era."[8]

Over the last decade, there has been a gradual shift in Japan's China policy from "a faith in commercial realism to a reluctant liberalism." This has been due in large measure to the generational change of politicians and fractured Japanese domestic politics since the early 1990s. At the same time, Tokyo is

Table 4.1 Power indicators: the United States, China, and Japan

Key Indicators	2004	2005	2006
GDP with PPP ($bn)			
United States	11,750.0	12,360.0	13,130.0 (13,210.0*)
China	7,262.0	8,859.0	10,000.0 (2,512.0*)
Japan	3,745.0	4,018.0	4,220.0 (4,911.0*)
GDP Growth Rate (%)			
United States	4.4	3.5	3.2
China	9.1	9.9	10.5
Japan	2.9	2.7	2.8
Trade Volume ($bn)			
United States	2,271.0	2,654.5	2,893.0 (est)
China	1,135.5	1,384.0	1,751.9 (est)
Japan	940.6	1,001.6	1,114.0 (est)
Foreign Exchange Reserve ($bn)			
United States			69.19
China			1,300.00
Japan			864.70
Defense Budget ($bn)			
Unites States	490.0	423.0	535.9
China	25.0	29.0	44.9
Japan	45.1	44.7	41.1
Population (m)			
United States	293.0	295.7	301.14**
China	1,298.8	1,306.3	1,321.8
Japan	127.3	127.4	127.4

Sources: The National Bureau for Asian Research, *Strategic Asia* database; The International Institute for Strategic Studies, *The Military Balance*, selected years; Central Intelligence Agency, *The World Factbook 2007*, https://www.cia.gov/cia/publications/factbook/index.html.

Notes: * Statistics based on official exchange rates. ** Estimates as of July 2007.

becoming increasingly wary of an emerging China with growing economic and military power.[9] The liberal assumption that China would become more accommodating as it became prosperous, hence necessitating a strategy of economic engagement through the Official Development Assistance (ODA) programs, trade and investment, has been gradually eroded as tensions began to build up between the two countries in the 1990s.[10] Public opinion polls conducted in Japan also depict a downward trend in Japanese attitudes toward China driven by uncertainty of that country's role in Asia Pacific and its impact on Japan.[11]

Four sets of factors have influenced the current state of Sino-Japanese relations. The first is the power shift in East Asia. Over the last two decades, the Chinese economy has registered an average of over 9 percent per annum in growth while that of Japan stagnated during the entire 1990s and it is only

Chinese perspectives on the US–Japan alliance

in recent years that the Japanese economy has shown signs of recovery. China's dramatic economic growth means that the gap between China and Japan has shrunk; at the same time, China's influence in the regional economy is expanding, especially in Southeast Asia where Japan used to hold a commanding position. Japan is beginning to feel that China may take over as the lead economy in Asia in the near future. There has begun an implicit competition for a regional leadership role if not hegemony or dominance.[12]

The second factor is that the end of the Cold War and the disintegration of the Soviet Union have removed the link that used to bind the two countries in common purposes—checking Soviet expansionism and threats to East Asian security. Third, there have been generational changes in the two countries' leadership. Older-generation Chinese and Japanese statesmen such as Zhou Enlai, Liao Chengzhi, Tanaka Kakuei, Ōhira Masayoshi, and Fukuda Takeo expended tremendous efforts at building such a bridge after China and Japan established diplomatic relations. Indeed, in the 1980s, Chinese and Japanese leaders Hu Yaobang and Nakasone Yasuhiro strongly promoted Chinese–Japanese youth exchanges. The current leaderships in both countries are held hostage to growing nationalism and are highly sensitive to public opinions at home. This creates enormous difficulties for policy flexibility and compromises.[13]

Finally, the international security environment has also changed. The nature and scope of the US–Japan alliance have changed, prompted by the United States' post-Cold War strategies of maintaining its primacy in the region and globally, and preparing for contingencies that require alliance systems to be more adaptable. The US–Japan alliance now goes beyond the original bilateral security arrangement to take on more regional and even global missions. This, to Beijing, poses the threat of infringing on Chinese sovereignty in particular where Taiwan is concerned.

These four sets of factors combined confront Beijing and Tokyo on how best to manage their bilateral relationship. Managed well, this could be turned into a realistic relationship based on mutual respect, acceptance, and power parity; it could also degenerate into open rivalry, fanned by history, nationalism, and the pursuit of dominance in the region.[14]

US–Japan security alliance: end of silver lining?

The changing US–China and China–Japan relations influence how Beijing views the US–Japan alliance. Chinese attitudes toward the US–Japan alliance have over the years shifted from outright condemnation and opposition in the 1960s, to tacit acquiescence in the 1970s and 1980s, to growing criticisms since the end of the Cold War. In the past the alliance in Beijing's eyes served a useful purpose of keeping Tokyo from seeking remilitarization and at worst it was more narrowly focused on defending Japan.[15] It is now increasingly viewed as a security threat as Chinese reticence is increasingly being replaced with publicly expressed concerns over the new direction of the alliance and especially the expanded role for Japan in the revised defense guidelines.[16] For

Beijing, the fundamental issue is whether the alliance will continue to serve as a useful means to keep a lid on Japan's military ambition or become a launching pad for Japan to justify the expansion of the JSDF's role in support of much-expanded alliance missions beyond the defense of Japan.[17]

China reacted negatively to the April 1996 US–Japan Joint Declaration on Security and the September 1997 US–Japanese Defense Cooperation Guidelines. The continued presence of US military forces in the region, and resilient US–Japan security ties at a time of much reduced security threats to the alliance only caused the Chinese to wonder about their true intentions and the implications for its own security.[18] First, Beijing considers the revitalized US–Japan military alliance as part of Washington's containment strategy against China. After all, the alliance was established during the Cold War years with the defense of Japanese territories as its primary mission. Now the Cold War has ended, the very raison d'être – protecting Japan from Soviet aggression – no longer exists. The alliance therefore reflects Cold War mentality and actually justifies and facilitates continued US military presence in the region with unmistakably clear objectives: to maintain American primacy and hedge against China as a potential future adversary.

Second, the revitalized alliance allows JSDF to take on additional responsibilities. Beijing has become increasingly worried that a more assertive Japan actively involved in the region's security affairs and seeking to be a "normal" power will emerge as a result.[19] The new defense guidelines in effect give Japan the green light to go beyond the original exclusive self-defense to a collective defense function, therefore providing justification for Japan to intervene in regional security affairs.[20] As Beijing sees it, Japan already has one of the largest defense budgets in the world and has a reasonably sized (given its peace constitution) but the best-equipped military in the region. In addition, Japan's industrial and technological wherewithal will provide it with the infrastructure and ready resources should it decide to become a military great power on short notice, including the acquisition of nuclear weapons.[21]

Chinese analysts point out that the revised defense guidelines provided a convenient pretext for Japan to undertake remilitarization away from the original "defense of Japan only" principles: that Japan would keep minimum self-defense forces; would not possess offensive weapons and power projection capabilities; would not launch preemptive military strikes and only engage in limited self-defense actions when directly attacked; the defense parameters would be surrounding air space, sea, and maritime territories; and Japan would refrain from extending intelligence gathering to others' air space. However, these have all been bypassed or modified.[22] Japan in particular needs the alliance to both address the concerns of Asian countries and enhance its military capabilities. The nature and parameters of the alliance and Japan's role within it have all undergone transformation: from a uni-dimensional US defense of Japan to joint security cooperation where Japan will play a greater supportive role. With regard to regional areas, the reinforced alliance is no longer confined only to the defense of Japan but extended to the

Asia-Pacific region. Japan is steadily moving toward becoming a normal country, having "breached" a number of previously established constraints—overseas dispatch of JSDF personnel, collective defense, and the use of force in self-defense.[23] And finally, the guidelines could be interpreted as extending the alliance's defense perimeter to include the Taiwan Strait. China is understandably concerned with the possible intervention of the US–Japan alliance in what it regards as its internal affairs and re-unification plans.[24]

US plan to develop and deploy theater missile defenses (TMD) in Northeast Asia and Japanese participation in their research and development programs raise another concern for China. While Beijing tacitly acknowledges the role of TMD in protecting US forward deployed troops from missile attacks, it objects to advanced TMD systems that could extend to Taiwan. In an interview with *Defense News* in February 1999, Sha Zukang, then director-general of the arms control and disarmament department in the Chinese Ministry of Foreign Affairs, said that China was not concerned about "what we call genuine TMD." Instead,

> what China is opposed to is the development, deployment, and proliferation of antimissile systems with potential strategic defense capabilities in the name of TMD that violate the letter and spirit of the Anti-Ballistic Missile Treaty and go beyond the legitimate self-defense needs of relevant countries.[25]

Chinese analysts point to a number of strategic motivations behind planned US TMD in East Asia. One is to continue its predominant position in the region. TMD deployment would enable the US to undertake military operations with little inhibition. Second, the US seeks to exploit allies' technical expertise and funding in missile defense R&D and increase allies' reliance on US security guarantees and protection by integrating their defense systems into US East Asian security architecture. Third, the decision to move forward with missile defenses demonstrates the rise of conservative forces in the US government dominating the defense and foreign policy agenda and leaning toward a more confrontational posture toward China and North Korea. Fourth, the US defense industrial complex could benefit from government contracts, and further consolidate its lead in the Revolution in Military Affairs (RMA). TMD, in particular its high-tier systems, such as the Theater High Altitude Area Defense (THAAD) and the Navy Theater Wide Defense (NTWD), could also form as a component of US overall ballistic missile defense (BMD) systems. And finally, TMD would force Beijing to increase defense expenditure, hence delaying China's economic development.[26]

In the context of Northeast Asian security, China has expressed a number of specific concerns over the development and deployment of theatre missile defense.[27] First, the Chinese see TMD as yet another deliberate step that the United States has taken to strengthen the US–Japan military alliance, hence enhancing its offensive as well as defensive capabilities. It has been reported that the US may begin deploying the TMD system as early as 2008.[28] In addition, China contends that TMD research and development encourage and provide a pretext for Japanese remilitarization. Beijing's suspicion of a post-Cold War assertive Japan is reinforced by Tokyo's reticence about its past history; its ambiguity regarding its defense perimeter; its potent and potential military capabilities; and its potential involvement in a Taiwan crisis.[29]

Third, Japan's participation in theater missile defense is also drawing increasing attention from China and elsewhere in Asia. Indeed, Beijing closely watches Japan's participation in TMD R&D.[30] Since the North Korean Taepodong missile launch in August 1998 and recent nuclear developments, Japan has speeded up steps to acquire and deploy missile defense systems in addition to its ongoing research and development collaboration with the United States.[31] According to Chinese estimates, the Japanese Self-Defense Agency began in 1995 a covert study of TMD technical feasibility and had spent 550 million yen between 1995 and 1998. In September 1998, the United States and Japan formally signed the MOU on joint TMD research and development.[32] Given Japan's current naval capability (it already possesses six *Aegis* destroyers and has the strongest naval fleet among Asian countries), TMD systems would equip Japan with both offensive and defensive capabilities. Soon after the passage of the UN resolution on maintaining the ABM Treaty in November 1999, the deputy director-general of Japan's Self-Defense Agency told reporters that it would not affect US–Japan joint research on TMD.[33]

Overall, since the Bush administration came into office, the US–Japan military alliance has been strengthened in a number of areas: the institution of a new military consultative mechanism to discuss long-term military strategies; closer cooperation in missile defense research and development; and the development of military contingency plans; and greater Japanese SDF rear area support for US military operations and defense of US military installations in Japan. Burden sharing aside, Washington wants to develop a special relationship with Tokyo similar to its relationship with London. The Armitage Report of 2000 argued that Japan's role in the alliance should be elevated, to follow the pattern of the special US–U.K. relationship. The Armitage/Nye Report of 2007 reaffirmed this position, calling for even closer security and military cooperation between the two allies.[34] The US is also encouraging Japan to discard the ban on undertaking collective defense functions so that it could fulfill its obligations such as rear area support as specified in the new defense guidelines. This is in line with the overall reorientation of the US strategic focus from Europe to Asia.[35]

Alliance and Japan's pursuit of hard power

One of the major concerns that Beijing has over the strengthening of the US–Japan alliance is whether Tokyo would take advantage of the requirements of the alliance, coupled with the changing international security environment, especially in the aftermath of the September 11 terrorist attacks, to introduce changes and amend the peace constitution so that Japan would legitimately rearm and step out of the postwar constitutional limitation on overseas deployment of military personnel. The 2001 National Defense Program Outline (NDPO) earmarked 25.16 trillion yen for the next five years, making Japan the second largest military spender after the United States and first in the world on a per soldier basis. Large allocations have been devoted to procuring major sea and air weapons systems and platforms.[36]

The 2004 Japanese Defense Guidelines introduced major changes, including expansion of the scope of national security interests from defense of Japan to global security. The latter in particular shifts the traditional emphasis from defense of Japan to abilities to respond to terrorism, ballistic missile threats, and proliferation of weapons of mass destruction, and to secure stability in regions critical to Japanese national interests. Second, Japan has undertaken measures to strengthen its defense capabilities through closer cooperation with the international community and allies, and self-help. Third, Tokyo is pursuing normal country status, including the right and ability to exercise collective defense and changes to the three nuclear principles and the arms export principles. Fourth, Japan is pursuing even closer coordination with the US strategic posture and expanding military interoperability. This includes building a more agile, flexible, multi-functional JSDF, shifting focus to areas spanning from the Middle East to East Asia, especially with respect to key sea lines of communication (SLOCs) vital to Japan's supplies of raw materials and resources. Lastly, the new defense guidelines pay greater attention to the growing threats from China and North Korea.[37]

In accordance with its new security policy and strategic orientation, Japan has undertaken to improve its military capabilities to meet new defense requirements and those of the alliance in the areas of interoperability, joint efforts in missile defense development, and greater rear area support of US and other allied operations. There has been a clear shift from the emphasis on cheque book diplomacy (official development assistance), to enhancement of its military and intelligence gathering capabilities, including power projection capabilities. In addition, the defense parameter has also been expanded to accord with the shift in objectives from the prevention of direct attack on Japan to active participation in the shaping of the international environment outside Japan's own territory.[38]

Chinese experts describe the 1990s in Japan as a "decade of conservative shift" in Japanese politics. Several pieces of legislation were passed in the decade and in years since, all in pursuit of normal country status. It was also the decade of "a leap forward" in defense policy, with the passage of the New Defense Guidelines of 1999. This was followed by the enactment of the special anti-terrorism bill in October 2001 and emergency measures bill in 2002. These bills have in effect resulted in three major breakthroughs: the first is the removal of geographic restrictions on overseas dispatches of JSDF personnel beyond the Far East and surrounding areas of Japan; the second is the right to use arms for self-defense and use of force; the third is the power of the Cabinet to dispatch SDF personnel overseas without prior parliamentary approval but only post-dispatch permission. Indeed, 9/11 provided the opportunity for Japan to take major strides in realizing its desire for normal country status, including the recent elevation of the JDA to the ministerial level.[39]

With regard to Japan's right to collective self-defense, two questions are especially important. One is whether Japan will render logistical support in the event of US involvement in a conflict with a third country not directly affecting Japanese interests. The second question is whether Japan would provide direct logistical support when allies close to Japan, including the United States, are under attack or involved in military conflicts. Either way, Japan will more than ever before get involved in participating in US-led military operations, including in the Taiwan Strait.[40]

Chinese analysts suspect that Tokyo may be seeking to acquire independent self-defense capabilities even as it strengthens its alliance with the United States. Whether or not Japan can achieve these objectives depends on how Washington handles the bilateral alliance that both serves as a cork in the bottle to prevent Japanese remilitarization and encourages Japan to play a more active role in regional and global contingencies.[41] Beijing is acutely attentive to the domestic debates on Japan's nuclear policy, Tokyo's intensifying efforts to move toward greater military integration with the US and missile defense deployments, and Japan's pursuit of greater autonomy in intelligence gathering, space capability, and potential relaxation of its arms export policy.

Nuclear debate

Perhaps the most serious concerns that Beijing has are those over Tokyo's potential reversal of its nuclear policy, especially the three non-nuclear principles—not to produce, not to use, and not to introduce nuclear weapons into Japan.[42] Chinese analyses focus on three sets of factors: (1) Japan's technical capabilities and material base for building nuclear weapons; (2) motivations for Tokyo to discard its non-nuclear principles and pursue the nuclear option; and (3) the obstacles, both domestic and international, to Japan's nuclear option, especially the role of the United States. In an article published in the *2006 Yearbook on International Arms Control and Disarmament*, three analysts from the Beijing Institute for Applied Physics and Computational Mathematics (IAPCM) carefully examine Japan's plutonium stockpiles and point out that while Tokyo in 1997 pledged to the International Atomic Energy Agency (IAEA) that it would not hold surplus plutonium, it had by the end of 2004 accumulated over 43 tons, enough for making 5,000 nuclear bombs. In addition, Japan is planning a new spent fuel reprocessing facility in Rokkasho-mura and will also introduce fast-breeder reactors.[43]

There is broad consensus among Chinese analysts that Japan has the necessary nuclear technologies, excessive quantities of plutonium potentially usable in making nuclear weapons, and computer techniques to simulate tests to derive relevant data for nuclear weapon designs, all of which would allow Japan to make nuclear weapons on very short notice.[44] One prominent Chinese Japan specialist points out that the current debate is based on a combination of factors: its desire to achieve greater independence of US control and to attain great power status, a growing emphasis on military power, fear of nuclear and missile threats in the region, as well as the rise of neighboring countries (such as China), and a revisionist approach to history.[45] Indeed, a number of Chinese analysts have suggested that North Korea's nuclear tests provide a convenient excuse and could prompt Japan to reconsider its options, including discarding its non-nuclear principles.[46] For stance, less than a week after the North Korean nuclear test, on October 15, 2006, Shoichi Nakagawa, Chairman of the ruling Liberal Democratic Party's (LDP's) policy research council, similarly suggested that Japan needed to discuss its nuclear options in response to North Korea's nuclear demonstration. He further argued that Japan's constitution did not prohibit the country from possessing nuclear weapons. Three days later, in a similar vein, Foreign Minister Taro Aso told a parliamentary committee that it was important to discuss the matter, which had long been considered off-limits.[47]

However, Chinese analysts also acknowledge that whether Japan will go nuclear will depend on several key factors: the US–Japan security alliance; the international environment; domestic developments; and Japan's strategic choice. Washington has strongly opposed any Japanese intention to acquire nuclear weapons and this will likely remain US policy. While the international nuclear nonproliferation regime has undergone significant strain over the last few years, the international community remains united in opposing further nuclear proliferation. Given Japan's reliance on overseas markets and resources, the consequences of its going nuclear would be very severe. Third, as Japan is the only country that has suffered nuclear attacks in the past, there is strong popular sentiment in Japan against acquiring nuclear weapons. Indeed, the Nakagawa Shōichi and Asō Tarō comments incurred immediate rebukes from the opposition parties and victims of nuclear bombs. Other LDP officials and Cabinet members, including the JDA Director General and the Chief Cabinet Secretary, expressed concerns over the more hawkish remarks of some diet members, considering them contradictory to Japan's domestic laws and international commitments and fearing that the remarks could send the wrong signals to other countries. The ultimate considerations would be if acquiring nuclear weapons, given the constraining factors listed above, would enhance Japan's security, and whether Tokyo remains confident in the US nuclear umbrella.[48]

The US attitude toward Japan's nuclear debates and its role in reining in Japanese nuclear ambitions are critical, according to Chinese analysts. Some Chinese reports describe Secretary Rice's trip to Japan right after the North Korean October 9, 2006 nuclear test as an effort to shore up Tokyo's confidence in the US nuclear umbrella as well as to secure pledges from the new Abe administration that Japan will not renege on its three non-nuclear principles. Asō pledged to Rice that Japan has no intention to acquire nuclear weapons, saying that Japan "is absolutely not considering" building a nuclear arsenal in response to the North Korean nuclear test. This has not passed unnoticed by the Chinese media, which implicitly gives a positive spin on the US nuclear umbrella as well as the US–Japan security alliance and their role in keeping a lid on Japan's nuclear aspirations. Chinese analysts note that the US military presence in Japan serves an important function in its strategy for East Asian security, that is, to allow Japan to play a more active role in regional security but at the same time to control Japan. In this context, a nuclear Japan will be detrimental to fundamental US strategic interests.[49]

Missile defense deployment and US–Japan military integration

Chinese analyses are focused most sharply on the implications of the ever-closer cooperation between Tokyo and Washington, as the two countries knit together missile defense networks and move toward the implementation of the United States–Japan Roadmap for Realignment to achieve closer operational coordination and improved interoperability between the US Forces in Japan and the JSDF. Chinese commentators and analysts have particularly scrutinized four sets of developments, because they are seen as reflecting not only Tokyo's sense of urgency in quickly deploying a working missile defense system, but also a carefully thought-out, long-term plan to transform Japan into a "normal" country by gradually chipping away at the constitutional and political obstacles to acquiring the customary trappings of military power.

Japan's Defense Agency (JDA; now Ministry of Defense) requested 219 billion yen (US$1.87 billion) in funding for missile defense for the 2007 fiscal year, an increase of more than 56 percent over existing spending. The money would be used for purchases and early deployment of both the land-based US Patriot Advanced Capability 3 (PAC-3) anti-missile system and sea-based US Standard Missile-3 interceptors. It would also be used for improvements in Japan's early warning systems, such as electronic surveillance and the introduction of unmanned aerial vehicles (UAVs). The sale to Japan of Standard-3 defensive missiles, worth $458 million, would be the first such US sales to a foreign country.[50]

A second major development being watched by Chinese analysts is the acceleration of Japan's missile defense deployment schedule, apparently prompted by North Korea's July 2006 missile tests. The United States and Japan had originally set 2011 as the year for deployment in Japan of defenses against theater-range missiles, although both countries also viewed 2006 as a critical year for aggressively advancing the joint missile defense efforts. Japan for its part decided to move its originally scheduled deployment of March 2008 ahead by several months to the end of 2007, with the initial units of PAC-3 interceptors slated for deployment at four bases around the Tokyo metropolitan area.[51]

The Chinese media have also focused on the US–Japan agreement to develop a joint center for missile defense intelligence gathering and information sharing, seeing it as an important new military link between the two countries. Once operational, it will become a core component of the US–Japan missile defense system, which will monitor and evaluate events such as future

North Korean missile tests. When Pyongyang conducted its missile tests in July 2006, the United States and Japan gathered and processed information independently, with little coordination.[52]

Finally, Japan's more active participation in US-led military exercises, such as the June 2006 "RIMPAC" exercise, has also come under the microscope of the Chinese media. In the maneuvers, the Japanese Maritime SDF destroyer *Kirishima*, equipped with the Aegis radar system, took part in a missile intercept by tracking the target missile. Meanwhile, the Chinese media have noted, Washington and Tokyo have moved closer toward development of unified military commands.[53]

For the time being, Beijing is less concerned with the effectiveness of these emerging missile defense capabilities than with what these developments indicate about the future direction of Japan's security policy and US strategic intentions.[54] Chinese analysts point out Japan has undergone major changes in its attitude toward missile defense, from a hesitant and lukewarm initial reception of the concept, to active participation and enthusiastic support.[55] And they conclude that Japan's core interest in speeding up missile defense deployment is directed toward China, despite Japan's claims that its objective is to defend itself against North Korea. Chinese commentators argue that Japan plans to deploy defenses on Okinawa, which would make them particularly useful in protecting the JSDF in their operations in the East China Sea, the Taiwan Strait, and the Diaoyu/Senkaku Island area, with China obviously in mind.[56]

Japan's interest in accelerated missile defense deployments, its growing integration into related US military operations, and its active participation with the United States in joint research and development activities raise serious questions, Chinese analysts say, about Tokyo's intentions. They see these actions as encouraging Japanese reconsideration of the long-standing restrictive interpretation of Article 9 of its constitution, which limits its right to collective self-defense, and as leading Tokyo to reexamine its ban on arms transfers to states that could become involved in regional conflicts, in particular missile-defense related technology transfers to the United States (which could potentially become involved in a conflict in the Taiwan Strait). Most troubling for Chinese analysts, it appears, is the possibility that Tokyo's missile defense activities could set the stage for Japanese involvement in a future conflict over Taiwan, with Japan's sea-based missile defense systems deployed to support Taiwan's defenses, as a counter to Chinese short-range missiles.[57]

Japan's military space policy

Chinese analysts are also paying growing attention to Japanese efforts to develop independent intelligence gathering and surveillance capabilities. Over the years, and in particular since the North Korean launch of the Taepodong missile, Tokyo has determined to acquire its own capacities in this critical area. On January 24, 2006, a Japanese Advanced Land Observation Satellite named *Earth* was launched by an H-2A rocket from the Yoshinobu space complex on

Tanegashima Island. A second satellite, a multi-purpose satellite MTSAT-2, was scheduled for launch in mid-February but malfunction forced its postponement. While Tokyo emphasizes that the satellite is for earth observation, Chinese media consider it a spy satellite, citing US news sources that the satellite carries three high-performance sensors that can detect objects of 2.5 m diameter size on earth and have surveillance over the entire Asia-Pacific 24 hours a day.[58]

Japan launched its first two spy satellites in March 2003, prompted largely by the need to have its own intelligence in response to growing concerns over North Korea's nuclear and missile developments. Indeed, according to one Chinese news source, a satellite intelligence center was set up within the Japanese Self-Defense Agency in early 2001, the first step in the country's intelligence satellite program.[59] Despite (and perhaps because of) the setback in late 2003 when two satellites broke up soon after launch and again in 2005 when launch had to be postponed, Tokyo is determined to acquire advance intelligence gathering and reconnaissance capabilities via satellites by allocating over 61 billion yen (approx $520 million) in a special appropriation in 2006 for satellite launches and maintenance.[60]

Chinese analyses focus on three worrisome trends in Japanese space policy as reflected in its satellite endeavors. The first is the Japanese government's effort to modify existing regulations governing peaceful use of space, which were promulgated in 1969. Chinese observers note that a special committee on space policy was established within the ruling Liberal Democratic Party to reassess current policy and make recommendations to the government for any necessary changes. The 1969 regulation prohibits JSDF from developing or using satellites for missile defense early warning purposes. One major change will be to modify the current, complete ban on the military use of space to allow so-called "non-offensive military use." The change would explicitly authorize the JSDF to develop and use space assets for defensive military purposes, including intelligence gathering.[61]

The second trend of concern to Chinese observers is Japan's interest in developing its military space capabilities to enable the SDF to expand the number and scope of their missions overseas. Japan is contemplating revising Article 9 of its constitution to pave the way, Chinese analysts believe, for rebuilding itself into a major military power. This would require Japan to develop its own military surveillance, reconnaissance, intelligence gathering, and communications capabilities. At the moment, Japan depends on the United States for support in these areas, due to Japan's lack of indigenous capabilities.[62]

Third, to Chinese observers, Japan's satellite program is strongly driven by Tokyo's vision of a future rivalry with the region's other major powers, China in particular. While Tokyo justifies its program as driven by concerns over North Korea's nuclear and missile developments, in reality it is seeking to develop counters to China, through satellites that can gather military intelligence using high-resolution imagery and early warning of missile launches, in support of Japan's emerging missile defense systems. Over time, Japan seeks to enhance its capabilities in the areas of force projection, precision positioning and targeting, and military surveillance.[63]

In May 2008, the Japanese parliament passed the Basic Space Law, replacing a 1969 law that confined Japanese space activities to strictly peaceful purposes. The new law would allow the government to develop "non-offensive" satellites to provide national security. The law also calls for the establishment of a "Strategic Space Development Headquarters" to be headed by the prime minister and subsequently a minister was appointed to lead a new ministry within the cabinet. Chinese media reports comment that this move would pave the way for Japan's military use of space and expand the authority of the Ministry of Defense.[64]

The alliance and the Taiwan issue

One important consideration when Beijing assesses the US–Japan alliance is how Washington and Tokyo approach their relationships with Taipei and to what extent such ties are consistently kept at the unofficial level as they both claim to uphold the "one China" policy and how the alliance's expanded missions can alter the security environment in the Taiwan Strait.

Despite the emerging common interests held by both Beijing and Washington in maintaining the status quo in the Taiwan Strait, the long-term stability of Sino-US relations will continue to be affected by their handling of cross-Strait relations.[65] The United States, while annoyed by Taipei's reckless and provocative postures when Chen Shui-bian was in power (2000–2008), which could disrupt the status quo and create unnecessary tension at a time when American capabilities are tied elsewhere, is nonetheless sympathetic to Taiwan's democratization and bound by the Taiwan Relations Act regarding the latter's defense. Within the United States, there are forces that are strongly pro-Taiwan and call for American support of the independence course.[66] Indeed, even as Washington was admonishing Taipei's referendum plan, officials in the Bush administration were also sending signals of reassurance to Chen's government.[67] The controversial re-election of Chen Shui-bian for a second term and a 2004 US announcement of the planned sale of long-range early-warning radar worth up to $1.78 billion to Taiwan reinforce this concern.[68]

Indeed, long-term US–Taiwan policy remains the most serious security concern for Beijing.[69] Since the mid-1990s, three trends have been particularly worrisome for the Chinese leadership. The first has been the US deviation in recent years from the "One China" principle set forth in the three Sino-US joint communiqués. Since the Bush administration came into office in 2001, the US has steadily upgraded its supposedly unofficial ties with Taiwan. The Bush administration also granted more transit stops to Chen Shui-bian (Taiwan's president) and Annette Lu (vice-president) than the Clinton administration.[70]

The second trend is the continuing US military sales to Taiwan, which are seen by China as contravening the spirit of the August 17, 1982 Sino-US Communiqué.[71] Over the last two decades since the communiqué was issued, the United States has provided Taiwan with a full spectrum of military equipment, including: F-16 air superiority fighters, Knox-class frigates, Kidd-class destroyers, anti-submarine S-2T, E-2T Hawkeye airborne early-warning aircraft, long-range early-warning radars, attack helicopters, Patriot-derived Modified Air Defense Systems, and Hawk and Chaparral ground-based air defense systems, among others. The US Department of Defense also runs exchange programs with Taiwan on C4I, air defense, and anti-submarine warfare (ASW).[72] In April, 2001, President Bush caused quite a stir when he gave the controversial "whatever it takes" comment in reference to the defense of Taiwan. Washington became increasingly frustrated as Taipei failed to push through a special defense procurement budget to purchase US arms approved by the Bush administration in 2001.[73]

Third and finally, there have been incessant congressional efforts at not only enhancing the US–Taiwan relationship, but also expanding it to include closer security cooperation.[74] The 1999 Taiwan Security Enhancement Act, which was passed in the House by a landslide, would require even closer defense cooperation between the United States and Taiwan in the areas of defense planning, threat analysis, training programs, and missile defense systems, all of which have been strongly opposed by Beijing.[75] The establishment of the Taiwan Caucuses in the US Senate and the House of Representatives is another major development. US–Taiwan military ties have moved beyond weapons sales to more frequent and official contacts. According to Chinese analysis, in recent years thousands of Taiwanese military officers from the rank of major and up to that of colonel have been sent to the United States for training.[76] The US position on the Taiwan issue over the next five years will be a critical element in both the stability of the Taiwan Strait and Sino-US relations.

Sino-Japanese relations experienced their most serious deterioration during 2001–6 when Koizumi Junichirō was the Japanese Prime Minister.[77] Three issues in particular strained the bilateral relationship: the historical legacy and growing nationalism in both countries; territorial disputes, especially in the context of Beijing–Tokyo competition for energy resources; and Japan–Taiwan ties, which Beijing views as blatant interference in its domestic affairs. These developments are taking place at a time when both countries are experiencing generational change in leadership transition against the dynamics of changing domestic politics and the external environment.

One worrying trend, as far as Beijing views it, is the growing ties between Taipei and Tokyo. While Japan officially has maintained its "one-China" policy ever since 1972, its position on Taiwan's legal status has always been ambivalent. When the Tanaka administration decided to normalize diplomatic relations with Beijing in September 1972, there was strong opposition from the pro-Taiwan Diet members and politicians within the ruling Liberal Democratic Party (LDP). In 1973, the LDP established a Diet Members' Japan–Taiwan Dialogue Group to maintain contact with Taiwanese politicians. The Democratic Party of Japan (DPJ) in 1997 also established a Diet Members' Japan–Taiwan Friendship

Association. The language that the Japanese government adopted in 1972 was that it "fully understands and respects" the position of the Chinese Government that "Taiwan is an inalienable part of the territory of the People's Republic of China."[78] During the so-called "golden era" of bilateral relations (1972–89), Beijing and Tokyo were able to handle the sensitive issue of Taiwan's status and the Japanese government for the most part kept Tokyo–Taipei ties strictly at the non-official level.

However, three developments have changed this relatively stable status. First, Taiwan has evolved from the KMT-controlled authoritarian regime to an emerging democracy. Especially since the former Taiwanese President Lee Teng-hui succeeded Chiang Ching-kuo in 1988, the process of democratization has picked up speed. In 1996, the first open presidential election was held in Taiwan and in 2000, the formerly banned Democratic Progress Party (DPP) won the election and its leader Chen Shui-bian took office as President.[79] He was re-elected in the controversial 2004 election. Lee Teng-hui in particular took the initiative to push for more and high-level official interactions between Taiwanese and Japanese officials. There is growing affinity between Taiwan and Japan as a result. Second, China's 1995–96 missile exercises in the Taiwan Strait raised the specter that Beijing might resort to the use of force to resolve the Taiwan issue. Given Taiwan's strategic location on the path of Japan's sea lines of communication (SLOC), Tokyo has become more attentive to cross-Strait developments and hence its interest in expanding interaction with Taiwan.[80]

Third, the East Asian regional economic transformation and growing economic interdependence have promoted greater Japanese–Taiwanese economic ties in that Japanese companies seek to use Taiwanese businessmen's connections to the mainland to gain access to markets and establish manufacturing facilities. Indeed, recent years have seen growing official interactions between Taipei and Tokyo, although these remain largely between legislators rather than high-level officials. While Tokyo still denies visas to Taiwanese officials holding the following five posts—president, vice-president, premier, defense and foreign ministers—it is reported that Taiwan's National Security Advisor regularly visits Japan for consultation with Japanese officials, although such reports have not been confirmed.[81] For instance, between January 2005 and July 2006, there were cumulatively more than 350 visits to Taiwan by Japanese Diet members in 21 groups. Japan has also granted Taiwanese visa waivers—against Beijing's strong protest and opposition—to facilitate tourism. In 2006, 1.2 million Taiwanese visited Japan while 1.18 million Japanese tourists visited Taiwan.[82] Indeed, it has been widely agreed that except for the official recognition, relations between Taipei and Tokyo have never been better even though Japan maintains that its "one-China" policy has not changed.[83]

As a result of these developments, the Japan–Taiwan ties have grown in recent years.[84] The Japanese government has granted visas to former Taiwanese President Lee Teng-hui to travel to Japan for medical treatment; former

Japanese Prime Minister Mori has visited Taiwan; and Chen Shui-bian even called on Tokyo to adopt a Japanese version of Taiwan Relations Act. Prime Minister Abe Shinzō's book during his 2006 campaign for the LDP leadership, *Changing Japan into a Beautiful Country*, called for closer cooperation between Japan and other democracies in the Asia-Pacific region, the so-called coalition of maritime democracies that presumably could also include Taiwan. Japan has publicly supported Taiwan's full membership in the World Health Organization, a move that even Washington has so far not undertaken.[85] Beijing therefore has plenty of reasons to be worried about the growing Tokyo-Taipei ties. Indeed, Chinese analysts suggest that Taiwan is more critical to Japan than it is to the United States. For the latter, Taiwan is merely a pawn in Washington's overall strategic game and a useful one for slowing down China's rise. But for Japan, the future of Taiwan could affect Japan's claims to the Diaoyu/Senkaku Islands, its sea lines of communication, and the East China Sea. Therefore, there are even more incentives for Tokyo to obstruct the eventual unification between the mainland and Taiwan.[86]

In harmony with growing activities related to the readiness of the US–Japan military alliance to intervene in case of contingencies in the Taiwan Strait, Japan has redeployed its SDF ground units to Okinawa and discussed constructing equipment depots on the island for US troops. The United States also plans to station F-22 fighter wings on Okinawa, which could arrive at the Taiwan Strait within 20 minutes.[87] More worrisome, from the Chinese perspective, is the increasing military-to-military contacts between Japan and Taiwan. In August 2006, Taiwan's Army Commander Hu Zengpu reportedly went to Japan to observe JSDF exercises under the guise of a "tourist excursion". The Japanese side declined comments on such reports. That controversy aside, it is known that Japan–Taiwan military ties have steadily expanded. According to Chinese analysts, four indicators mark this trend. First, retired high-ranking military officers are now appointed to key positions in the quasi-official representative offices in each other's capital. Second, retired Japanese military officers are increasingly engaged in bilateral security dialogues with serving Taiwanese military personnel. Third, there is even discussion of retired JSDF personnel serving as advisors to the Taiwanese armed forces on military exercises. And finally, there is reported intelligence-sharing between the two. With the introduction of PAC missile defense systems to Taiwan, it can be expected that more intelligence sharing could take place among Washington, Tokyo, and Taipei.[88]

China has clearly been upset by and deeply concerned with the alliance's potential impact on the Taiwan issue. The most significant development was the joint statement released at the end of the February 2005 US–Japan Security Consultative Committee meeting (the so-called 2+2 meeting), as noted earlier.

The joint statement drew strong condemnation from the Chinese government. Its Foreign Ministry spokesman stated at a press conference that Beijing "resolutely opposes the United States and Japan in issuing any bilateral document concerning China's Taiwan, which meddles in the internal affairs of China, and hurts China's sovereignty."[89] The Chinese objection came on the heels of its protest in response to Director of US Central Intelligence Agency Porter Goss's testimony at the Senate Select Committee on Intelligence where he pointed out that "Beijing's military modernization and military buildup is tilting the balance of power in the Taiwan Strait" and that "improved Chinese military capabilities threaten U.S. forces in the region."[90] Defense Secretary Donald Rumsfeld, at another hearing before the Senate Armed Services Committee, also voiced concerns over the expansion of China's navy.[91]

What alarmed Beijing is what it views as the unprecedented clarity with which Washington and Tokyo define their security interests and perimeter in the region, which now clearly includes the Taiwan Strait. This is seen by China as exceeding the scope of a bilateral security pact. While the US–Japan joint statement also made a point to "develop a cooperative relationship with China, welcoming the country to play a responsible and constructive role regionally as well as globally," the spat and misunderstanding that could arise from this development could cast a shadow over the long-term stability in the region.[92]

Soft vs. hard power: Beijing's balancing act

Chinese responses to the strengthening of the US–Japan alliance and the security challenges it faces in Asia have alternated between the pursuit of hard power and the exercise of soft power. China's own experiences with pursuing hard vs. soft balancing in this new but uncertain international security environment have informed Beijing's policymakers as well as security analysts that realpolitik hard power may not be as effective as soft power in helping to achieve China's ultimate objectives of peace and development, and national unification. In the early 1990s, China's assertiveness in territorial disputes with its Southeast Asian neighbors and its display of coercive pressure over Taiwan actually undermined its long-term security interests as the latter moved closer to the United States and echoed the "China threat" rhetoric. Indeed, the strengthening of the US–Japan alliance followed the 1995–96 Chinese missile exercises in the Taiwan Strait, which provided the rationale for the alliance's revitalization as both Washington and Tokyo reacted to the growing Chinese power.[93]

Indeed, China's pursuit of hard power capabilities in the early 1990s—calls for building up the country's comprehensive national power, growing defense spending and major weapons procurement – coupled with Beijing's strong anti-hegemony rhetoric and its demonstrated reluctance in endorsing and participating in regional security dialogues, turned out to be rather counterproductive. Since then, Beijing has made significant policy adjustments to better serve its national interests, namely, to preserve a peaceful external environment for continued economic developments, to assure neighboring countries and the world of its peaceful intentions even as its power increases, and to find ways to soft balance the United States or at least to foil Washington's efforts in weakening, encircling, or containing China. What evolved is the so-called new security concept in that Beijing not only endorses multilateral security dialogues, it actively participates in developing such mechanisms as alternatives to military alliances, and it even begins to take the lead in establishing, nurturing, and promoting regional politico-security arrangements such as the Shanghai Cooperation Organization (SCO).[94]

In the Asia-Pacific, Beijing's public denouncement of the US–Japan alliance and Cold War mentality are increasingly replaced with calls for diplomacy, dialogue, and the development of regional institutions. These efforts apparently are paying off. Indeed, many are surprised at the gains China has made in the region that only a short time ago had harbored strong suspicions of Chinese intentions and ambitions, which had been amply displayed in the construction on the Mischief Reef in the South China Sea and the PLA's missile exercises adjacent to Taiwan. The "China threat" was then a popular selling point and had a more receptive audience. But Beijing's leadership has since dramatically modified its tactics if not the essence of its policy objectives. Beijing has put forward a New Security Concept that appeals to and is compatible with the ASEAN Way of working on security issues, and has become an active participant in the region's only multilateral security arrangement—the ASEAN Regional Forum, or ARF—something that it had shunned in the early 1990s. In earlier years China considered the ARF a thinly veiled attempt by the region's states to gang up against China. Beijing's diplomacy has become more proactive, confident, and skilled as China's power and influence continue to rise in regional and global contexts.[95]

Not only has China embraced multilateralism—with ASEAN characteristics, of course—but Beijing has now actively promoted its virtues as a preferred alternative for regional security architecture to what it considers the Cold War relics, i.e., the hub-spokes type bilateral military alliances led by the United States. Beijing has also significantly moderated its approaches to territorial disputes, by signing a declaration on the code of conduct in the South China Sea that commits it, in principle at least, to peaceful solutions to the disputes. It has also acceded to the ASEAN Treaty of Amity and Cooperation, the first major power to do so, effectively accepting the organization's principles of respect for sovereignty, non-interference in domestic affairs, and the code of consensus in reaching decisions.[96]

Indeed, China–ASEAN relations have evolved from enmity and suspicion to amity and greater cooperation on a broad range of issues. Joshua Kurlantzick captures this dramatic development in a recent book that records China's "charm offensive" as he terms it. Beijing's exercise of its new found "soft power"—cultural connections between China and many of the Southeast Asian countries, efforts to show respect for the region's medium and small powers and hence assuage concerns about power bullying by China, and the ability to use economic largess in investment and trade arrangements – presents a China as a benign, non-threatening power that offers many opportunities.[97] Having established a strategic partnership, the two sides are working toward building a stable, long-term relationship for the future. Beijing's efforts to assure its neighbors through the so-called new diplomacy have paid off in winning confidence from its smaller neighbors if not completely erasing disputes between them. The 1997 Asian financial crisis hit ASEAN really hard. Chinese responses to the crisis, including its pledge of $1 billion to help Thailand and not to devaluate the Renminbi, won the good will of ASEAN countries. Beijing also emerged more confident of its own potential leadership role in the region, although it allows ASEAN to take the lead.[98]

China began to publish a defense white paper in 1998. Now published every two years, the document has also moved from a mere exposition of general principles to some elementary explanations of defense budgets, modernization programs, and doctrinal issues. While still far from ideal, at least some modest steps have been made to enhance transparency. China also put forward the "New Security Concept" at the meeting of the ARF Inter-Sessional Support Group (ISG) on Confidence Building Measures that China co-hosted with the Philippines in Beijing in March 1997. The NSC emphasizes cooperative security, confidence building, peaceful resolution of disputes, and multilateral dialogue.[99] In November 2004 China hosted the ARF Security Policy Conference in Beijing. This particular initiative was clearly an effort to counter the US-centered military alliances in Asia by presenting an alternative model of security building. Conscious of ASEAN countries' hedge strategies and their desire to see the US remain engaged in the region to counter China's rise, Beijing has hinted it has no intention to oust the United States from Asia; in fact, it has even acknowledged that the US presence could play a stabilizing role.[100] Within a decade, growing interdependence and skillful Chinese diplomacy have sustained a steady improvement in the relationship between China and ASEAN, allowing Beijing to exercise greater influence in the region.[101]

China and ASEAN are also expanding their areas of cooperation, in particular in the non-traditional security areas, including securing sea lanes of communication, anti-terrorism, anti-piracy; ecological issues related to the Greater Mekong River project and other environmental issues; responses to the outbreak of SARS (for instance, the first China-ASEAN summit on SARS); transnational organized crime and money laundering.[102] Chinese Premier Wen Jiabao has proposed *mulin, anlin, fulin* ("friendly neighbors"— peaceful coexistence, regional stability and harmony; "secure neighbors"— regional peace and stability through dialogue, negotiation to resolve disputes; and "rich neighbors"—develop and deepen regional and sub-regional economic cooperation, and promote regional integration).[103]

These are all significant achievements that extend China's reach and influence in the region. More important, these achievements also reflect Beijing's focused strategy of building up and using its growing soft power to win friends and foil undesirable actions by hostile powers, including perceived missions of the enhanced US–Japan alliance.[104] The case of China's evolving relationship with ASEAN demonstrates that Beijing is increasingly aware of and consciously nurturing its soft power assets, which can be put to diplomatic use to consolidate China's place in Asia and deflect any negative impacts of the US–Japan alliance on its security interests. These soft power assets include the promotion of non-military approaches to security issues, where Beijing is putting forth the concept of a harmonious world that draws on traditional Chinese culture of modesty and harmony; the "Beijing consensus" of economic development model that balances growth and politico-social stability that appeals to many developing countries; more active defense of the interests of smaller countries at international forums and within international organizations, especially against the tyranny of great power politics, hegemony, and use of sanctions; and a willingness to make economic sacrifices and/or reject use of economic power for political interference in dealing with other countries.[105]

Soft power remains a new concept in the Chinese discourse of international relations and there is recognition that China's soft power assets are yet to be developed. Chinese analysts suggest that for China to continue to raise soft power must be an important ingredient. There are several aspects to it, which range from identifying the country's core values, raising the overall quality of the nation and its citizenry, and promoting the nation's image.[106] Some describe the attributes of China's soft power as residing in its diplomatic practices and behavior, including the growing influence of the so-called "Beijing consensus" as a model of socio-economic development, especially for developing countries; its endorsement and practices of multilateralism; economic diplomacy; and the good-neighbor policy. In some instances, the exercise of China's soft power refers to what Beijing does not do—for instance, keep a low profile in diplomacy—as contrasted to the blatant US display of hegemony and hence its abuse of hard power.[107]

Clearly, Chinese understanding of soft power and especially its own is rather modest, obviously not the kind that Joseph Nye describes. Indeed, these are the limitations of Chinese soft power assets. For instance, a number of Chinese analysts compare US and Chinese soft power and conclude that there remains a significant gap between the two countries in their abilities to appeal and attract followers, and to mobilize international and domestic support for particular policy initiatives. The sum total of these indicators continues to favor the United States, although China is gradually catching up and the United States is going down, not because of the attributes of its soft power but rather the exercise (or abuse) of its hard power over the last few years.[108] Beijing can exercise certain influence and some of its proposals can be appealing, but one is hard put to establish the cause–effect relationship and make the case that it will continue its trajectory and become more formidable. Kurlantzick, for instance, introduces a dose of caution about China's charm and soft power even as he describes how China has increased and benefited from it.[109] This conclusion corresponds to the similar findings of a recent study by the Chicago Council on Global Affairs, where the assessment is that "China still has a way to go to claim the world's full recognition as a multifaceted power."[110]

While not directly engaged in a contest with the United States, China does have different interests in the region's development in terms of security architecture, economic interdependence and integration, and political systems. Beijing promotes ARF and multilateral security dialogues as alternatives to what it considers as the Cold War relics—military alliances. China puts a high premium on sovereignty and non-interference in domestic affairs while the United States seeks to promote democracy and challenge the legitimacy and hold on power of authoritarian and repressive regimes such as the military junta in Myanmar.[111] However, in the case of Southeast Asia and increasingly even in Northeast Asia, China's soft power has played out better and apparently have an edge over the United States and Japan, not so much because it has greater assets but because Washington and Tokyo either have been negligent of the region, or—and this was particularly true with the Bush administration—appeared too heavy-handed and overtly uni-dimensional in pursuing the anti-terrorism agenda.

Within this larger context, the US–Japan alliance represents one of the three contending regional security architectures in the post-Cold War Asia-Pacific. One is multipolarization, promoted by countries such as China and Russia, and to some extent it provides opportunities for ASEAN to act as an important player. The second is the common security and multilateralism endorsed by ASEAN, which seeks to establish a regional security architecture that is not dominated by any great power and that gives small countries a voice in regional security affairs. ARF is the product of such an approach. And finally there is the model of bilateral military alliances, of which the US–Japan alliance is the most important and prominent. While the alliance has served useful purposes in the past and, if functioning properly, can continue to play a positive role in regional security, it increasingly is seen by the region's other powers, China in particular, as having a negative impact on the region's balance of power and even threatening China's core security interests such as sovereignty and unification of Taiwan and the mainland.[112]

Others see friction in the US–Japan military alliance. This has been reflected in US global military transformation and Japan's pursuit of permanent membership in the United Nations Security Council. Japan has been less than forthcoming to US adjustment in military deployment and its consultation with Tokyo. Washington seeks to consolidate its position in East Asia by using Japan while Tokyo wants to elevate its position as an equal partner in the alliance and strengthen its own military capabilities. In addition, the US has not shown determined support for Japan's bid for a permanent seat on the UN Security Council.[113]

Some Chinese analysts suggest that Japan's path to normal country status can be bolstered by its continued pursuit of peace and development, giving up the right to war and collective defense, upholding the three principles on arms exports and space non-weaponization, economic assistance to neighboring countries, and peaceful partnership with its neighbors. Indeed, they acknowledge that pacifism is widely accepted by the Japanese people, and that opposition to nuclear weapons, support of nuclear disarmament, and interest in environmental protection are deeply rooted in the Japanese society.[114] Instead of making the best of its soft power assets, Tokyo in recent years has presented itself as a country singularly preoccupied with the pursuit of hard—and in its case, predominantly military—power; one that refuses to face history and constantly irritates and worries its neighbors with such issues as textbooks, comfort women, and the Yasukuni Shrine visit, and its widely perceived obstructionist stand on the abduction issue within the Six-Party Talks process and hawkish positions regarding sanctions on North Korea.

China, on the other hand, has acted rather strategically and in a diplomatic savvy way with regard to the North Korean nuclear issue. Beijing in effect has turned the nuclear crisis into a platform to convince Washington of its irreplaceable role, gain the latter's consent if not trust in how the crisis should be resolved and, in the process, demonstrate how multilateral diplomacy, not military alliances, is the way to go about achieving de-nuclearization on the Korean Peninsula.

Ironically, the soft power aspects of the US–Japan alliance—its continued utility as a cork in keeping the Japanese military power in check and within the alliance framework, its assurance to the region's small countries of its peaceful intentions, and its role in securing sea lanes of communication and combating regional terrorist activities – have not been fully exploited. This explains the continued wariness of countries in the region to fully embrace the alliance and in particular the military approaches that it embodies and favors and the failure of Japan to leverage its alliance affiliation to achieve its objective of transforming itself into a politically acceptable great power, and recognized as such, with the permanent Security Council membership as a token of that recognition, despite its significant financial contribution and growing active participation in UN-sponsored peacekeeping operations.

Interestingly, had China pursued hard-power approaches to the strengthening of the US–Japan alliance—from strong rhetoric and military buildup of its own—this could only have further strengthened the alliance without necessarily addressing China's core concerns effectively. At the same time, such hard-nosed approaches, while intended primarily to counter the US–Japan alliance, could just as well appear threatening to the region's medium and small powers, in addition to providing the very rationale for Washington and Tokyo to give new lease of life to the alliance in the first place. Indeed, Beijing has been promoting its "peaceful rise" over the past few years precisely out of the concern that it should address the apprehension of other countries about the implications of China's growing economic power and political influence.[115] However, by adopting a soft power approach, where Beijing appears more receptive to multilateralism, advocates alternative security architecture, and acts responsibly to confronting real security threats in the region such as the North Korean nuclear issue, China at least avoids the mistake of playing into the hands of proponents of the US–Japan alliance.

Conclusion

Beijing's perspectives on the evolving US–Japan alliance are being shaped by how alliance developments would affect vital Chinese security interests, especially with respect to the Taiwan issue and Japan's pursuit of normal power status in terms of its military buildup. Granted, China's own dramatic rise as a major economic and military power increasingly wielding greater political influence in the region in turn provides justification for Washington and Tokyo to redefine their security relationship and look beyond Japan's defense to hedge against future contingencies. These dynamics, both determined by structural factors—relative positions of the three in the pecking order of the current international system and assessments of capabilities – could lead to intense rivalry for regional dominance, worsen security dilemmas, and result in much less security for all concerned. Within this context, the policy issues relevant to China and the US–Japan alliance would be whether better communication and strategic dialogue could help remove misperceptions and misunderstandings, or, alternatively, arms control and conflict management would be the more appropriate mechanisms for managing the evolving power shift in the region.

Of the four factors that I raised at the beginning of the chapter, Beijing's relationships with Washington and Tokyo, and in particular with the former, would be the most important factor in China's assessment of how, where, and to what extent the alliance would likely affect its security interests negatively. While there are still some uncertainties in Sino-US relations, there are common interests and, equally important, sufficient stakes and costs, which would provide incentives for both Beijing and Washington to manage, if not eliminate, frictions. Clearly, Washington and Beijing could make greater efforts to promote common interests and minimize their differences. This scenario would be conducive to continued regional peace and stability and Sino-US cooperation. Alternatively, the two powers could easily follow the tragic path of great-power rivalry despite their economic interdependence and the enormous setback their open confrontation would cause to progress and prosperity in bilateral, regional, and global terms. A stable and working relationship between Washington and Beijing, based on growing common interests and the mutual desire to minimize instability and conflict, would go a long way toward keeping the Taiwan issue and a potential Sino-Japanese rivalry in check.

While Beijing is wary of the US global strategy, its responses have been measured, low-key, and pragmatic. China recognizes its own limitation and the need to avoid direct confrontation with the United States. At the same time, there is also the recognition that the reach and application of US global strategy will be limited in scope and to only a few exceptional cases simply because such a posture cannot be sustained long with domestic and international opposition. Beijing seized the opportunity provided by 9/11 and the changing focus of US security policy to expand areas of common interest while minimizing the impact of differences. To a significant extent, how US global strategy will affect China's interests in the future will likely depend on how well the two manage their increasingly complex relationship.

Sino-Japanese ties were seriously strained during the Koizumi administration of 2001–6. While serious structural problems remain—from power transition, historical issues, to territorial disputes driven increasingly more by economic interests—the recent thawing of bilateral relations as exemplified by the resumption of summit meetings and more official exchanges, including those between the two militaries, offer both Beijing and Tokyo an opportunity to at least keep their disputes on the backburner while looking for long-term solutions. Beijing and Tokyo are making serious efforts to restore the political trust that was lost during the administration of Koizumi Junichirō, when summit meetings were indefinitely suspended due to his controversial visits to the Yasukuni Shrine. Former Prime Minister Abe Shinzō's "ice-breaking" trip to China in October 2006, right after he assumed office and broke the tradition of Japanese prime ministers always undertaking their first visits to the United States, paved the way for the two countries to re-engage each other at the highest political level. Premier Wen Jiabao's "ice-thawing" trip to Japan in April 2007 further consolidated the rapprochement. With Chinese President Hu Jintao's visit to Japan in April 2008, a "spring time" in bilateral relations seems to have arrived. This would have an important impact on Chinese perspectives on the alliance.

Japan's pursuit of hard power over the past decade, while worrisome in the eyes of Chinese analysts, has not earned it good standing in the international community. Its failure to gain significant support for the UNSC bid is a case in point. At the same time, by forfeiting its soft power potentials—its steadfast position on nuclear disarmament and its three non-nuclear principles—it has earned the image of a power aligned to the United States under the latter's nuclear umbrella. At the same time, and unlike other western powers such as Britain and France, Japan has continued with a more responsible nuclear policy.

While the Japanese government has conducted a series of studies over the years on the feasibility of pursuing nuclear weapons, Tokyo has in the end upheld the three non-nuclear principles. Its international standing also rose in the postwar years, from that of a militarized aggressive imperial state to one that has achieved its economic superpower status through industrialization, innovation, and the maximization of its comparative advantage. It became one of the most generous, if not *the* most generous country providing official development assistance and technical help to developing countries. It has adopted an economic development model that was the envy of many countries in the 1970s and 1980s. While these soft power assets remain at Tokyo's disposal, and indeed, there is continued fascination with things Japanese (from electronic gadgets to cartoon characters), where Japan puts its priorities and define its identity will have a great impact on how these resources will be used. It remains to be seen if the pursuit of normal state status by building hard power will in the end pay off.

China's pursuit of soft power approaches to regional security issues since the late 1990s has registered an initial payoff in winning friends in the region, expanding influence, and developing alternative security models to counter the US-centered alliance systems. However, Beijing continues to be concerned with the future direction and developments of the US–Japan alliance. The most recent developments, with the realignment of US forces in Japan, combined with greater integration and interoperability between the US military and the JSDF, suggest further expansion of the alliance. Public statements by US and Japanese officials on the Taiwan issue and the alliance's relevance in securing peace and stability in the Taiwan Strait reinforce Beijing's concerns over sovereignty issues. In the long run, how the US–Japan alliance evolves and the extent to which it poses serious security implications for China would be contingent on how US–China and China–Japan relations evolve. One note for cautious optimism is that extensive interdependence between the three powers—in political as well as economic terms—makes the stakes large enough that all have incentives to avoid a slippery slide toward confrontation.

Notes

1 For an overall assessment of the current state of bilateral relationship, see John D. Negroponte, Deputy Secretary of State, "The Future of Political, Economic and Security Relations with China," testimony before the House Committee on Foreign Affairs, May 1, 2007, http://www.state.gov/s/d/2007/84118.htm.
2 Banning Garrett, "US–China Relations in the Era of Globalization and Terror: A Framework for Analysis," *Journal of Contemporary China* 15:48 (August 2006), pp. 389–415.
3 Aaron L. Friedberg, "The Future of U.S.–China Relations: Is Conflict Inevitable?" *International Security* 30:2 (October 2005), pp. 7–45; Wang Jisi, "China's Search for Stability with America," *Foreign Affairs* 84:5 (September/October 2005), pp. 39–48; Evan S. Medeiros, "Strategic Hedging and the Future of Asia-Pacific Stability," *The Washington Quarterly* 29:1 (Winter 2005–6), pp. 145–67.
4 Jia Qingguo, "The Impact of 9–11 on Sino-US Relations: A Preliminary Assessment," *International Relations of the Asia-Pacific* 3:2 (August 2003), pp. 159–77; David M. Lampton, "Small Mercies: China and America after 9/11," *The National Interest* (Winter 2001/2002), pp. 106–13.
5 Wang Jisi, "Xinxingshi de zhuyao tedian he zhongguo waijiao [Main Characteristics of the New Situation and China's Diplomacy], *Xiandai guoji guanxi* [*Contemporary International Relations*], No.4 (April 2003), pp. 1–3; Liu Jianfei, "Zhanlue jiyuqi yu zhongmei guanxi [The Period of Strategic Opportunity and Sino-US Ties]," *Liaowang* [*Outlook Weekly*], January 20, 2003, pp. 56–57; Yuan Peng, "9.11 shijian yu zhongmei guanxi [September 11th and Sino-U.S. Relations]," *Xiandai guoji guanxi* [*Contemporary International Relations*], No.11 (November 2001), pp. 19–23, 63.
6 Zalmay Khalilzad *et al.*, *The United States and a Rising China: Strategic and Military Implications.* MR-1082-AF (Santa Monica: RAND, 1999); Zalmay Khalilzad *et al.*, *The United States and Asia: Toward a New U.S. Strategy and Force Posture.* MR-1315-AF (Santa Monica: RAND, 2001).

7 Reinhard Drifte, *Japan's Security Relations with China since 1989: From Balancing to Bandwagoning?* (London: Routledge, 2003); Wan Ming, *Sino-Japanese Relations: Interaction, Logic, and Transformation* (Stanford: Stanford University Press, 2006).
8 Yoichi Funabashi, 'Tokyo's Depression Diplomacy', *Foreign Affairs* 77:6 (November/December 1998), p. 2.
9 Michael Green, "Managing Chinese Power: The View from Japan," in Robert Ross and Alastair Iain Johnston, *Engaging China* (London and New York: Routeledge, 1999), pp. 152–75; The National Institute for Defense Studies, *East Asian Strategic Review 2007* (Tokyo: NIDS, 2007), http://www.nids.go.jp/english/index.html.
10 Christopher B. Johnstone, "Paradigms Lost: Japan's Asia Policy in a Time of Growing Chinese Power," *Contemporary Southeast Asia* 21:3 (December 1999), pp. 376–78; Tsukasa Takamine, "A New Dynamism in Sino-Japanese Security Relations: Japan's Strategic Use of Foreign Aid," *The Pacific Review* 18:4 (December 2005), pp. 439–61.
11 Masaru Tamamoto, "How Japan Imagines China and Sees Itself," *World Policy Journal* 22:4 (Winter 2005/2006), pp. 55–62; Yoshihisa Komori, "The True Character of the Japan–China Friendship," Tokyo Shōkun in Japanese, November 2000, pp. 92–101. FBIS; Neil E. Silver, *The United States, Japan, and China: Setting the Course* (New York: Council on Foreign Relations, 2000), pp. 19–25.
12 Aurelia George Mulgan, "Why Japan Still Matters," *Asia-Pacific Review* 12:2 (November 2005), pp. 104–21.
13 Mike M. Mochizuki, "China–Japan Relations: Downward Spiral or a New Equilibrium?" in David Shambaugh, ed., *Power Shift: China and Asia's New Dynamics* (Berkeley, CA: University of California Press, 2005), pp. 135–50.
14 Mochizuki, "China–Japan Relations."
15 Wang Jianwei and Wu Xinbo, *Against Us or with Us? The Chinese Perspective of America's Alliances with Japan and Korea* (Stanford: The Asia/Pacific Research Center, 1998).
16 Wu Xinbo, "The End of Silver Lining: A Chinese View of the U.S.–Japanese Alliance," *The Washington Quarterly* 29:1 (Winter 2005–6), pp. 119–30; Paul Midford, "China Views the Revised US–Japan Defense Guidelines: Propping the Cork?" *International Relations of the Asia-Pacific* 4 (2004), pp. 113–45.
17 Liu Jiangyong, "Rimei tongmeng zhuanxing jiqi dui zhongguo de yingxiang [The Transformation of the U.S.–Japan Alliance and Its Impact on China]," *Guoji guancha* [*International Observation*], no. 1 (2006), http://www.sinoir.com/power/ShowArticle.asp?ArticleID = 1649
18 Thomas J. Christensen, "China, the U.S.–Japan Alliance, and the Security Dilemma in East Asia," *International Security* 23:4 (Spring 1999), pp. 49–80.
19 Lu Zhongwei, "Riben de guojia zuoxiang yu rizhong guanxi [Japan's Course of Direction and Its Relationship With China]," *Xiandai guoji guanxi* [*Contemporary International Relations*] (July 2001), pp. 2–7.
20 Liang Ming, "Rimei xin fangwei jihua yinren zhumu [The New US–Japan Defense Guidelines Attracts Attention]," *The PLA Daily*, December 22, 2000 (internet version).
21 "Opposition Leader Ozawa Says Japan Could Produce Nuclear Weapons," *Kyodo* in English, April 6, 2002. FBIS-JPP20020406000056.
22 Yang Bojiang, "Qianghua rimei tongmeng: riben mianxiang 21 shiji de zhanlue qitiaoban [Strengthening the U.S.–Japan Alliance: A Launching Board for Japan in the 21st Century]?" *Xiandai guoji guanxi* [*Contemporary International Relations*], No. 6 (1999), pp. 24–28.
23 Ji Xide, "Rimei tongmeng de 'zaidingyi' jiqi weilai qushi [The Re-Definition of the U.S.–Japan Alliance and Its Future Trends]," *Shijie Jingji yu Zhengzhi* [*World Economics and Politics*], No.7 (2000), pp. 13–18.

24 Liu Jiangyong, "Xin 'rimei fangwei hezuo zhizhen' heyi lingren youlu [Why the New US–Japanese Defence Cooperation Guidelines Arouse Concerns]?" *Xiandai guoji guanxi* [*Contemporary International Relations*], no.11 (November 1997), pp. 7–12.
25 Sha Zukang, "Some Thoughts on Nonproliferation," address give at the 7th Carnegie International Nonproliferation Conference, January 11–12, 1999, Washington, D.C. http://www.ceip. org/programs/npp/sha/html; Howard Diamond, "China Warns U.S. on East Asian Missile Defense Cooperation," *Arms Control Today* 29:1 (January/February 1999), p. 27.
26 Zhu Feng, *Dandao daodan fangyu jihua* [*Ballistic Missile Defenses*] (Shanghai: Shanghai renmin chubanshe, 2002), chapter 9; Yan Xuetong, "Theater Missile Defense and Northeast Asian Security," *The Nonproliferation Review* (Spring–Summer 1999), pp. 65–74; Jin Xin, "Meiguo yanfa TMD de yitu jidui quanqiu he woguo anquan de yingxiang [The Intent of US TMD R& D and Its Impact on Global and Chinese Security]," *Guoji Guancha* [*International Observation*], no.4 (1999), p. 22–25.
27 Medeiros, *Ballistic Missile Defense and Northeast Asian Security*, and *Missiles, and Theatre Missile Defense, and Regional Stability*.
28 "U.S. Informs Japan Joint Missile Shield To Be Deployed in 2008," *Kyodo News*, November 10, 2002.
29 Hong Yuan, "The Implications of a TMD System in Japan to China's Security," Nuclear Policy Project Special Report, August 1999; Sun Cheng, *Riben yu yatai – shiji zhijiao de fenxi yu zhanwang* [*Japan and Asia Pacific – Analysis and Prospect at the Turn of the Century*] (Beijing: Shijie zhishi chubanshe, 1997).
30 Michael Swaine, Rachel Swanger, Takashi Kawakami, Japan and Ballistic Missile Defense (Santa Monica: RAND, 2001); Norimitsu Onishi, "Japan Support of Missile Shield Could Tilt Asia Power Balance," *New York Time*, April 3, 2004; Kori J. Urayama, "Chinese Perspectives on Theater Missile Defense: Policy Implications for Japan," *Asian Survey* XL: 4 (July/August 2000), pp. 599–621.
31 "Japan Adopts Missile Defense System," *Mainichi Daily News*, December 19, 2003 <http://mdn.mainichi.co.jp/news/archive/200312/19/20031219p2a00m0dm007000c.html>.
32 Meng Xiangqing, "Juxinguoce de zhanlue jucuo – riben canyu TMD de Beijing yu qitu [Strategic Move with Ulterior Motives: Backgrounds and Intentions of Japanese Participation in TMD," *Shijie zhishi* (*World Affairs*), February 1999, pp. 18–19; Zhu Feng, "TMD yu dangqian dongbeiya 'daodan weiji' [TMD and Current 'Missile Crisis' in Northeast Asia]," *Dangdai yata* [*Contemporary Asia-Pacific*], no.5 (1999), pp. 3–10.
33 Liang Ming, "Meiri jiyu tuifan 'fandao tiaoyue' [US, Japan Eager to Annul 'ABM Treaty']," *Jiefangjun bao* [*PLA Daily*], November 14, 1999, p. 5.
34 Richard L. Armitage *et al.*, *The United States and Japan: Advancing Toward a Mature Partnership*. INSS Special Report, National Defense University, October 2000. http://www.ndu.edu/inss/strforum/SR_01/SR_Japan.htm; Richard L. Armitage and Joseph S. Nye, *The U.S.–Japan Alliance: Getting Asia Right through 2020*. Center for Strategic and International Studies, February 2007.
35 Zhao Jieqi, "Meiguo junshi zhanlue tiaozheng yu rimei tongmeng tizhi [U.S. Military Strategic Adjustments and the U.S.–Japan Alliance]," *Heping yu fazhan* [*Peace and Development*], No. 4 (2001), pp. 36–39; Gao Hong, "Tangxiang zai zhongri guanxi de lishi yu xianshi zhijian [Between History and Reality of Sino-Japanese Relations]," *Riben Yanjiu* [*Japanese Studies*], No.1 (2005), pp. 21–26.
36 Liang, "New US–Japan Defense Guidelines."
37 Hu Jiping, "Cong xinfangwei dagang kan riben anquan zhanlue de tiaozheng fangxiang [On Japanese Adjustments in Its Security Strategy via Its New Defense Program Guidelines]," *Xiandai Guoji Guanxi* [*Contemporary International Relations*], January 2005, pp. 48–49, 52.

38 Christopher W. Hughes, "Japanese Military Modernization: In Search of a 'Normal' Security Role," in Ashley J. Tellis and Michael Wills, eds., *Strategic Asia 2005–06: Military Modernization in An Era of Uncertainty* (Seattle, WA: The National Bureau of Asian Research, 2006), pp. 105–34.
39 Zhang Chunyan, "Meiri anquan guanxi de bianhua ji zoushi [US–Japan Security Ties: Changes and Trends]," *Xiandai Guoji Guanxi [Contemporary International Relations]* (September 2002), pp. 43–47, 36; Lu Zhongwei, "Bawuo bianhua, zhongshi weilai—zhongri jianjiao sanshi zhounian huigu yu qianzhan [Keeping Abreast of Changes with a View to the Future—Sino-Japanese Relations in the 30th Anniversary: Retrospect and Prospect]," *Xiandai Guoji Guanxi [Contemporary International Relations]* (August 2002), pp. 1–6; Pan Xiaoying, "Be Vigilant against Japanese Desire to Establish a Ministry of Defense," Beijing *Renmin ribao* in Chinese, December 11, 2000, p. 2. FBIS-CPP20001211000026.
40 Li Xiushi, "'Xingshi jiti ziweiquan' yu riben fangwei zhuanxiang ['The Right of Collective Self-Defense' and the Changing Direction of Japan's Defense," *Xiandai Guoji Guanxi [Contemporary International Relations]* (June 2005), pp. 14–18.
41 Guo Lili, "Riben de 'zizhu fangwei' yu rimei tongmeng fazhan qushi [Japan's 'Self-DeterminedDefense' and Development Trends in the U.S.–Japan Alliance]," *Guoji Wenti Yanjiu [International Studies Quarterly]* No. 2 (2005), pp. 52–55.
42 Huang Dahui, "Lun riben de wuhehua zhengche [On Japan's Non-Nuclear Policy]," *Guoji Zhengzhi Yanjiu [International Politics]*, no.1 (2006), pp. 155–73.
43 Sun Xiangli, Wu Jun, and Hu Side, "Riben de buwenti jiqi guoji guanqie [Japan's Plutonium Issue and International Concerns," in China Arms Control and Disarmament Association, *2006: Guoji Junbei Kongzhi yu Caijun Baogao [2006 Yearbook on International Arms Control and Disarmament]* (Beijing: Shejie zhishi chubanshe, 2006), pp. 83–91.
44 Duan Wei, "Zhanlue guancha: riben hewuqi shengchan qianli jiemi [Strategic Survey: Disclosing Japan's Nuclear Weapons Production Capabilities]," *Junshi Wenzhai [Military Digest]*, April 3, 2006.
45 Jin Xide, "Shiping: jingti riben 'chihelun' hungshui muyu [Commentary: Beware of Japan Fishing in Trouble Water for Nuclear Weapons Possession]," *Guoji xianqu daobao [International Herald Leader]*, October 20, 2006.
46 Gu Shan, "Fenxi renshi: chaoxian heshiyan keneng tuidong riben fazhan hewuqi [Analysts: North Korean Nuclear Test Could Motivate Japan to Develop Nuclear Weapons]," Zhongguo xinwenwang [Chinanews.com], October 9, 2006.
47 Reuters, "Japan Should Reexamine Its Nuclear Weapons Ban, Ruling Party Official Says," *Washington Post*, October 16, 2006, p. 16.
48 Jin Xide, "Beware of Japan"; Gong Chang, "Meiguo danxin riben 'hewuzhuang' [U.S. Concerned over Japan's Going Nuclear]," *Huanqiu shibao [Global Times]*, October 18, 2006, p. 2.
49 Geng Xin et al., "Laisi mengya riben hechongdong [Rice Supresses Japan's Nuclear Urge]," *Huanqiu shibao [Global Times]*, October 19, 2006. See also, Kessler, "Japan, Acting to Calm U.S. Worries."
50 Dongfangwang (Eastday), "Meiguo jiangxiang riben tigong 80 duomei aiguozhe-3xing daodan [U.S. to Supply 80 PAC-3s to Japan]," August 24, 2006; Gao Yong, "Richeng zhongri lingtu jufen shijushi jizhang, yuzeng daodan fangyu yusuan [Japan to Increase Budget for Missile Defense Due to Heightened Tension Caused by Sino-Japanese Territorial Dispute]," Renmin ribao wangzhan (www.people.com.cn), September 1, 2006; Dongfangwang, "Ri fangweiting jiang zhiding 227 yi riyuan yingdui chaoxian daodan yusuanan [JDA Budgets $22.7 Billion in Response to North Korean Missile Tests]," August 23, 2006.Gao Yong, "Richeng zhongri lingtu jufen shijushi jizhang, yuzeng daodan fangyu yusuan [Japan to Increase Budget for Missile Defense Due to Heightened Tension Caused by Sino-Japanese Territorial Dispute]," Renmin ribao wangzhan (www.people.com.cn), September 1,

2006; Dongfangwang, "Ri fangweiting jiang zhiding 227 yi riyuan yingdui chaoxian daodan yusuanan [JDA Budgets $22.7 Billion in Response to North Korean Missile Tests]," August 23, 2006.
51 "Riben tiqian bushu daodan fangyu xitong queli juedui junshi yushi [Japan to Deploy Missile Defense Ahead of Schedule to Establish Absolute Military Superiority]," August 15, 2006; Zhongguo xinwenwang, "Riben ni tizao yinian bushu sizuo aiguozhe-3xing daodan fashejia [Japan to Complete Four PAC-3 Deployment One Year Ahead]," July 10, 2006.
52 "Meiri daodan fangyu hezuo mabutingti, lianguo tisheng qingbao fenxiang [U.S. and Japan Missile Cooperation Without Halt, Enhance Joint Information Sharing]," September 9, 2006.
53 "Japan to Deploy Missile Defense Ahead of Schedule."
54 "CCTV-7 'Defense Review Week' 26–27 Aug 06 Discusses US–Japan TMD System," Open Source Center, CPP20060828133001/002, August 26, 27, 2006.
55 Zhang Hao, "Riben daodan fangyu fazhan zuji [The Evolution of Japanese Missile Defense Development]," in China Arms Control and Disarmament Association, *2006: Guoji Junbei Kongzhi yu Caijun Baogao* [*2006 Yearbook in International Arms Control and Disarmament*] (Beijing: Shijie zhishi chubanshe, 2006), pp. 174–85; "Rimei daodan fangyu xitong jiasu zhupao [US–Japan Missile Defense Speeds Up]," *Huanqiu* [*Globe Biweekly*] February 20, 2006.
56 Dongfangwang, "Meiri dazao dongya dandan fangyuwang mingfang chaoxian shiji zhendui zhongguo [U.S. and Japan Deploy Missile Defense Nets Ostensibly Against North Korea But In Fact with China as Target]," July 3, 2006.
57 Zhang, "The Evolution of Japanese Missile Defense Development."
58 Ye Lian and Sima Hangren, "Spy Eyes Hidden in Japanese Satellite," *China's National Defense*, February 7, 2006, http://www.chinamil.com.cn/site1/zbx1/2006–02/07/content_401384.htm.
59 Li Wentao, "Japan Speeds Up Building All-Dimension Intel Networks," *Global Times*, January 16, 2006, p. 8. http://military.people.com.cn/GB/1077/52987/4036891.html
60 "At 61 Billion Yen, Japan Set to Launch Two Additional Spy Satellites," Xinhua, January 7, 2006, http://military.people.com.cn/GB/1077/52987/4006621.html.
61 You Wenhu, "Japanese Space Policy Going Through Significant Change," Renminwang Military Channel, January 11, 2006, http://military.people.com.cn/GB/1078/4017365.html; Qiu Yongzheng, "Unbinding 'Non-Militarization' Ban: JSDF Poised for Space Charge," *Youth Reference*, January 10, 2006, p. 5, http://military.people.com.cn/GB/1077/52987/4010693.html.
62 "Japan Spends Huge Amounts on Spy Satellites: Paying the Way for Major Military Power Status?" *Xinhua*, January 25, 2006, http://news.xinhuanet.com/mil/2006–01/25/content_4095876.htm.
63 "Japan Covertly Develops Military Space Capabilities," *Xinhua*, January 28, 2006, http://news.xinhuanet.com/mil/2006–01/28/content_4110297.htm.
64 Kazuki Shiibashi, "Japan OKs New Space Law," *Aviation Week*, internet version, June 18, 2008, at: www.aviationweek.com, accessed on July 13, 2008. For Chinese commentaries, see, Huang Jun, "Ri tongguo 'yuzhu jibenfa' [Japan Pass 'Basic Space Law']," *Jiefang ribao* [*Liberation Daily*] (Shanghai), May 11, 2008, http://mil.eastday.com/eastday/mil1/m/20080511/u1a3582523.html.
65 Editorial, "Taiwan Issue Core of Sino-U.S. Ties," *People's Daily*, February 28, 2004; Michael D. Swaine, "Trouble in Taiwan," *Foreign Affairs* 83:2 (March/April 2004), pp. 39–49.
66 William Kristol and Ellen Bork, "The Bush Administration, Taiwan, and China: Why is the Bush administration siding with Beijing against Taiwan's democratic referenda?" *The Daily Standard*, February 10, 2004. <http://www.weeklystandard.com/Content/Public/Articles/000/000/003/719aazqc.asp>.

67 See, for instance, statements by Richard Lawless, Deputy Assistant Secretary of Defense and Randy Schriver, Deputy Assistant Secretary of State at the US–China Economic and Security Review Commission hearing on Military Modernization and Cross-Strait Balance, February 6, 2004.
68 John Ruwitch and Jim Wolf, "China Scolds U.S. for Radar Sales to Taiwan," Reuters, April 1, 2004.
69 Andrew Bingham Kennedy, China's Perceptions of U.S. Intentions toward Taiwan: How Hostile a Hegemon?" *Asian Survey* 47:2 (March/April 2007), pp. 268–87.
70 See Robert Sutter, "Bush Administration Policy toward Beijing and Taipei," *Journal of Contemporary China* 12:36 (August 2003), pp. 477–92.
71 Wei-Chin Lee, "US Arms Transfer Policy to Taiwan: from Carter to Clinton," *Journal of Contemporary China* 9:23 (March 2000), pp. 53–75; John P. McClaran, "U.S. Arms Sales to Taiwan: Implications for the Future of the Sino-U.S. Relationship," *Asian Survey* 40:4 (July/August 2000), pp. 622–40.
72 East Asia Nonproliferation Program, Center for Nonproliferation Studies, "Arms Sales to Taiwan: Statements and Developments 1979–2003 <http://www.nti.org/db/china/twnchr.htm>. Additional information regarding US arms sales to Taiwan can also be found at: <http://taiwansecurity.org/TSR-Arms.htm>.
73 Alice Hung, "Time Running Out as Taiwan Wrings Hands over US Arms," Reuters, October 2, 2005.
74 James Mann, "Congress and Taiwan: Understanding the Bond," in Ramon H. Myers, Michel C. Oksenberg, and David Shambaugh, eds., *Making China Policy: Lessons from the Bush and Clinton Administration* (Lanham: Rowman & Littlefield Publishers, Inc., 2001), pp. 201–19.
75 Julian Baum, "Silent Running," *Far Eastern Economic Review*, July 1, 1999, p. 28; George Gedda, "China Warns Against Sales to Taiwan," Associate Press, October 14, 1999 <http://www.washingtonpost.com/wp-5 … ne/19991014/aponline163839_000.htm>.
76 Xiao Kang-kang, "Meiritai junshi hudong guanxi de xinfazhan [New Developments in U.S.–Japan–Taiwan Military Interactions]," *Guoji Ziliao Xinxi* [*International Information*], no. 9 (2007), pp. 15–19.
77 "So Hard to be Friends," *The Economist*, March 23, 2005; James Brooke, "Japan's Ties to China: Strong Trade, Shaky Politics," *New York Times*, February 22, 2005; Michael Yahuda, "The Limits of Economic Interdependence: Sino-Japanese Relations," in Alastair Iain Johnston and Robert S. Ross, eds., *New Directions in the Study of China's Foreign Policy* (Stanford: Stanford University Press, 2006), pp. 162–85.
78 Sadako Ogata, *Normalization with China: A Comparative Study of U.S. and Japanese Processes* (Berkeley: Institute of East Asian Studies, University of California, 1988); Philip Yang, "Japanese–Taiwanese Relations and the Role of China and the U.S.," *NBR Analysis* 16:1 (October 2005), p. 94.
79 Shelley Rigger, *From Opposition to Power: Taiwan's Democratic Progress Party* (Boulder, Colo.: Lynne Rienner Publisher, 2001).
80 Yoshihide Soeya, "Changing Security and Political Contexts of Japan-Taiwan Relations: A View from Japan," *NBR Analysis* 16:1 (October 2005), pp. 39–56; Yang, "Japanese–Taiwanese Relations," pp. 97–98.
81 Author interviews, Tokyo and Taipei, March 2007.
82 Author interview, Taipei, March 2007. Zheng-Jia Tsai, "Jingji nenggou dapu zhengzhi de fanlima: 2000 nian zhihou tairi guanxi de zhuanbian [Can Economy Break the Political Hedge: The Transition of Relationship between Taiwan and Japan after 2000]," *Yuanjing Jikan* [*Prospect Quarterly*] (Taipei) 7:3 (2006), pp. 75–104.
83 Author interviews, Tokyo and Taipei, March 2007.
84 Since 2002, the Foundation on International and Cross-Strait Studies in Taipei and the Institute for International Policy Studies in Tokyo have co-sponsored the

annual Taiwan–Japan Forum, attended by both officials and academics from the two sides.
85 Agence France Presse, "Japan and China Lock Horns Again over Visa for Ex-Taiwan President," December 16, 2004, http://www.channelnewsasia.com/stories/afp_asiapacific/view/122613/1/.html; Hiroyasu Akutsu, "Tokyo and Taipei Try to Tango," *Far Eastern Economic Review* (January/February 2007), pp. 31–35.
86 Zhao Jieqi, "Riben duitai zhengce dongxiang zhide zhuyi [Japan's Policy toward Taiwan Deserves Attention]," *Heping yu Fazhan* [*Peace and Development*] 4 (2004), pp. 51–54; Yu Yongsheng, "Taihai wenti: meiri yinsu you chayi [The Taiwan Strait: The Difference between the U.S. and Japanese Variables]," *Shijie Zhishi* [*World Affairs*], 4 (2006), pp. 28–29.
87 Zhang Zhuo, "Jiedu meiri beizhan taihai celue [Interpreting U.S.–Japan War Preparation for Taiwan Strait Contingencies]," China Radio International Online, January 31, 2007.
88 Interviews, Tokyo, Taipei, March 2007. Wu Jinan, "Ritai junshi hudong de xianzhuang, beijing ji weilai zoushi [Japan-Taiwan Military Interaction: Current Status, Background, and Future Direction]," *Xiandai Guoji Guanxi* [*Contemporary International Relations*] (September 2006), pp. 56–63.
89 "U.S.–Japan statement on Taiwan opposed," China Daily, February 20, 2005, http://www.chinadaily.com.cn/english/doc/2005-02/20/content_417717.htm.
90 Bill Gertz, "Chinese Military Buildup Assessed As Threat to U.S.," *Washington Times*, February 18, 2005, http://www.washtimes.com/national/20050217-114812-3737r.htm.
91 Jane A. Morse, "U.S. Monitoring China's Military Improvements, Rumsfled Says," U.S. Department of State International Information Program, February 18, 2005.
92 Hu Jiping, "Meiri 'gongtong zhanlue mubiao' yu riben shetai lichang bianhua [U.S.–Japan 'Common Strategic Objectives' and Changes in Japan's Stance on Taiwan]," *Xiandai Guoji Guanxi* [*Contemporary International Relations*], No. 3 (2005), pp. 35–36, 38.
93 Aileen San Pablo-Baviera, "The China Factor in US Alliances in East Asia and the Asia Pacific," *Australian Journal of International Affairs* 57:2 (July 2003), pp. 339–52.
94 These developments are discussed in details in Bates Bill, *Rising Star: China's New Security Diplomacy* (Washington, D.C.: The Brookings Institution, 2007).
95 On China's changing diplomacy and growing influence, see David Shambaugh, ed., *Power Shift: China and Asia's New Dynamics* (Berkeley, California: University of California Press, 2005); Yong Deng and Fei-ling Wang, eds., *China Rising: Power and Motivation in Chinese Foreign Policy* (Lanham: Rowman & Littlefield Publishers, Inc., 2005); Robert Sutter, *China's Rise in Asia: Promises and Perils* (Lanham: Rowman & Littlefield Publishers, Inc., 2005); Bates Gill, *Rising Star: China's New Security Diplomacy* (Washington, D.C.: The Brookings Institution, 2007).
96 Jing-dong Yuan, *China–ASEAN Relations: Perspectives, Prospects and Implications for U.S. Interests* (Carlisle, PA: Strategic Studies Institute, U.S. Army War College, October 2006).
97 Joshua Kurlantzick, *Charm Offensive: How China's Soft Power Is Transforming the World* (New Haven and London: Yale University Press, 2007); Seth Mydans, "China's 'Soft Power' Winning Allies in Asia," *International Herald Tribune*, July 11, 2007, http://www.iht.com/articles/2007/07/11/news/timor.php.
98 Jürgen Haacke, "Seeking Influence: China's Diplomacy Toward ASEAN after the Asian Crisis," *Asian Perspective* 26:4 (2002), pp. 13–52; Alice D. Ba, "China and ASEAN: Renavigating Relations for a 21st-Century Asia," *Asian Survey*, vol. 43, no. 4, September/October 2003, pp. 622-647, at," pp. 637–38.
99 "Summary Report of the ARF ISG on Confidence Building Measures, Beijing, 6–8 March 1997," http://www.aseansec.org/3605.htm.

116   *Jing-dong Yuan*

100 Gill, *Rising Star*, chapter 2.
101 Chairman's Summary of the First ASEAN Regional Forum Security Policy Conference, Beijing, 4–6 November 2004," from the ASEAN Secretariat website; Evan S. Medeiros and M. Taylor Fravel, "China's New Diplomacy," *Foreign Affairs* 82: 6 (November/December 2003), pp. 22–35; Brantly Womack, "China and Southeast Asia: Asymmetry, Leadership and Normalcy," *Pacific Affairs* 76:3 (Winter 2003–4), pp. 529–48; Denny Roy, "Southeast Asia and China: Balancing or Bandwagoning?" *Contemporary Southeast Asia*, vol. 27, no. 2, 2005, pp. 305-22, at p. 309.
102 Cai Peng Hong, "Non-Traditional Security and China-ASEAN Relations: Co-operation, Commitments and Challenges," in Leong and Ku, eds., *China and Southeast Asia*, pp. 146–69; Zhai Kun, *1991—2020: Zhongguo jueqi yu zhongguo dongmeng guanxi de fazhan [1991—2020: The Rise of China and China-ASEAN Relations]*, unpublished manuscript, 2005.
103 Lu Shiwei, "Zhongguo de dongmeng shijiao [China's ASEAN Perspective]," *Liaowang [outlook weekly]*, October 13, 2003, pp. 6–9.
104 There is a growing literature on the rise and limitation of China's soft power. See Kurlantzick, *Charm Offensive*; Bates Gill and Yanzhong Huang, "Sources and Limits of Chinese 'Soft Power'," *Survival* 48:2 (Summer 2006), pp. 17–36; Yanzhong Huang and Sheng Ding, "Dragon's Underbelly: An Analysis of China's Soft Power," *East Asia* 23:4 (Winter 2006), pp. 22–44.
105 Chinese scholars and analysts have only recently begun to pay more attention to soft power and are now engaged in discussions of soft power as a concept in general and what China needs to do to enhance its soft power assets.
106 Kong Hanbing, "Ranshili yu zhongguo jueqi [Soft Power and China's Rise]," *Zhongguo pinlun [China Review]*, No. 6 (2007), online at: http://gb.chinareviewnews.com, accessed on July 23, 2007; Yu Yongsheng, "Tisheng zhongguo xingxiang yao jiangjiu celue [Promoting China's Images Requires Tact]," Guoji zaixian [China Radio International], July 31, 2007, at http://gb.cri.cn/12764/2007/07/31/342@1699266.htm, accessed on August 2, 2007.
107 Zheng Yongnian and Zhang Chi, "Guoji zhengzhi zhongde ranliliang yiji dui zhongguo ranliliang de guancha [Soft Power in International Politics and the Observation of China's Soft Power]," *Shijie Jingji yu Zhengzhi [World Economics and Politics]*, No. 7 (2007), pp. 6–12.
108 Fang Changping, "Zhongmei ranshili bijiao jiqidui zhongguo de qishi [A Comparison of Chinese and U.S. Soft Power and Its Implication for China]," *Shijie Jingji yu Zhengzhi [World Economics and Politics]*, No. 7 (2007), pp. 21–27; Yan Xuetong and Xu Jin, "Zhongmei ranshili bijiao [A Comparison of Chinese and US Soft Power]," *Xiandai Guoji Guanxi [Contemporary International Relations]*, No. 1 (2008), pp. 24–29.
109 Kurlantzick, *Charm Offensive*, chapter 11.
110 The Chicago Council on Global Affairs, *Soft Power in Asia: Results of a 2008 Multinational Survey of Public Opinion*. Asia Soft Power Survey 2008, p. 2.
111 Wayne Bert, "Burma, China and the U.S.A.," *Pacific Affairs* 77:2 (Summer 2004), pp. 263–82.
112 Ni Feng, "Meiri tongmeng yu diqu anquan [US–Japan Alliance and Regional Security]," *Taipingyang Xuebao [Asia-Pacific Journal]*, No. 2 (June 1999), pp. 65–76.
113 Zhang Kexi, "Dui rimei junshi tongmeng lingyi cemian de chubu tantao [A Preliminary Analysis of the Other Aspect of U.S.–Japan Military Alliance]," *Waiguo Wenti Yanjiu [Comparative International Studies]*, No. 78 (January 2005), pp. 43–48.
114 Lu Zhongwei, "Riben de guojia zouxiang yu zhongri guanxi [Japan's National Orientation and Sino-Japanese Relations]," *Xiandai Guoji Guanxi [Contemporary International Relations]*, July 2001, pp. 2–7.
115 Yu Xintian, "Ranshili jianshe yu zhongguo duiwai zhanlue [The Development of Soft Power and China's Foreign Strategy] *Guoji Wenti Yanjiu [International Studies Quarterly]*, No. 2 (2008), pp. 15–20.

5 North and South Korean views of the US–Japan alliance

Daniel A. Pinkston

Introduction: Korean views of "soft power"

North and South Korea have been engaged in a "soft power" battle of persuasion since the peninsula was divided after World War II. This battle has been waged in the shadow of hard power, but given the robustness of mutual deterrence on the Korean peninsula, Koreans have looked for any advantage in inter-Korean competition. In the early days of national division, these efforts could be described as a crude propaganda war, but in recent years both governmental and nongovernmental actors have recognized the existence and value of soft power, and both tend to believe that soft power can be harnessed or manipulated—within limits—to further national goals.

The two Koreas have different views on their national soft power resources and how these assets should be utilized. North Korea tried hard power to resolve national division in June 1950 but ultimately failed. And although the threat of a second Korean War has never completely disappeared, the cost of war has made it almost unthinkable to any rational government. National division has forced Pyongyang and Seoul to focus on inter-Korean relations and national unification policy, and the power of persuasion is very important in inter-Korean competition.

Most people would agree that South Korean soft power has been increasing in recent years as Seoul has assumed a greater role in global affairs and in the international economy. However, North Korean soft power is not necessarily in the same type of free fall that the national economy experienced in the 1990s. Pyongyang has been adjusting its soft power tactics, which are mostly targeted at South Koreans and Koreans overseas, but the nuances and sophistication of North Korea's recent propaganda efforts are essentially unnoticed by non-Korean audiences.

Until the early 1970s, North Korea's superior economic performance made the North an attractive alternative to South Korea's endemic corruption and economic ineptitude. When Syngman Rhee's (Yi Seung-man) First Republic collapsed in April 1960 and the Second Republic's parliamentary democracy was ousted by a military coup d'état in May 1961, North Korea confidently presented positive images of its approaches to economic development and national unification. North Korea's appeal played a prominent role in convincing about 70,000 Koreans in Japan to return to North Korea during 1960–61, and most of those repatriated originated from the southern part of the Korean peninsula.[1] During the Cold War period Pyongyang also used positive North Korean images to court allies in the Third World's Nonaligned Movement in an effort to isolate Seoul and to win supporters for the North's unification policy.

By the 1990s, most of North Korea's previous soft power assets had disappeared. However, Pyongyang has been reassessing the transformation of its soft power resources, the media through which North Korean soft power is conveyed, and the recipients or potential recipients of North Korean images. North Korea's international image is generally negative, except for fringe "true believers" who have few remaining "communist" countries to cite as models of political development. However, Pyongyang now makes very few references to Marxism-Leninism or international socialism, and instead invokes slogans such as "our style socialism (*urisik sahoejuui*)" and "our people together (*uri minjokkiri*)," which carry a nationalistic message targeted at Koreans in the North, South and abroad.

Former President Roh Moo-hyun's National Security Council believed that the ROK has "plenty of 'soft power' resources such as the experience of successful democratization, rich cultural creativity, and national self-confidence as illustrated during the 2002 FIFA World Cup."[2] The Lee Myung-bak government is now trying to focus on enhancing public diplomacy and coupling it with the country's soft power resources to achieve national goals. After a series of perceived blunders and large-scale street protests during Lee's first months in office, the government officials have realized that soft power alone is not sufficient; how soft power resources are utilized also matters.

South Korea's soft power assets are found within its vibrant civil society and the country's growing economic clout around the world. Scholars and pundits praise South Korea's rising soft power resources, and many advocate the use of soft power to avoid military conflict and big power rivalry while increasing Korea's regional and global influence. For example, Professor Lee Geun of Seoul National University asserts that soft power has become more important in world affairs and South Korea should cultivate and utilize its soft power in order to play a significant role in global governance.[3]

Many South Koreans are also upbeat about the so-called "Korean wave (*hanryu*)" of pop culture that has become popular in East Asia in recent years. This phenomenon is mainly manifested in Korean pop songs and television dramas with translations or subtitles for foreign audiences, mainly in Japan and Southeast Asia.[4] Koreans probably overestimate the impact of the "Korean wave" and it would certainly be an exaggeration to say it has any foreign policy influence on its own. However, the South Korean private sector views it as a positive development and conducive to creating a good international image or "branding" of Korea that could generate positive externalities for private firms seeking to enter markets or expand their market share abroad.

Korean views of the US–Japan alliance

Korean views of the US–Japan alliance are affected by a number of complex variables: the historical legacy of the Japanese colonial period and World War II, the global and regional security environments, economic relationships, domestic politics, the status or conditions of the US–Japan alliance and the US–South Korea alliance, and North Korea's alliance relationships with China and Russia. Korean opinion of the US–Japan alliance varies, more so in South Korean society than in the north. North Korean views of the alliance are relatively straightforward; Pyongyang views Washington and Tokyo as having hostile intent towards the DPRK, and the alliance is considered an aggregation of capabilities that can be arrayed against Pyongyang.

North Korea views the US–Japan alliance through the prism of hard power and power politics, but South Korean perspectives are more complex and nuanced. Realism would predict that relations between Seoul and Tokyo would be close since the onset of the Cold War. Both countries faced the threat of communism and the two countries formed alliances with the United States to face that common threat. Furthermore, realism would predict that Seoul and Tokyo would balance against the persistent North Korean threat and the rise of Chinese power. However, relations between South Korean and Japan often have been rocky even though both countries could enhance their security by forming an alliance against common threats.

Some realists predicted the end of the Cold War meant that Asia was "ripe for rivalry" and that arms races loomed in the region,[5] but that has yet to materialize. Some realists counter that it is only a matter of time before an arms race is triggered, or that American hegemony has temporarily prevented it. Some scholars and analysts have argued that Asia might be different, and that Western theories of international relations might not apply to the region.[6]

Various forms of democratic peace theory are correct in predicting hostile relations between Pyongyang and Tokyo, but they would also predict a warming of relations between Tokyo and Seoul as the two countries democratized. Liberal theories based on neo-classical economics would predict warmer relations between Seoul and Tokyo, as well as warmer relations between Tokyo and Pyongyang since Japan is the third largest trading partner of the DPRK. Japan has been a source of significant North Korean imports and an important source of foreign exchange.[7] However, North Korea–Japan trade and cash remittances to Pyongyang have recently declined drastically and trade has plummeted in the wake of sanctions imposed following the DPRK's missile exercise and nuclear test in 2006. North Korea has also been involved with illicit trade and smuggling activities in Japan, infuriating the Japanese people and government.[8]

Constructivist approaches to international relations provide little insight into Korea–Japan relations. Despite centuries of interaction, relations have varied considerably. The relationship has generally been antagonistic, and there has been little convergence of interests and identity. Furthermore, Japanese relations with the two Koreas are quite different, although both North and South Koreans still have feelings of animosity towards Japan for the colonial period (1910–45).

Koreans often cite *han* as a unique Korean sentiment of resentment and hatred felt by victims of injustice. And Koreans often refer to several historical instances of Japanese injustice towards Korea such as the Hideyoshi Toyotomi invasions of the 1590s, the Treaty of Kanghwa in 1876,[9] the Taft–Katsura Agreement of 1905, and Japanese imperialism in the twentieth century. Most Koreans feel that Japan has not addressed these injustices adequately, and thus interactions with Japan are conducted in a *han*-tainted atmosphere. Many Koreans feel that Japan's failure to show sufficient contrition for past injustices is an indication of malicious intent in the present or future. On the other hand, many Japanese feel that Koreans are overly emotional and obsessed with the past, or that Koreans emphasize past injustices in an attempt to extract concessions from Japan.

Historical legacies are important in the formation of social perceptions; however, it is difficult to construct formal historical models or historical explanations to account for all outcomes in Korea–Japan relations. While history matters, many analysts rely upon history as an ad hoc explanation to account for current outcomes or anomalies. Victor Cha's analysis is correct in that history is a necessary variable, but not a sufficient one to explain relations between Korea and Japan. Feelings of enmity have been constant; therefore, history cannot explain cooperation between the two countries.[10]

Another problem with historical analysis is that it is impossible to identify the point in time where the series of events is triggered to generate a particular outcome. However, World War II and the Korean War are prominent historical events that left Japan and the Koreas weak and insecure. Given the international security environment at the time, Japan, North Korea, and South Korea formed security alliances to address their insecurity.

All security alliances are characterized by the fears of abandonment or entrapment, and these fears have driven the alliances dynamics in East Asia for the last half-century. From the Korean perspective, those fears have oscillated alongside their *han* towards Japan and suspicions about Japanese intentions to once again seek hegemony in East Asia. Korean fears of a Japanese military resurgence have been mitigated by Japan's close alliance ties with the United States, but many Koreans now believe that paradoxically, increasingly closer ties with the United States in recent years could result in fewer constraints against Japanese hard power. Instead, this common argument posits that closer ties and greater Japanese burden sharing in its alliance relationship with the United States give Tokyo greater maneuverability under the wing of its superpower patron.

After Korean liberation in 1945, Koreans were very concerned about the possible remilitarization of Japan, but these fears were mollified somewhat by the Yoshida Doctrine whereby the Japanese government under Prime Minister Yoshida Shigeru made the strategic choice of aligning itself with the United States in the early period of the Cold War. Under the grand bargain of the doctrine, Japan signed a peace treaty with the United States in 1951 and agreed to provide military bases to US Forces for the security of Japan and US allies in East Asia.[11] The Yoshida Doctrine enabled Japan to focus on economic recovery and development, but Japan and South Korea were unable to normalize diplomatic relations until 1965 after several years of contentious negotiations.

Tokyo and Seoul were able to overcome lingering animosity and normalize relations because of the common threats of the Soviet Union and North Korea during the Cold War. However, with the disappearance of the Soviet threat and with an emerging divergence in South Korean and Japanese views regarding the North Korean threat, relations between Tokyo and Seoul have deteriorated. Many South Koreans believe that during the Roh Moo-hyun administration (February 2003–February 2008) bilateral relations deteriorated to their lowest level in forty or fifty years.[12]

In recent years, Korean views of Japanese intentions have become more complicated and sensitive because of Japan's increasing "hard power" capabilities. Japanese and Americans are more likely to view Japan's increasing capabilities and its trajectory towards becoming a "normal state" as natural and desirable developments commensurate with Japan's economic power. This increase in Japanese hard power is viewed as necessary for dealing with emerging threats in the new security environment after the end of the Cold War and the terrorist attacks against the United States in September 2001. Both Japan and South Korea have provided support for US-led combat operations in Iraq and Afghanistan, and both countries desire global stability and harmonious relations with the United States. Nevertheless, Tokyo and Seoul have provided this support independently and without any bilateral collaboration despite their common objectives.

End of the Cold War and emergence of the DPRK threat

In the early 1990s, North Korea's nuclear and missile programs emerged as the most immediate security threat to Japan. However, Japan had little choice but to rely upon the United States for its security against the North Korean threat. Japan's social pacifism and domestic legal constraints limited Tokyo's capacity to balance internally by building up its indigenous military capabilities. These domestic constraints were revealed when many in the United States and elsewhere perceived Tokyo as having responded weakly to the 1991 Gulf War in what became known as "checkbook diplomacy." International criticism motivated Tokyo to avoid a recurrence and move towards becoming a "normal state" capable of contributing to the provision of international public goods in the security realm.

After the Soviet threat had vanished, Japan also had to be concerned with China's increasing power. The Senkaku/Diaoyutai Islands, which are claimed by both China and Japan, could be a flashpoint between the two countries. China's missile tests in 1995 and 1996 in an effort to intimidate Taiwan's perceived moves towards independence also raised questions in Tokyo regarding Chinese intentions for the region.[13] Japan responded by moving closer to the United States, particularly in missile defense cooperation, for two main reasons: (1) domestic constraints against an aggressive military buildup; and (2) Tokyo's desire to avoid antagonizing Beijing.

The domestic push moving Japan closer to the United States coincided with Washington's pull for closer cooperation and a greater contribution from Tokyo to deal with contingencies surrounding the Korean peninsula in the wake of the first North Korean nuclear crisis. In 1995, the US Defense Department released its "United States Security Strategy for the East Asia-Pacific Region," or so-called "Nye Report," which recommended the continued deployment of 100,000 US troops in the region and close security cooperation with Japan.[14] In the same year, Japan issued a revised National Defense Program Outline that included "areas surrounding Japan" as part of Tokyo's national defense strategy.[15]

In 1997, the two countries revised the Guidelines for US–Japan Defense Cooperation, which moved Japan closer to embracing collective defense.[16] The new guidelines expanded the geographic scope of US–Japan security cooperation, but the guidelines were ambiguous in defining the geographic area.[17] North Korea responded negatively to this development as Pyongyang perceived the revised guidelines as aimed at the DPRK, but the South Korean overall response was ambivalent since the guidelines were seen as improving the capabilities to respond to the North Korean nuclear threat. On the other hand some South Koreans view the guidelines as part of power politics and an American strategy to enlist Japan in the containment of China in order to maintain US hegemony in the western Pacific.[18]

After the terrorist attacks against the United States in September 2001, Japan responded quickly and passed the Anti-Terrorism Special Measures Law in November 2001 to enable Japanese Self Defense Forces (JSDF) to support coalition forces in Afghanistan against Taliban and Al Qaeda elements.[19] In January 2004, JSDF were deployed to Iraq to participate in humanitarian and reconstruction missions.[20] The barrier against Japanese military deployments overseas had already been breached when Japan passed legislation in June 1992 for the deployment of JSDF to Cambodia to participate in non-combat missions as part of United Nations Peace Keeping Operations.[21] While Japan emphasizes these activities as contributions to international peace and security, many Koreans view them as the first steps in establishing a capability to deploy military forces for malign reasons.

In December 2004, Japan's National Defense Program Guidelines (NDPG) recognized the significance of non-state actors in international security and that traditional deterrence might not always be effective in the new international security environment. The NDPG named North Korea's programs to develop WMD and ballistic missiles as threats to Japan's peace and stability, and the document also stated that Japan must pay attention to the rise of Chinese power. In particular, Tokyo is concerned about Beijing's modernization of its nuclear weapons and missile forces, as well as the Chinese military's increasing capability to expand its operations at sea.[22]

According to the NDPG, Tokyo has two basic national defense objectives: preventing direct threats against Japan; and improving the international security environment. To achieve these objectives, Japan plans to use a combination of three methods: increasing Japan's indigenous military capabilities; maintaining cooperation with its allies; and cooperating with the international community.[23] While the first two approaches are based on hard power, Japan's approach to international cooperation includes elements of soft power. Japan's Defense White Paper for 2005 summarizes a number of "soft power activities" designed to improve the international security environment. These efforts include diplomatic initiatives, humanitarian assistance, reconstruction efforts in Iraq, medical services, water supply, the provision of transport services, etc.[24]

While Japan must be commended for the amount of soft power resources expended to enhance the international security environment, few Koreans recognize these efforts. Dr Kim Gyeong-soon of Korea National Defense University recognizes there are positive security externalities from the few cases of Korea–Japan cooperation. She cites the conclusion of a communications agreement between the two air forces in 1995, and combined search and rescue exercises by the ROK Navy and Japan Maritime Self Defense Forces in the area around Cheju Island in 1999. The two sides have been holding bilateral military talks since 1994, but Kim also admits that security relations between the two countries are weak in the area of policy and they lack strategic focus.[25]

President Lee Myung-bak campaigned on a platform that included a pledge to improve relations with Japan and neighboring countries after Lee and his Grand National Party (GNP) asserted that relations had deteriorated significantly under former President Roh. On 21 April, 2008, President Lee visited Tokyo where he and Prime Minister Fukuda agreed to establish a more "future-oriented" relationship.[26] One week later, the ROK Ministry of National Defense (MND) announced that Seoul was considering signing a military cooperation agreement with Tokyo that had first been proposed in 2005, but was shelved because of bilateral tensions surrounding Dokto and disputed claims over economic zone sea boundaries.[27] However, on 18 May, Japanese media reported that a new middle school handbook will include Japanese sovereignty claims over Dokto, which resulted in ROK Foreign Minister Yu Myung-hwan summoning Japanese Ambassador Toshinori Shigeie the next day.[28] Seoul also recalled its ambassador from Tokyo in protest. In sum, bilateral relations can worsen despite the intentions of political leaders. History, perceptions, domestic politics, and civil society matter in Japan–South Korea relations. Soft power resources and how they are used can also affect the relationship.

Given the historical legacy and the emotionally charged issue of Dokto, Koreans are very sensitive about Japanese efforts to enhance its indigenous military capabilities. Korean scholars and journalists often cite defense budget figures or weapons acquisition plans, and then proclaim that Japan is already a "normal country" and a large military power. At the very least, most Koreans are convinced that Japan is well on its way to becoming a military power that can directly challenge or affect Korea's national interests. For example, tensions mounted in April 2006 when Japan announced its intention to survey the seabed in the area around the Dokto islets, but Tokyo ultimately withdrew its plan.[29] Nevertheless, President Roh Moo-hyun responded by criticizing Japan for its "criminal history of waging wars … as well as 40 years of exploitation, torture, imprisonment, forced labor and sexual slavery."[30]

The friction over Dokto in 2006 caused ROK defense officials and analysts to review the balance of naval forces between the two countries, leading ROK officials to realize that Japan had a considerable advantage and that South Korea could not prevail in a naval conflict.[31] Many ROK government officials believe the country is not strong enough militarily, but the US–ROK alliance is weakening while the US–Japan alliance is getting stronger. The Lee Myŏng-bak government has made an effort to improve alliance ties with the United States, but Washington remains committed to disbanding the US–ROK Combined Forces Command in 2012. President Lee and former President Bush agreed to upgrade the alliance to deal with twentieth-first-century threats beyond the geographic range of the Korean peninsula, but the global interests of the two countries are not always congruent, and the dispatch of ROK troops abroad requires National Assembly approval, and therefore, public support. There are many reasons for Seoul and Washington to maintain their alliance relationship, but if an imbalance between the US–Japan alliance and the US–ROK alliance continues to grow without the development of a multilateral security institution in East Asia, South Korea will respond with an even greater military buildup.

A South Korean military buildup might be counter-intuitive for some analysts since bandwagoning through alliances is considered a method of signaling one's benign intent. Takafumi Ōtomo argues that alliances can be divided into three functional categories: control, voice, and reassurance. In Ōtomo's framework powerful states can control and reassure weaker states through alliances, and weaker states can express their concerns to the stronger alliance partner. Furthermore, alliances can be a signaling mechanism whereby allied states can demonstrate their benign intentions or restraint towards third parties.[32] Ōtomo and others argue that Japan's alliance with the United States constrains Tokyo and/or signals benign intent towards Japan's neighbors. However, the US–Japan alliance is not sufficient in alleviating South Korean suspicions, and North Korea views the alliance as a real threat.

Many South Koreans share the contrarian view that the US–Japan alliance and Washington's requests for greater burden-sharing by Tokyo give cover for

Japanese intentions to remilitarize. Kim Seong-cheol of the Sejong Institute has written that domestic forces in Japan have used US requests for increased Japanese military capabilities as a type of *gaiatsu* or "foreign pressure" to push military reforms in a particular direction.[33] Both North and South Koreans are concerned that Japan could be manipulating its alliance relationship with the United States to increase its military capabilities, which could be turned against other countries in the future. Many Koreans also hold the very cynical view that the US–Japan alliance (along with increasing cooperation between Washington and New Delhi) will be utilized in Washington's geopolitical strategy of containing China.

Japan's virtual nuclear weapons

North and South Koreans both tend to believe that the United States has enabled Japan to develop a latent nuclear weapons capability. In the realm of nuclear policy, South Koreans view the two alliances as inequitable. South Koreans resent the fact that Washington has permitted Tokyo to have a complete nuclear fuel cycle while Washington opposes Korean acquisition of uranium enrichment or spent fuel reprocessing facilities. Many South Korean journalists and scholars criticize the international concern over North Korea's small stock of plutonium while Japan continues to amass tons of plutonium.[34] Not all Koreans recognize that Japan's plutonium is not weapons grade, but even those who do acknowledge this fact also believe that political obstacles are the only real barriers to Japan developing nuclear weapons. Kim Gyeong-min has written that Japanese society's "nuclear allergy" is a significant barrier that non-Japanese fail to appreciate, but Kim also agrees with the common Korean view that Japan has achieved a special status as a "virtual nuclear power."[35]

South Korean society is strongly opposed to the opening of Japan's spent fuel reprocessing facility at Rokkasho-mura. In December 2005, 67 South Korean NGOs and 121 university professors released a declaration demanding that Japan immediately cancel its plans to operate the facility.[36] But on the other hand, according to a poll taken between August 31 and September 16, 2005, about two-thirds of South Koreans believe that South Korea should possess nuclear weapons.[37]

South Korea's bilateral nuclear agreement with the United States and the DPRK–ROK Joint Declaration on the Denuclearization of the Korean Peninsula prohibit Seoul from obtaining uranium enrichment or spent fuel reprocessing facilities. However, the bilateral nuclear agreement with Washington expires in 2014 and must be renegotiated. In 2005, South Korea's National Intelligence Service commissioned a study on whether South Korea needs those capabilities, and if so, how Seoul should work to obtain them. The authors of the study agreed that Seoul should acquire both uranium enrichment and spent fuel reprocessing capabilities, but that South Korea must improve its ties with the United States and work with

ROK hard power response to an uncertain security environment

In the 1970s, the South Korean government became concerned that the United States would not honor its alliance commitments in the case of another North Korean military attack. The late 1960s and early 1970s were characterized by frequent North Korean provocations, including the capture of the *USS Pueblo* off the North Korean east coast, the shooting down of a US reconnaissance plane, the infiltration of commandos in an attempt to assassinate South Korean President Park at the Blue House, and another assassination attempt against Park that claimed the first lady's life.

North Korea's armed provocations occurred when the United States was embroiled in Vietnam and subsequently trying to extricate itself from a lost cause. President Nixon's "Guam Doctrine," which called for Asian allies to share more of the burden in human resources so that the United States could reduce its troop commitments, alarmed the South Korean government. Fears of US abandonment led President Park to implement a "self-reliant" national defense policy that included an aggressive import-substitution program in armaments as well as crash programs to develop nuclear weapons and ballistic missiles. Park dropped his nuclear weapons program under strong US pressure and Washington's promise to shore up the alliance.

South Korea's efforts to increase its "hard power" capabilities in the 1970s were a function of abandonment fears and the North Korean military threat. The Roh Moo-hyun government implemented a policy of "self-reliant national defense," but with different motivations and objectives compared to the Park Chung-hee policy of the 1970s. President Roh's "self-reliant national defense policy" was pursued with the intention of maintaining a close alliance relationship with the United States, albeit when the alliance was experiencing strains.

South Korean defense policy is primarily concerned with the North Korean threat, but the balance of conventional forces has steadily been shifting against Pyeongyang over the past two decades. North Korea's WMD and missile programs are a major concern, but many South Koreans feel that North Korea would never use such weapons against fellow Koreans. Furthermore, many defense planners are looking ahead to the military needs of a unified Korea in an uncertain future security environment. Whether the region drifts towards "realist power balancing" or develops a cooperative security mechanism, the consensus in Seoul is that greater military capabilities will serve the national interest.

South Korea's greatest fear is to be drawn into regional big power conflict or being forced to "chose sides" in a big power clash over issues such as Taiwan. Seoul has no territorial ambitions beyond the Korean peninsula, but it seeks to develop and maintain a minimal conventional deterrent against any potential foes in the region. Most South Koreans are concerned about Chinese and Japanese intentions as the two countries modernize and build up their military forces. In particular, more and more South Koreans subscribe to the view that the US–Japan alliance is a mechanism for Japan to remilitarize and potentially use its capabilities against Korean interests.

Soft power for persuasion or coercion?

Joseph Nye describes soft power as being distinct from hard power—military force or the threat of its use against an adversary. Soft power is difficult to grasp or operationalize, but critics of Nye's approach cannot deny the existence of the power of persuasion. Soft power deals with human psychology and intangibles, and even the most powerful states are concerned with their image in the world. Soft power can help states achieve desired policy outcomes, but soft power and its effectiveness are difficult to measure.

While Japan is increasing its hard power capabilities, many scholars and analysts believe the US–Japan alliance operates as a constraint as well as a signal of Japan's benign intentions. Tokyo is using its soft power assets to reassure other states that Japan has no hostile intent and is only interested in helping provide public goods in the realm of international security. But Koreans see little of Japan's soft power, so Tokyo's efforts do not reassure Koreans about Japanese intentions.

Tokyo seems to ignore the soft power issues that would assuage Korean suspicions: compensation for the comfort women; dealing with the Yasukuni Shrine issue; and controversies over some Japanese textbooks, for example. Many Koreans believe that Japan's failure to deal with such issues indicates that Japan does not respect China or Korea at all. Many Koreans also feel Tokyo is a hypocrite on human rights. While South Koreans are sympathetic towards the abduction victims and their families, most of them do not believe North Korea's past abductions of Japanese citizens should be on the agenda of the Six-Party Talks, which were convened to address the North Korean nuclear program. South Koreans condemn North Korea's behavior, but the number of South Koreans kidnapped by the North is much greater, and Japan's past atrocities and human rights violations are worse. Most South Koreans believe Japan's introduction of the abduction issue at the talks is selfish, and they view Japan's foreign policy as awkward.[39]

Soft power can be used to persuade, but it can also be used for coercion. The former Bush administration's strategy in convening the Six-Party Talks was to establish a coalition for applying pressure against North Korea until Pyongyang abandons its nuclear ambitions. An assessment of this strategy is beyond the scope of this chapter, but the administration increasingly used soft power as a form of pressure or coercion against North Korea when the Six-Party Talks became stalled. As the Japanese government moved closer to the United States, Tokyo cooperated with Washington in using soft power of coercion against Pyongyang.

Coercive soft power aimed at North Korea includes pressure on human rights, economic sanctions, the freezing of North Korean financial assets, economic sanctions against third parties for dealing with Pyongyang, increasing safety inspections and insurance requirements for North Korean ships, and increasing pressure against the pro-Pyongyang General Association of Korean Residents in Japan. It is unclear whether these efforts will be successful in resolving the North Korean nuclear issue, but they run the risk of increasing regional tension and alienating South Korea. According to a senior official at South Korea's Ministry of Unification, "attacks by the US and Japan against North Korea through human rights and other issues are also *attacks against us.*"

Notes

1 Tessa Morris-Suzuki, "A Dream Betrayed: Cold War Politics and the Repatriation of Koreans from Japan to North Korea," *Asian Studies Review*, Vol. 29, December 2005, pp. 357–81. For a personal account of a family's return to North Korean and tragic internment in a labor camp, see Chol-hwan Kang and Pierre Rigoulot, *Aquariums of Pyeongyang* (New York: Basic Books, 2002).
2 ROK National Security Council, "Peace, Prosperity and National Security: National Security Strategy of the Republic of Korea," May 1, 2004, p. 17.
3 Lee, Geun, "Hanguk Oegyojeongchaek Paereodaimeul Bakkwora," *Shindonga*. No. 556, January 2006, pp. 90–99.
4 For example, see Seiko Yasumoto, "The Impact of the 'Korean Wave' on Japan: A Case Study of the Influence of Trans-border Electronic Communication and the Trans-national Programming Industry," a paper presented to the 16th Biennial Conference of the Asian Studies Association of Australia, June 26–29, 2006.
5 Aaron Friedberg, "Ripe for Rivalry: Prospects for Peace in a Multipolar Asia," *International Security*, Vol. 18, No. 3, Winter 1993/1994, pp. 5–33.
6 David C. Kang, "Getting Asia Wrong: The Need for New Analytical Frameworks," *International Security*, Vol. 27, No. 4, Spring 2003, pp. 57–85; Peter J. Katzenstein and Nobuo Okawara, "Japan, Asia-Pacific Security, and the Case for Analytical Eclecticism," *International Security*, Vol. 26, No. 3, (Winter 2001), pp. 153–85.
7 In particular, cash remittances from the pro-Pyongyang General Association of Korean Residents in Japan (GAKRJ, commonly known as *Chōsen Sōren* in Japanese, or *chochongnyon* in Korean).
8 Mark E. Manyin, "Japan–North Korea Relations: Selected Issues," CRS Report for Congress, November 26, 2003, http://fpc.state.gov/documents/organization/27531.pdf.
9 The Treaty of Kanghwa, or the Korea–Japanese Treaty of Amity, was signed in 1876 and was designed to open Korean ports to Japanese trade. The treaty was drafted by Japan along the lines of the unequal treaties thrust upon China by the western powers in the 19th century.
10 Victor D. Cha, *Alignment despite Antagonism: The United States–Korea–Japan Security Triangle* (Stanford: Stanford University Press, 1999).
11 Christopher W. Hughes, "Japan's Post-War Security Trajectory and Policy System," Chapter One in Hughes, *Japan's Re-emergence as a 'Normal' Military Power*, Adelphi Paper 368–69, 2004.
12 Author interview data, Seoul, May 2006.
13 For details on the crisis surrounding the missile tests, see Robert S. Ross, "The 1995–96 Taiwan Strait Confrontation: Coercion, Credibility, and Use of Force," *International Security*, Vol. 25, No. 2, Fall 2000, pp. 87–123.

14 For a critique of the report, see Chalmers Johnson and E.B. Keehn, "East Asian Security: The Pentagon's Ossified Strategy," *Foreign Affairs*, July/August 1995.
15 For an unofficial English translation, see Japan Defense Agency, "National Defense Program Outline in and after FY 1996," adopted by the Security Council and by the Cabinet on November 28, 1995, http://www.jda.go.jp/e/defense_policy/japans_defense_policy/4/ndpof1996/index.htm.
16 For a Korean view of the 1997 guidelines and corresponding Japanese legislation, see Yoon Hong-suk, "Japan's Legislation on the New Defense Guidelines: Building a Normal State?" *East Asian Review*, Vol. 11, No. 3, Autumn 1999, http://www.ieas.or.kr/vol11_3/yoonhongsuk.htm. The new guidelines revised the previous guidelines issued in November 1978. See Japan Ministry of Foreign Affairs, "Joint Statement U.S.-Japan Security Consultative Committee Completion of the Review of the Guidelines for U.S.-Japan Defense Cooperation," September 23, 1997, http://www.mofa.go.jp/region/n-america/us/security/defense.html; Japan Ministry of Foreign Affairs, "The Guidelines for Japan-U.S. Defense Cooperation," http://www.mofa.go.jp/region/n-america/us/security/guideline2.html.
17 For analysis and details on the functional areas of cooperation unde the guidelines, see Christopher W. Hughes, "Forging a Strengthened US–Japan Alliance," Chapter 4 in Hughes, *Japan's Re-emergence as a 'Normal' Military Power*, Adelphi Paper 368–69, 2004.
18 Ahn Byung-joon and Konstantin Sarkisov, "Korean Peninsula Security and the U.S.–Japan Defense Guidelines," IGCC Policy Paper # 45, October 1998, http://www-igcc.ucsd.edu/pdf/policypapers/pp45.pdf; Lim, Eul-cheol, "Miguk, Horangisaekki Kiunda," *Hankyoreh 21*, No. 391, January 2, 2002.
19 Christopher W. Hughes, "Japan, Regional Cooperation, Multilateral Security and the 'War on Terror'," Chapter 5 in Hughes, *Japan's Re-emergence as a 'Normal' Military Power*, Adelphi Paper 368–69, 2004; Nam Chang-hee, "Mi-il Dongmaengui Ganghwawa Juilmigun Jaebaechiui Jeonlyaggudo: Hankookui Jungjanggi Dongmaengjeonlyage Daehan Hamui," *Gukgajeonlyag*, Vol. 11, No. 3, 2005, pp. 74–75.
20 Nam Chang-hee, "Mi-il Dongmaengui Ganghwawa Juilmigun Jaebaechiui Jeonlyaggudo: Hankookui Jungjanggi Dongmaengjeonlyage Daehan Hamui,", pp. 74–75.
21 Hughes, "Japan, Regional Cooperation, Multilateral Security and the 'War on Terror'."
22 Japan Ministry of Defense, *Defense of Japan 2005*, http://www.mod.go.jp/e/publ/w_paper/2005.html; Park Young-jun, "Ilbonui Anbojeongchaekgwa Mi-il Dongmaeng Byeonhwa: 21segi Dongasia Anbojillseoui Jigakbyeongdonggwa Gukgadaejeonlaygui Mosaek," *Miraejeonlyagyeonguwon Issuewa Daean*, March 24, 2005.
23 Park Young-jun, "Ilbonui Anbojeongchaekgwa Mi-il Dongmaeng Byeonhwa: 21segi Dongasia Anbojillseoui Jigakbyeongdonggwa Gukgadaejeonlaygui Mosaek," *Miraejeonlyagyeonguwon Issuewa Daean*, March 24, 2005.
24 Other activities include "friendly relations with local people in Iraq" by "teaching them origami paper folding and holding music concerts." See *Defense of Japan 2005*, p. 57.
25 Kim Gyeong-soon, "Han-mi-il Gunsaanbohyeopryeok," *Hapcham*, No. 25, (no date), available at: http://www.jcs.mil.kr/main.html.
26 "Lee Urges Japan to Grant Korean Residents Voting Right," *The Korea Times*, April 21, 2008, http://www.koreatimes.co.kr/www/news/nation/2008/08/113_22885.html; "Korea, Japan Agree to Strengthen Ties," *Chosun Ilbo*, April 22, 2008, http://english.chosun.com/w21data/html/news/200804/200804220013.html.
27 Jung Sung-ki, "South Korea Seeks Closer Military Ties with Japan," *The Korea Times*, April 28, 2008, http://www.koreatimes.co.kr/www/news/nation/2008/08/113_23280.html.

28 Jung Sung-ki, "Seoul Slams Tokyo Over Dokdo," *The Korea Times*, May 19, 2008, http://www.koreatimes.co.kr/www/news/nation/2008/08/113_24427.html.
29 "Japan Agrees to Withdraw Survey Plan in Disputed Waters," Xinhua News Agency, April 22, 2006, http://news.xinhuanet.com/english/2006-04/22/content_4461384.htm; Mark J. Valencia, "Japan and Korea: Between a Legal Rock and a Hard Place," Nautilus Institute Policy Forum Online 06-37A, May 11, 2006, http://www.nautilus.org/fora/security/0637Valencia.html.
30 B. J. Lee, "A New Kind of Pride," *Newsweek*, May 8, 2006, in Lexis-Nexis, http://www.lexis-nexis.com.
31 Interview with ROK Ministry of Unification official, Seoul, May 12, 2006.
32 Takafumi Ōtomo, "Bandwagoning to Dampen Suspicion: NATO and the US–Japan Alliance after the Cold War," *International Relations of the Asia-Pacific*, Vol. 3, 2003, pp. 29–55. For a brief discussion on multilateralism as a binding mechanism for a hegemonic power, see David A. Lake, "The Self-Restrained Superpower," *Harvard International Review*, Fall 2000, pp. 48–53.
33 Kim Seong-cheol, "Mi-il Dongmaenggwa Ilbonui Oegyo-anbo Jeongchaek," *Tongilgyeongjae*, Spring 2005, pp. 22–32.
34 Kim Chang-suk, "Ilbon Haekpoktanui Kkumul Gyeonggyehara," *Hankyoreh21*, No. 596, February 8, 2006.
35 Kim Gyeong-min, "Mi-il Daebukjeongchaek Donghyanggwa Han-mi-il Jeongchaek Gongjo," *Hanbando Anbojeongsebyeonghwawa Hyeopryeokjeok Jajugukbang* [Guknae Anbohaksulhoehu (2004.5.11) Balpyononmumjip] (Seoul: Korea Institute of National Unification, 2004), pp. 35–52. For anther example of the "virtual nuclear power" view, see Kim Jang-sook, "Ilbon Haekpoktanui Kkumul Gyeonggyehara," *Hankyoreh21*, No. 596, February 8, 2006.
36 Daniel A. Pinkston, "Japanese, South Korean Plutonium Plants Raise Security Concerns in Region," *WMD Insights*, February 2006, http://www.wmdinsights.com/Old_EastAsia/Feb06/I2_EA1_Rokkashos.htm.
37 Daniel A. Pinkston and Dave H. Kim, "South Korean Opinion Polls: Majority Favors Nuclear Weapons; 1980s Generation Question U.S. Ties," *WMD Insights*, December 2005–January 2006, http://www.wmdinsights.com/Old_EastAsia/DecJan/I1_EA1_SouthKoreanOpinion.htm.
38 Interview with ROK government official, Seoul, May 14, 2006.
39 Interview with Dr. Han Yong-seop, Director of the Research Institute on National Security Affairs, Korea National Defense University, in Seoul, May 10, 2006.

6 Russian perspectives on the US–Japan security alliance

Sergey Sevastyanov

Introduction

This chapter examines Russia's perspectives on the changing US–Japan alliance. To understand them properly several critical considerations should be taken into account.

First, Moscow clearly distinguishes the US as a leading partner in the US–Japan alliance, and thus considers Washington's global policy priorities as a defining factor that may affect Russian security interests in the Asia-Pacific. In this context it is worth mentioning that though Russian–American interests mostly coincide in this part of the world, bilateral differences and growing conflicts elsewhere, especially in Europe, may impede their security and economic cooperation in East Asia.

Second, Russian–Japanese ties are characterized by a controversy: on one hand, during the last fifteen years a network of bilateral contacts (political and economic ties, military and cultural exchanges, etc.) has been gradually growing. On the other hand, a long-term territorial dispute has prevented any substantial breakthrough in bilateral relations. That is why it is important to clarify whether Tokyo's pursuit of the so-called "normal state" status and more offensive capabilities for the Japanese Self-Defense Forces (JSDF) may become a threat to Russia's interests in the region.

From this author's point of view, the complex state of Russian–American relations that is poisoned by such issues as the NATO enlargement, Washington's abrogation of the Antiballistic Missile Treaty, American plans to install National Missile Defense (NMD) in Eastern Europe informs Moscow's perspective on the American role in the US–Japan alliance. This analysis will examine how the American use of hard power as well as soft power has changed Russia's post-Cold War policy, and what that experience says about the effectiveness of the use of those two components of "smart" power. The chapter then discusses differences in Russian and Japanese approaches to the territorial dispute and the latest changes in bilateral economic ties as a precursor of a possible Moscow–Tokyo compromise to support further strengthening of bilateral relations. This will be followed by a discussion of Russia's assessment of the main components of Japan's soft power, developments surrounding the JSDF, and the evolution of the US–Japan security alliance.

Russian security interests and threat perception in Northeast Asia

Russia perceived the main regional security threats to its Far Eastern territories in the 1980s and early 1990s to be: potential armed conflict on the Korean Peninsula; the military growth of China and its potential conflict with Taiwan; tension with Japan over unresolved territorial disputes; proliferation of weapons of mass destruction (WMD) and the illegal arms trade; and potential development of the US theater missile defense (TMD) systems.

Over the last thirty years, Russia changed its assessment of the US–Japanese security alliance according to Russian internal policy priorities. During the Cold War period, Russia considered the alliance as a critical threat to security in Northeast Asia (NEA). During Gorbachev's "perestroika" years (1986–90), Russia praised the alliance as contributing to regional security. During the last years of the twentieth century through the early years of the twenty-first, Moscow gave the alliance a neutral assessment; that is, Moscow neither praised nor criticized the alliance.

Since the end of the Cold War, Moscow has emphasized diplomacy, not raw power, as an effective means to counter the above mentioned threats and to support stability in the Asia-Pacific. In view of the absence of any full-scale Track-I (state-level) security mechanism in NEA, Russia has been doing her best to achieve regional stability on a bilateral and a multilateral basis. In 1996 Russia became a full participant of the ASEAN Regional Forum (ARF) and in 1998 joined the Asia Pacific Economic Cooperation (APEC). In 1996 Russia was admitted into the Western Pacific Naval Symposium. The main goal of that forum is to build confidence and to intensify cooperation among Western Pacific navies.

From 2003 Russia has been taking part in the Six-Party Talks on the Korean security problem. The recent war in Iraq demonstrated that America's declarations concerning the so-called "Axis of Evil" countries were not mere rhetoric, but a substantive part of the new Bush Doctrine. In view of the fact that the DPRK, with which Russia has a common border and where Moscow has legitimate interests, is on the list of such countries, it is of critical importance for Russia to prevent the United States from using the Iraqi model to solve the Korean Peninsula issue.

At the same time, during the last eight–ten years the spectrum of security threats in the territories of the Russian Far East (RFE) has become more diversified. The most urgent security concerns in the region are now considered either internal or of non-military character, e.g., negative demographic trends, terrorism, illegal migration, and criminal fishery activities.

For example, the situation with criminal fishery activities in the vicinity of southern Kurile Islands has reached a dangerous point. It is impossible for Russia to maintain control over every fishing vessel, especially given the inadequate funding available for law enforcement. As a result, only 15–20 percent of valuable seafood species, mostly crabs, are taken legally. The rest (worth billions of dollars annually) is illegally exported to Japan and the Republic of Korea.

Several of the above mentioned changes in security threat assessments and new concepts on how to use the navy and other "force structures" more effectively to counter threats have been incorporated into practice during strategic exercises conducted in the Russian Far East since 2003. Interestingly enough, in some of the exercises only 25 percent of tactical episodes have been devoted to conventional military issues, such as the bombing of surface combatants, marine landing operations, etc. Most of the episodes have been devoted to countering paramilitary threats, such as fighting terrorists, piracy, poaching in the economic zone, and ecological threats as a consequence of accidents at sea, etc.

Russian–American global "coopetition"[1]

A principal feature of the Russian–American relationship is that US policies in East Asia do not seem to contradict any critical interests of Russia in regional security. In fact, on a number of diplomatic issues, the two countries' interests have effectively converged. Moscow highly appreciated US financial help in dealing with the nuclear submarine waste of Russia's Pacific fleet, as well as Washington's not much publicized rejection of a Japanese proposal to remove part of the US military presence from Okinawa to Hokkaido. Moscow has never called for the dismantling of America's Cold War-era treaties with Japan and South Korea, and Russia's only visible issue with America's bilateral ties in Asia is the US–Japanese joint effort to develop a TMD system. As far as mutual economic ties between Russia and the United States are concerned, US involvement in the Russian Far East had been at low levels and mostly limited to the development of gas and oil in the Sakhalin Island shelf area.

During the last fifteen years Russian–American military contacts in the Asia-Pacific have been very positive, including a series of search-and-rescue and amphibious disaster relief exercises, and numerous naval port calls. The centerpiece of those events was *Cooperation from the Sea*, a series of exercises that took place annually in 1994–98. The theme of those exercises was the coordination between the Russian Pacific fleet and the American Pacific fleet in joint disaster relief operation. Staff personnel, surface combatants and amphibious ships as well as Marines and Naval infantry detachments participated in four exercises of that type. So far, they are the only series of bilateral naval exercises between Russia and the United States in the post-Cold War era.

However it is of principal importance that the above mentioned Russian–American military cooperation in the Asia-Pacific had always played a secondary role to the Russian–American relationship in Europe, and several times the worsening of bilateral relations in Europe negatively affected their ties in the Pacific. The Kosovo crisis, the NATO enlargement, and other events effectively blocked Russian–American military cooperation in the Asia-Pacific. For example, in spring 1999 the post-Kosovo effect put *Cooperation from the Sea* indefinitely on hold.

To understand the dynamics and trends in the post-Cold War Russian–American relations we will rely on the concept of "soft power," as developed by Joseph Nye. We will also attempt to discover what component of American power (hard or soft) has been the more effective in changing Russian security policy.

According to Nye, coercion and payments are the main elements of hard power, while persuasion is the basic way to exercise soft power. The latter resource base is composed of a county's culture, political values, and foreign policies.[2] There is no consensus among scholars on what type of relationship exists between soft power and hard power. Joseph Nye states that soft power does not depend on hard power, while Samuel Huntington insists that the former requires a foundation of the latter.[3] The critical question for every nation is to seek an optimal balance between hard and soft power to maximize its influence over other nations' preferences.

Further developing the "soft power" concept, Nye states that in international dialogue all messages go through "cultural filters," and that messages are very seldom interpreted in the same way as their authors intend.[4] Soft power can be exercised through the "fine-tuning" of messages to facilitate their recipient's acceptance and comprehension of the intended effect of the messages.

In this context, semiotics (the science of symbols and signs) offers a very useful toolkit for analyzing Russian–American relations since the end of the Cold War. Semioticians refer to communication as a process that involves "encoding" and "decoding". Each state, when communicating with other states (both through texts and actions) employs a particular system of codes that is not necessarily shared by message recipients, and thus the latter often fail to grasp the intended meaning of the original message. For example, the United States and its closest European allies exist in a joint semiotic space, and their interpretative codes practically coincide. On the contrary, Russian–American interaction is occurring in a very rare semiotic space, while Russian interpretative codes often do not coincide with American ones due to differences in history, political values, etc. As a result, a political action implemented by or political concept introduced by Washington is interpreted in Moscow in a non-American system of coordinates and given a different understanding than intended that by the United States.

Russian scholars Igor Zevelev and Mikhail Troitsky have singled out several components of the American foreign policy that could be regarded as means of the US soft power destined to influence the Russian system of interpretative codes as follows: democratization, market reforms, and geopolitical pluralism on post Soviet (CIS) territories, human rights promotion, and the American approach to fighting terrorism and non-proliferation of WMD. American hard power in interactions with Russia in the twenty-first century materialized in such foreign policy actions as: NATO enlargement, abrogation of the Antiballistic Missile Treaty, American military deployments in Central Asia, plans to install several elements of the National Missile Defense (NMD) system and to deploy troops in Eastern Europe, a military operation against Iraq in 2003, etc.[5]

Most Russian foreign policy experts agree that Vladimir Putin's Presidency could be clearly defined in two periods. During the first term (2000–4) Putin's ultimate goal was to integrate Russia as a modern competitive state into the world community led by the United States. During the second term (2004–8) Moscow's view of the world and Russia's place in it has undergone dramatic changes. Due to acute disagreements with the West on the situation in the CIS territories and in Eastern Europe, increased Russian wealth based on high oil prices, and American failure in Iraq, Moscow began to position itself as an independent center of power in a multipolar world, and an energy superpower that rightfully became a very influential player on the international political and economic scene.

To understand the role, if any, that American soft power may have played to facilitate those critical changes in Russian foreign policy, we should consider several policy messages sent by Washington to Moscow in 2000–2007, and analyze how those messages have been interpreted in Moscow, and whether the messages may have changed Russia's interpretative codes.

The Russian code of the war against international terrorism – as a main threat to national security – happened to be similar to the American code. However, that code was not imposed on Moscow by Washington, because it had been formed in Russia as a result of a prolonged war in Chechnya much earlier than the source of anti-terror code in the United States post 9/11. However, in most cases American political messages were interpreted by Russia in codes that did not coincide with Washington's vision. For example, we can look at the Russian discussion of the second phase of NATO enlargement and the US abrogation of the Antiballistic Missile Treaty among other developments.

For the United States, NATO enlargement is a part of American strategy to support market economies and promote democratic governments in Eastern Europe and it is a part of US global mission. Moscow considers NATO enlargement in an entirely different way – as an anti-Russian project, and interestingly enough, Baltic states share Moscow's view, interpreting NATO enlargement as a means of collective defense against Russia. Most recent American plans to install elements of the NMD system and to deploy troops on the territory of four Eastern European countries are interpreted in opposite ways by Washington and Russia.

In 2001, Washington unilaterally abrogated the Antiballistic Missile Treaty (ABM), believing that American nuclear strategy was of the highest priority for US national security and that it was free of any limits imposed by international treaties. Obviously enough, such an American approach was interpreted by Moscow in an entirely opposite way – as an intention to belittle the importance of the Russian nuclear arsenal and to draw Moscow into a new round of arms races.

In both cases (second phase of NATO enlargement and the abrogation of ABM Treaty) American soft power did not work. Washington could not impose on Moscow its interpretation of those actions, and resorted to a unilateral exercise of hard power. Upset with the American plans to install the NMD and to deploy troops in Eastern Europe, President Putin in February 2007 made his famous Munich speech in which he tried to impose on the United States and other Western countries his own counter-hegemonic code to interpret the above mentioned events and plans.

Speaking in Munich about American plans to install TMD in Eastern Europe, Putin mentioned that North Korean and Iranian threats were not critical enough to justify such radical changes in strategic stability. According to Russian military experts, American NMD components in Alaska and California are capable of defending the United States from the North Korean missile threat, while Iran needs 15–20 years to acquire a technical capacity to produce any real missile threat against Europe.

The only way for Washington to use its soft power in an attempt to change the Russian interpretation of NATO's further enlargement and NMD installment in Eastern Europe is to propose Russia as an equal partner in constructing the NMD system. Trying to initiate such a change in the American position, in his latest speeches and at a summit meeting with President Bush in Kennebunkport in July 2007 President Putin proposed Russian help in defending Europe from the Iranian missile threat. He said that if the US would not deploy NMD and troops in Eastern Europe, Russia would offer NATO full access to and joint use of the Gabalinskaya radar station that Moscow is renting in Azerbaijan, and also for the new radar that is under construction in southern Russia in the Armavir area (slated for full operation in 2008). Both radars are situated in geographically advantageous positions to track missiles that could be launched to Europe from the Middle East and South Asia. According to Putin, "[S]uch cooperation would lead to gradual development of Russian–American partnership in the security area ... leading to an entirely new level of trust."[6]

Unfortunately, those proposals did not receive a positive response from Washington, and after two weeks Putin signed a decree suspending Russian participation in the Treaty on Conventional Armed Forces in Europe. The document noted that this step was taken as a result of exceptional circumstances affecting the security of the Russian Federation and requiring immediate action.[7]

Russian–Japanese ties and the territorial dispute

During the last fifteen years the Russian–Japanese relationship has been characterized by obvious contradictions. On the one hand, the geopolitical interests of both countries depend on radical improvements in bilateral relations. On the other hand, Moscow's proposal for joint economic development of the southern Kurile Islands, without the transfer of sovereignty to Japan, did not get a positive reply from Tokyo, and thus economic exchanges between the two countries remained limited. Overall, the bilateral relationship has been composed of two unequal elements: a slowly widening network of cooperation in various fields and a long-term territorial dispute over the southern Kurile Islands.

During the 1990s Japan's desire to support reforms in Russia was constantly reaffirmed by policies of three prime ministers (Hashimoto Ryutaro, Obuchi Keizo, and Mori Yoshiro). Positive changes in Tokyo's policies toward Moscow were explained by some experts not only as a reflection of Japan's desire to solve the territorial dispute, but also as a consequence of improvements in Sino-Russian relations. According to this explanation, the warming relations between China and Russia induced Tokyo's policy change aimed at increasing Japan's own diplomatic maneuverability.

As a result, the paradigm of bilateral military cooperation had changed in a positive way. In 1996 a Japanese Maritime Self-Defense Force (MSDF) ship paid a visit to Vladivostok – the first visit to Russia by an MSDF ship since the end of the Cold War. In 1997 Russia reciprocated with an official naval visit to Tokyo – 104 years after the last port visit of this kind. In 1998, the first joint Russian–Japanese search-and-rescue naval exercise was held in the Vladivostok area. In 1998, the then Japanese Minister of Defense Norota Hosei paid an official visit to the Russian defense minister and signed an important memorandum of understanding on military cooperation. Another breakthrough happened in September 2000 when MSDF ships (the first foreign Navy ships in the recent Russian history) visited the Kamchatka peninsula. Additionally, in August 2003, the MSDF took part in a strategic exercise held in Russian Far Eastern waters. Military ties and exchanges between the Russian Armed Forces and the Japanese SDF also improved and expanded between other military services (Army and Air Force).

Reflecting those trends, the Japanese government approved a new National Defense Program Outline (NDPO), covering a ten-year period starting in 2005, proposing to cut by one third the number of SDF tanks and artillery units. That meant that Tokyo was shifting its military focus from Cold War threats, and that for Japan "a scenario of a full-scale invasion of Hokkaido by Russian ground forces" no longer existed.[8]

For Russians it was obvious that ground forces on Hokkaido could have been substantially reduced long ago, during the Gorbachev years, without compromising the security of Japan. Such a long delay in adapting to profound changes in the neighboring country was a clear example that confidence building among nations "requires a significant amount of time. The planned reduction of the SDF regiments stationed on the island of Hokkaido will certainly improve mutual trust between Russia and Japan, both military and political."[9]

In fact, even during the Cold war decades Russia did not consider Japan itself as a conventional military threat; Moscow's main concern was American military bases on Japanese soil. Though Japanese territorial claims seriously affected bilateral political ties, Moscow had every reason to believe that, while implementing a cautious and sensible policy, Tokyo would never try to capture southern Kurile Islands by force.[10]

After a century of war and confrontation, Russia and Japan have practically demilitarized their relations. In modern Russia a majority of experts abandoned the Soviet-era approach toward Japan as a real threat to the security of the Russian Far East, and did not belong any longer to the old style "rising Japanese militarism" school of thought. They believe that a military conflict between Russia and Japan is just as inconceivable as a conflict between Russia and Germany, for example. Moreover, the strategic challenges facing Moscow and Tokyo objectively force them to view each other not only as security and economic partners, but also, first and foremost, as a resource to be exploited for mutual development.[11]

As already mentioned in this chapter, during the first presidential term (2000–2004) Putin's ultimate goal was to integrate Russia into the world community led by the United States. To realize that plan in the Asia-Pacific, Putin decided to amend Moscow's relations with Tokyo, and to rely on Japanese money and modern technologies to improve the situation in the Russian Far East.

At that time Moscow considered Tokyo as a very prospective partner and during the first year of the first term Putin publicly mentioned Japan 195 times (the most mentioned country). During his visit to Tokyo in 2000 Putin proposed a grand plan to extend the Trans-Siberian railway to Japan. The plan incorporated the idea of joint construction of two tunnels: between the Russian main land and Sakhalin island, and between Sakhalin and Hokkaido. Joint use of an extended Trans-Siberian railway could help Tokyo to more than halve the time taken to transport cargo to European countries (from 35 days by sea to 15 days by land), and to make the transportation of Russian natural resources to Japan a more cost-effective operation. Putin's second proposal was to build an energy bridge between the two countries. He proposed that Japanese businessmen participate more actively in the Eastern Siberia and Sakhalin gas and oil extraction and transportation projects.

Due to a steady growth of the Russian economy Japan began to demonstrate more interest toward its northern neighbor. Mutual trade turnover between the two countries increased from the decent level of $5 billion in 2003 to a record $14 billion in 2006. Giant automobile producer Toyota Motor Company's decision in 2005 to construct an assembly plant near St Petersburg got much publicity in Russia.

A positive trend in Russia's economic relations with Japan has not yet been matched by any progress on the issue of the sovereignty dispute over the so-called "Northern Territories," which has led Japanese businessmen to believe that the solution to it would neither help nor hinder bilateral economic ties. The changed attitude in Moscow to a possible compromise with Japan on this thorny issue has been reflected in the fact that during the first year of Putin's second term, Japan was not even among the ten countries most mentioned by the President.

Neither side appeared ready to soften its position, and a trip to view several of the islands by Prime Minister Junichirō Koizumi on a patrol boat in September 2004 did not improve the atmosphere. In 2005 the two countries celebrated the 150th anniversary of the establishment of Russian–Japanese diplomatic relations. In Tokyo there had been anticipation of the historic date and a planned visit to Japan by Putin could become the occasion for a softening of the Russian position. But Moscow believed it had already taken a step toward solving the issue through Putin's November 2004 proposal to settle the dispute on the basis of the Joint Declaration signed by Japan and the Soviet Union in 1956. Under the terms of the agreement, two islands (Shikotan and Habomai) were to be transferred to Japan upon the conclusion of a peace treaty. According to Yury Alekseyev, Russian deputy foreign minister in charge of Asian affairs, both sides have "diametrically opposite" perspectives on a peace treaty. The foreign ministers of both countries pledged to try to bridge the gap in their perspectives.[12]

Bridging the differences on the territorial issue and concluding a peace treaty are not easy, but also not impossible. Let us try to uncover the critical difference in perceptions of those issues in the two countries. A well-known Japanese scholar of Russia, Kimura Hiroshi, in his recent book suggested that there was a wide gap between President Putin's diplomatic objectives vis-à-vis Japan and his real behavior. Kimura formulated his key argument as follows: "If the Putin government assigned the conclusion of a peace treaty through the solution of territorial disputes the highest priority in its Japan policy, it is difficult to understand why it actually adopts an all or nothing diplomatic behavior vis-à-vis Tokyo," and does not make great efforts toward narrowing the gap over the territorial row with Tokyo to the maximum extent possible.[13] In reality Kimura misread Moscow's priorities regarding the peace treaty issue. First of all, according to public opinion polls conducted in 2006, 73 percent of Russians consider that a transfer of Russian territories to any foreign country cannot be tolerated and that Moscow should stop any negotiations on the fate of the southern Kurile Islands that belong to Russia. Second, the financial situation in the RF has changed in a very positive way, and thus there is no urgent need for foreign investments in Russia as it had been the case in 1990s. Finally, the peace treaty with Japan has little practical importance for Russia's security, and Moscow's real interest is to develop economic ties with Tokyo and acquire Japanese advanced technologies.

A final border demarcation with China that had been achieved during President Putin's visit to Beijing in October 2004 facilitated a new wave of discussion about the fate of the southern Kurile Islands, especially when the Russian leader hinted that it could be solved in a similar way when both sides were ready for a compromise. In November 2004 Russian Foreign Minister

Sergey Lavrov publicly formulated Moscow view on a possible settlement with Tokyo. He made it clear that an atmosphere for a real peace treaty should be created, and it could be concluded only when relations between the two countries reached the level of a mature economic and strategic partnership. At the same time, he referred to the Soviet Union–Japan Joint Declaration of 1956 as a basis for compromise in the framework of a comprehensive peace treaty.[14]

In other words, Russia is interested in developing a bilateral partnership with an emphasis on economic ties, and dealing with the territorial dispute later when a favorable atmosphere would be created. During the last several years Moscow decided to "fine-tune" its message to Tokyo by sending several straightforward signals to clarify its priorities in developing mutually advantageous economic ties with Japan.

In an address to the first Russian–Japanese Investment Forum in September 2006, Deputy Minister of the Russian Ministry of Economic Development and Trade Kiril Androsov mentioned that Japanese companies already invested about $5 billion in the Sakhalin oil and gas projects, but what Russia really wanted now was Japanese investment in other industrial sectors, and that Moscow was very encouraged by Nissan and Toyota's decisions to build automobile plants in Russia.[15] Such a clear policy message confirmed Moscow's new approach toward foreign investments, which had been demonstrated earlier by President Putin's personal attendance at the ceremony held by Toyota Motor Company to mark the start of the plant construction in St Petersburg in June 2005.

It is important to consider positive changes in the financial situation in Russia. In summer 2007 the RF foreign exchange reserves and stabilization fund reached record levels of $400 billion and $110 billion, respectively, and both (reserves and fund) are quickly growing. As a result, Moscow is not so eager for Japanese FDI, especially in the development of natural resources. Overall, as one Russian diplomat stated,

> [T]he government of Japan still displays assertiveness in territorial matters. Russia hopes that Tokyo's position will become more balanced, and that efforts to settle the territorial question will be accompanied by steps to broaden Japan's relations with the Russian Federation.[16]

Recent statements by then–Japanese Prime Minister Shinzō Abe indicated that after some hesitation at least part of the Japanese political and economic elite interpreted the above mentioned Russian signals in the same way Moscow intended for Tokyo. In June 2007 during a meeting with President Putin at the J-8 Summit in Germany, Abe offered Moscow help in developing the Russian Far East, including cooperation in the construction of nuclear power stations, laying optical cables for Internet communications to connect Asia and Europe, joint projects in infrastructure development, tourism and ecology. Moscow's positive reaction was very quick, and during a visit to

Japan in July 2007 the then Russian Deputy Prime Minister Sergey Narishkin officially accepted Tokyo's offer of help in jointly developing the Russian Far East based on latest Japanese technologies.[17]

Sources and effectiveness of Japanese soft power

The image of Japan in Russia may be considered as a mixture of politics, economics, culture, art, history, etc. Strange as it may seem, most Russians, while aware of modern Japan's economic and technological prowess, still cultivate an image of the samurai-era Japan as a distinctly eastern civilization. That kind of image is very attractive and exotic, but in fact it does not correspond much with the real situation in modern Japan that has accumulated many of the aspects of western civilization: progress, culture, and traditions.

Nye defined the main components of soft power as follows: culture (if attractive to others), political values (when it behaves consistently with those values), and foreign policies (when others see it as legitimate and moral).

Japanese foreign policy historically received a negative evaluation in Russia. There are several stereotypes that Russians resort to in characterizing Japan. One of them is represented by historical images connected to the Russian–Japanese war of 1904–5 and to memories of World War II. They may be stated as "our proud cruiser *Varyag* did not surrender to the enemy" and "being an accomplice of fascist Germany, Japan got a well-deserved punishment, and thus Tokyo cannot not raise any territorial claims against Russia as a winner in World War II". The modern-day image of Japanese foreign policies in Russia is also mostly negative, because Tokyo is considered as not being free to choose its own political course, and openly positioning itself as a faithful, junior partner of the United States in world and regional affairs.

Two other aspects of Japanese soft power (values and culture) are much welcomed in Russia. Japanese positive images represent a mixture of romantic history (samurais, geishas, kimonos, etc.) and different elements of Japanese modern culture, known as "Japanese cool" (anime, fashion, sushi, the famous writer Haruki Murakami, etc.). Modern electronics and popular cars can be added to this list.

Public opinion polls conducted recently in forty-six provinces (*oblast*) of Russia, including the Russian Far East, show that the majority of Russians feel very positive about Japan and expanding relations with this country. Across the country, Russians show a pragmatic approach to Japan, and for them the image of this country is associated with electronics (48%) and cars (36%). For most of them (54%) modern Japan is a vivid example of economic success and positive experience for Russians to study. Fifty-one percent of the respondents to the polls regarded Japan as an important economic and trade partner for Russia. In this context it is instructive to compare the attitudes of

Russians toward China and Japan. Although Russian attitudes were more positive for Tokyo than for Beijing, most of those polled view China (33%) and not Japan (21%) as Russia's leading prospective partner in the Asia-Pacific.[18]

According to another recent poll, Japan remains the most "likable" country for a very significant part of the population in the Russian Far East. Forty-five percent of them have the strongest positive feelings toward Japan, followed by ROK (12%), China (9%), and DPRK (3%). No other country in the world can rival Japan's popularity in the region. Among the reasons for Japan's popularity are its economic achievements (53% of those polled) and its unique culture (42%). A significant number think that Russia–Japan ties are in good shape: 29% call them "good" and "very good", and 52% "satisfactory". The respondents are even more optimistic about future prospects.[19]

Most Russians obtain information and form impressions about Japan not by visiting the country but through indirect sources: media, literature, films, cultural events, different types of imported goods, etc. Japan generates its soft power in Russia through its official state channels, business companies, NGOs, and individual citizens. For example, the Japanese embassy and consulates-general in Russia exercise soft power by arranging academic[20] and citizen exchanges, film festivals, music concerts, theatre performances, exhibitions featuring different aspects of Japanese culture. The Japanese Ministry of Foreign Affairs has formed in Russia a network of Japanese Centers to offer training programs for local businessmen and facilitate the development of regional economies. For ten years the Japanese Center in Vladivostok, for example, arranged different types of training programs, seminars, etc. for more than 7,500 Russian participants.

Overall, the majority of Russians consider Japan an important economic partner, a country with a very attractive culture and not a security threat, although we should not forget that Russians still view one component of Japanese soft power (foreign policy) in a negative way. Latest events in Russian foreign policy suggest that Moscow attached much more attention to hard power than to soft power, and thus the clear and strong attraction of Russians toward Japan so far has not become a decisive factor in settling the territorial dispute. On the other hand, according to the above mentioned recent polls, the population of the Russian Far East did not demonstrate such strong positive feelings toward China, but nevertheless a final border demarcation between Russia and China had been successfully achieved in 2004.

This comparison helps us to answer a critical question – whether the emotional likes and dislikes of the Russian population affect the ability to settle territorial disputes. And the answer is that in practice they do not affect this ability much. In other words, in such cases population likes could be considered as a desirable but not a sufficient condition, and what really matters is the real status of comprehensive bilateral relationship between countries.

Thus this example demonstrates confusion in the soft power concept over the recipient of this power. As stated by Ogura Kazuo, sovereign nations in the international community act not on the basis of likes and dislikes, but in accordance with their own interests. No matter how attractive a given country may be, other countries will not accept its attractive power if it obstructs their freedom of action or adversely affects their economic interests.[21]

Russia's stance toward changing US–Japan alliance

In May 1997 the then Russian Defense Minister Igor Rodionov became the first Russian defense chief to visit Japan since the Soviet era. He called the US–Japan security treaty a stabilizing factor in Northeast Asia, and agreed to start a wide variety of defense exchanges, including mutual visits by the SDF chiefs of staff, and military researchers, joint participation in military exercises, etc.

These days Russian diplomacy does not regard the US security treaties with Japan, South Korea, and Australia

> as a direct threat to its interests, and recognizes that they played a certain stabilizing role in the past. At the same time, we believe that these political and military ties should act as a safety net or an emergency means of precaution, but nothing more.[22]

In other words, in principle Moscow is against revisionism in regional security politics, and thus it would not encourage any measures that could trigger a new round of regional armed races, or which are aimed at facilitating Tokyo's more aggressive posture in the framework of the US–Japan security alliance.

Considering the US–Japanese effort to install TMD in Northeast Asia, from Moscow's standpoint any attempt to create closed ABM systems would involve colossal military expenditures and may bring instability in the regional balance of power. Joint deployment of a US–Japanese TMD system to defend Japan is approaching its final stage. Its first echelon will consist of SM-3 complexes installed on US Navy and Japanese MSDF cruisers and destroyers equipped with AEGIS systems, which are capable of intercepting ballistic missiles with a flight range of up to 5,000 kilometers at the medium stage of trajectory. Its second echelon will be composed of ground-based Patriot PAC-3 complexes capable of intercepting ballistic missiles with a flight range of up to 1,000 kilometers at the final stage of trajectory.[23]

American NMD and TMD systems' operational tasks in various parts of the world are tightly interconnected. For example, American Navy and Japan MSDF cruisers and destroyers equipped with AEGIS systems when deployed in the Sea of Japan could successfully solve two operational tasks: to defend American and Japanese military objects from medium-range ballistic missiles as a part of the TMD system, and also to intercept intercontinental ballistic missiles (ICBMs) at the initial stage of their flight trajectory as a part of the American NMD system.

The TMD system in Northeast Asia could effectively intercept Chinese ICBMs at the initial stage of their trajectory, thus substantially degrading Beijing's nuclear deterrence potential. Eventually installation of the TMD system may add strategic uncertainty to the security situation and stimulate a new wave of arms races in the region.

Generally, the Russian leadership considers the American decision to deploy a global NMD system, including a TMD component in Northeast Asia, as a new round of arms races, and Moscow plans to increase its defense budget to modernize its strategic missile force and to strengthen its conventional forces in the western part of the country. That was why in July 2007 Moscow suspended Russian participation in the Treaty on Conventional Armed Forces in Europe.

The most worrisome scenario for Russia would be if Japan decided to acquire nuclear weapons. This option would be absolutely unacceptable for Moscow, because it would break the military balance of power in the region and inevitably accelerate nuclear arms races, especially involving China. That is one of the reasons why Russia is actively participating in the Six-Party Talks in an attempt to eliminate the DPRK nuclear threat and not to give Tokyo any reason to choose this dangerous option.

At this point it makes sense to analyze Japan's moves and intentions in the realization of its desire to become a "normal state" capable of exercising not only soft power but also hard power capabilities expected of a major power. From the author's standpoint, at this time in history Tokyo, with sufficient public support in the country, has the right to revise Article 9 of the Japanese constitution; otherwise its goal to become a "normal state" would be unreachable.

Considering Japan's military capabilities, Tokyo has already undertaken some measures to shed the constitutional restraints on the SDF's operational use, and actively discussed several options aimed at substantially increasing the nation's offensive capabilities, which go far beyond the framework of the Japanese constitution. The Russian view concerning those measures and options deserves a more detailed evaluation.

Japan's 241,000-strong military with its $40 billion military budget has ranked amongst the world's top five. From Micronesia to Iraq, Japan's military has been rapidly eliminating operational use restraints placed on it since World War II. Most visible examples include the dispatch of SDF personnel to Iraq in support of the US-led international coalition, MSDF ships' refueling of US Navy ships in the Indian Ocean, etc. The recent exercise in Guam involved the dropping of 500-pound live bombs on Farallon de Medinilla, a tiny island in the western Pacific, clearly demonstrated Japan's capability to surgically attack a target in North Korea. For this bombing run, Tokyo deployed its newest fighter jets, the F-2s, developed by Japan with technology transfers from the United States. Japan is also purchasing two aircraft carriers that operate helicopters and vertical take off and landing aircraft. Both the F-2 fighter and those light aircraft carriers are dual-purpose weapons that blur the line between offensive and defensive weaponry.[24]

In its SDF arsenal Japan still lacks strategic offensive weapons, such as nuclear submarines, long-range missiles or large aircraft carriers that amount to real power projection. At the height of the fear of the rising China in recent years, Taiwan, Australia and some Southeast Asian countries have encouraged Japan to take up a more proactive role in East Asia. However, when Washington goes ahead to push Japan towards remilitarization, China and South Korea publicly and strongly express their fear of a Japanese military buildup.[25]

Moscow's approach to the SDF's strategic weapons acquisition is a more nuanced one, and at this point in time it is a "tough sell" for the Russian political elite. Overall, the Russian position will depend on several factors, including: the level of American military presence in the region (Moscow is apprehensive about a militarily fully independent Japan and the growing military potential of China), the future state of Russian–Japanese relations, etc.

Some Russian scholars believe that on condition of Japan's agreement to the compromise option in settling the territorial dispute, Moscow could offer Tokyo a "package decision" based on "Two Plus ... " approach. The "two" reflects the idea proposed by Moscow to solve the dispute via the 1956 Declaration by transferring Habomai and Shikotan Islands to Japan, and after that to sign a comprehensive peace treaty. The "plus" reflects the non-territorial benefits that Moscow could provide Tokyo in exchange for adopting the compromise option. As a part of this "package decision" Moscow could support Japan's movement toward expanding the scope of SDF application (a wider use of the SDF abroad and acquisition of dual purpose weaponry), and introducing the respective amendments to the constitution. Moreover, Moscow could do its best to actively cooperate with both Japan and China in establishing a reliable and predictable hydrocarbon market in East Asia. Moscow may also provide consistent support for Tokyo's bid for a permanent seat on a reformed UN Security Council.

For Moscow such an approach would be helpful in acquiring a powerful "Japanese resource" for the development of the Eastern Siberia and the Far East thus preserving the integrity of the Russian state. As far as Washington is concerned, the countries in the Russia–Japan–USA triangle no longer see each other as a military threat, but on the contrary could use each other assets as mutually beneficial economic and political resources. Given its changing security interests in NEA Washington could benefit from a resolution to the territorial dispute and the complete normalization of Russian–Japanese relations.[26]

Considering the roles that Tokyo and Washington may play vis-à-vis each other in the framework of the US–Japan security alliance during its ongoing changes, as already mentioned above, Moscow does not want Tokyo to become fully independent in its military strategy and SDF operational application. On the other hand, expanded scope of the SDF application, and more independence from the US in producing high-tech weaponry (for example, Japan expressed a desire to develop its own, next generation stealth fighter jet), may lead to an expanded role for Tokyo in the alliance and gradually reduce Japan's military dependence on the United States.

Another critical issue is how far Japan will go in changing its strategy concerning the role of the SDF in future deployments overseas, especially taking into account the recent experience in Iraq where the SDF provided no direct support for US combat operations. One Japan policy expert believes that the suggestion that Japan will become the "Britain of Asia" in its support of US policy is off the mark. He thinks Japan's public, long considered a non-factor in policymaking, will play a significant role in determining how "normal" is defined, while accepting "a defensive realist view that recognizes military power as useful primarily for homeland defense." He suggests the Japanese are strengthening the SDF in order to deter "a North Korean attack or Chinese infringement on Japanese territory."[27]

In reviewing the Russian stance toward the US–Japan alliance, it is worth mentioning the recent case of Russia's successful interaction with the United States and Japan in solving a nuclear safety issue. A great number of decommissioned Russian Pacific Fleet nuclear submarines – remnants of the Cold War – were slated for dismantlement and deactivation in the 1990s and posed a serious ecological threat to the surrounding areas. The United States and Japan offered help and allocated funds to solve the problem. In 2003 the whole complex became operational, with the US Department of Defense funding a technical shore base and the Japanese funding a floating filtration plant. The implementation of the joint project has led to several positive outcomes. According to Russian Rosatom Head Sergey Kirienko, all decommissioned submarines will be utilized by 2010, thus improving the safety of the Russian Far East's territories as well as the ecological situation of the Sea of Japan. Second, the international cooperation had a profound socio-economic impact, the creation of new jobs in the city of Bol'shoi Kamen, where the Zvezda ship repair yard was the largest industrial enterprise.[28]

Finally, considering Russia's approach toward the ongoing changes in the US–Japan security alliance, one Russian expert suggests that though "a new relationship between Russia and the US has been established with its positive dynamics," for the sake of a more stable security situation in the Asia-Pacific, Moscow, however, prefers "more emphasis in Japan on the rising economic importance of East Asia rather than strategic relations with Washington." Besides, "[A]n expansion of the SDF's role far beyond the Japanese borders may provide new opportunities for bilateral cooperation with Russia in global peacekeeping operations"[29] under the auspices of the UN, and for regional interaction in various areas, including anti-terrorist operations, defense of sea lines of communications, etc.

Conclusion

Misinterpretation of each other's actions and words has been typical of the Russian–American post-Cold War relationship. It occurred in many cases, including the NATO enlargement, the abrogation of the ABM Treaty, and most recently the American decision to deploy an NMD system and troops in Eastern Europe. Over that period Washington tried to use its soft power to influence Russian interpretative codes but failed to achieve any tangible results. Moscow continued to grasp American actions in an anti-hegemonic code, and Washington unilaterally resorted to hard power. But the more the United States achieved by means of hard power, the smaller became the role of American soft power in US–Russian relations.[30]

Further exercise of hard power would lead to a situation where American soft power would be completely irrelevant in relations with Russia. However, a long-term bilateral partnership would be unsustainable unless the two countries' interpretative codes can be drawn nearer. In his speech in Munich and at the summit meeting with President Bush in Kennebunkport in 2007, President Putin clarified the seriousness of the situation, and attempted to improve it by discussing those interpretative codes and trying to exchange them with his American counterpart. Recent decisions by the American President Barak Obama not to proceed with previously declared plans to deploy the US NMD components in Poland and Czech Republic manifested that to some extent Russian arguments have been taken into account. Generally Russia's perception of the Washington's diplomatic initiatives in East Asia and the American role in the changing US–Japan alliance would continue to be affected by the overall state of Russian–American relations defined by acute differences in approaches toward various international security issues, especially in Eastern Europe.

Differences in perceptions on the territorial issue and peace treaty continue to stay at the centerpiece of Russian–Japanese relations, although it is unlikely that the long-term dispute will pose a serious challenge to regional stability. Tokyo has tried to impose on Moscow its interpretative code as follows: a solution of the territorial dispute is a major prerequisite for a peace treaty. In spite of the strong attraction many Russians feel toward Japan (up to 50% of the population), Japanese soft power has not become a decisive factor in settling the dispute. That example demonstrates that in the international community states act not on the basis of likes and dislikes, but in accordance with their own interests.

Russia continues to send Japan its own message: a peace treaty can be concluded when bilateral relations reach the level of a mature economic and strategic partnership. During last few years Moscow fine-tuned its message to Tokyo by sending straightforward signals to clarify its priorities in developing mutually advantageous bilateral ties: to redirect Japanese investment flows and the latest technological innovations from natural resource sectors to other value-added production-oriented sectors of the Russian economy.

Recent events demonstrate that to some extent those signals have been interpreted in Tokyo as intended by Moscow. In summer 2007 the then Prime Minister Abe officially offered Japanese assistance in the development of the Russian Far East, on the basis of latest Japanese technologies, in such fields as nuclear energy, communications, infrastructure development, tourism, ecology, and Moscow readily accepted the offer. These events reflect new trends that may lead to a strengthening of bilateral ties and eventually to a peace treaty between Moscow and Tokyo.

At the same time we should consider that although Japan enjoys a very positive image in Russia, Japan is losing to China, when comparing Russian perceptions of its prospective partners in East Asia. Overall, on the one hand, the successful final demarcation of the Russian–Chinese border demonstrated that there was nothing impossible in international politics; on the other hand, it is clear that, due to absolutely different state of bilateral Russian–Japanese ties, in the near term Russian–Chinese border demarcation model could not be used to solve territorial dispute with Japan.

Japan's pursuit of the status of "normal" state" and more offensive capabilities for the JSDF does not pose a direct threat to Russia in the region. Provided Tokyo will agree to compromise solution in its territorial dispute with Moscow, Russia may support Japan's move toward amending its constitution.

Expansion of the SDF's roles and activities and greater independence from the United States in producing high-tech weaponry may lead to an enhanced role for Tokyo in the US–Japan alliance, and gradually reduce Japan's military dependence on the United States. This will facilitate a more confident Japan with a more independent foreign policy. A simultaneous pursuit of soft and hard power would make Japan a more reliable, trustworthy, and capable partner; and the overall implications for its alliance with the United States will also be positive. On the other hand, there is no indication that the Japanese people will fully endorse a more active SDF role in overseas deployments. A defensive realist view that recognizes the JSDF military power as useful primarily for homeland defense will be more likely to prevail.

As far as security threats posed by the US–Japan alliance in the region are concerned, Moscow considers two of them as most critical: the already running US–Japanese program to establish a TMD system in Northeast Asia and possible Japanese decision to acquire nuclear weapons. Both of these developments are unacceptable to Moscow, because they will destroy the military balance of power in the region, and inevitably accelerate conventional and nuclear arms races, especially involving China.

Russia enjoys a positive experience of interaction with both members of the US–Japan security alliance in solving the nuclear safety problem of the Russian Far East. However, Moscow's general approach to the American-led security alliances in NEA is very cautious. Although they do not pose any direct threat to Russia's security, Moscow is not a part of this system and thus its options in championing its interest in the region are limited. That is why Russia is keen on complementing American regional alliances with a new international governmental organization to deal with security issues in Northeast Asia that could be formed, for example, on the basis of the Six-Party Talks mechanism. Moscow also welcomes the activities of the ASEAN Regional Forum and other multilateral security architectures, proposing to "move in this direction in a step-by-step manner, with the goal of establishing an integrated system that covers the entire Asia-Pacific."[31]

Notes

1. This author proposed this term ("coopetition") to characterize the state of modern Russian–American relations as a mixture of cooperation and competition.
2. Joseph Nye, Jr., *Soft Power: The Means to Success in World Politics*, New York: Public Affairs, 2004, p. 11.
3. Samuel Huntington, *The Clash of Civilizations and the Remaking of World Order*, New York: Touchstone, 1996, p. 92.
4. Nye, Jr., p. 111.
5. Igor Zevelev and Mikhail Troitsky, *Power and Influence in U.S.–Russian Relations*, Moscow: Oblizdat, 2006, pp. 15–16.
6. Joint Press Conference with President of the United States George Bush, July 02, 2007.
7. President of Russia official website, July 14, 2007.
8. *The Japan Times*, December 12, 2004; *The New York Times*, February 13, 2005.
9. Viacheslav Amirov, "Japan and the Asia-Pacific: A Russian Perspective," in Rouben Azizian, ed., *Russia, America, and Security in the Asia-Pacific*, Honolulu: APCSS, 2006, p. 115.
10. Viktor Pavlyatenko, "Security of Russia in the Asia-Pacific Region: A Dander of Isolation," in Andrey Zagorsky, eds., *Security of Russia: XXI Century*, New York, East–West Institute, 2000, pp. 184–85.
11. Dmitri Trenin and Vasily Mikheyev, *Russia and Japan as a Resource for Mutual Development: A XXI Century Perspective on a XX Century Problem*, Moscow: Carnegie Moscow Center, 2005, pp. 4–6.
12. http://www.mid.ru. March 26, 2005.
13. Hiroshi Kimura, "Putin's Policy Toward Japan: Eight Features," in Hiroshi Kimura, ed., *Russia's Shift toward Asia*, Tokyo: SPF, 2007, p. 117.
14. http://www/strana.ru, November 15, 2004.
15. RIA Novosti, September 2006.
16. Alexander Ignatov, "Russia in the Asia-Pacific," in R. Azizian, ed., *Russia, America, and Security in the Asia-Pacific*, Honolulu: APSCC, 2006, p. 3.
17. AFP, July 25, 2007.
18. All-Russian Center to Study Public Opinion (VCIOM) polls results, October 15–16, 2005, p. 49.
19. Trenin and Mikheyev, p. 11.
20. In most cases preference is given to Russians who speak Japanese and to students interested in studying Japanese language and culture.
21. Ogura Kazuo, "The Limits of Soft Power," *Japan Echo*, Tokyo, October 2006.
22. Ignatov, p. 9.
23. "U.S. in Final Stages of Installing Missile Defense System in Japan," Defencetalk. com, March 10, 2006.
24. "Japan's Military Shedding Its Restraints," *Straits Times*, July 24, 2007.
25. "Japan's More Provocative Military Makes Neighbors Nervous," *International Herald Tribune*, July 22, 2007.
26. Trenin and Mikheyev, pp. 17–22.
27. Paul Midford, "'Realist View' of Defense May Be Viewed Differently in Tokyo and Washington," The East West Center website, Honolulu, January 31, 2007.

28 Sergey Sevastyanov, "The Russian Far East's Security Perspective: Interplay of Internal and External Challenges and Opportunities," in *Siberia and the Russian Far East in the 21st Century: Partners in the "Community of Asia" Proceedings*, Sapporo, Japan, February 2005, pp. 35–38.
29 Amirov, pp. 115–16.
30 Zevelev and Troitsky, pp. 61–62, and 70.
31 Ignatov, p. 15.

7 European views of a changing US–Japan alliance
Declining prospects for "civilian power" cooperation?

Christopher W. Hughes

European and Japanese responses to US hegemony

The resurgence of the United States's hegemonic "hard" and "soft" power since the mid-1990s, and the unrivalled hegemonic position and degree of freedom of international action that this has gifted to the United States, has posed major questions for its allies, let alone its foes, with regard to how to manage relations with the sole superpower (Krauss, Hughes and Blechinger-Talcott 2007). For the United States' allies, although difficulties were clearly emerging under the Clinton administration, it is the advent of the George W. Bush administration and the events post-September 11, 2001 that have thrown into sharpest relief the problems of potentially unbridled US hegemony, and the risks of the United States functioning more as a predatory than a benign hegemon. There has been speculation that the United States may in fact be proving to be the "world's dispensable nation" (Lind 2005), increasingly preoccupied with its own unilateralist, or even "military-imperial", agenda, and thus risking irrelevance in the eyes of other regions more intent on building common institutions (Johnson 2004). There are also indications that the United States' current "hyper-power" status (Malone and Khong 2003: 421–22) may prove transitory and limited, as revealed by the aftermath of the Iraq war, the continuing rise of China and India, and renewed power of Russia. Nevertheless, mainstream allied opinion in Europe and Asia still regards the United States' hegemonic presence as the essential underpinning force for the international system (Allin, Andréani, Errera and Samore 2007).

Indeed, it is notable that even in the United States the emphasis has been not upon evading alliance commitments, but on how to better activate alliance relationships to complement its attempts to restructure the post-Cold War international system. Hence, the principal challenge for US allies has been not to find ways to reject outright (at least not beyond the rhetorical level, or in the medium term) US hegemony and alliance ties. Instead, for allies the imperative has been to search for strategies to improve their management of US power and to address issues of bilateral or broader international concern where the United States occupies a central position; whether these relate to the response to threats of transnational terrorism and weapons of mass destruction (WMD) post-September 11, political economy, or climate change. These strategies to manage US power may include the adjustment and strengthening of existing bilateral alliances ties in the security and economic domains; the strengthening of multilateral political, economic and security frameworks to defuse, dilute and deflect US power; and the fostering of regional ties in order to leverage the collective power of states against an over-mighty US (Krauss, Hughes and Blechinger-Talcott 2007).

Japan and Europe, as the two principal alliance partners that have facilitated US trans-Pacific and trans-Atlantic hegemony in the postwar period, have faced similar challenges in managing their respective alliance relationships with the United States, and especially since the start of the Bush presidency. Japan, as observed in other chapters of this book, faced with demands for an enhanced contribution to international security from its US ally post-September 11, and set against the context of the perception of its own economic decline and continued military limitations relative to a resurgent United States and a rising China, has responded by strongly re-adhering to US hegemony. Japan, first under the leadership of Prime Koizumi Junichirō, then Abe Shinzō, Fukuda Yasuo, and now under Asō Tarō, has invested its policy energy in strengthening bilateral security cooperation, thereby diffusing potential conflicts with the United States' evolving security strategy that increasingly seeks to utilize its regional allies and bases to respond more flexibly to regional and now global military contingencies (Hughes 2005). In the meantime, the United States, in identifying Japan as the key bastion for the maintenance of its military hegemony in East Asia vis-à-vis China, has largely subordinated economic to security ties, thereby alleviating the potential for economic conflict that has afflicted US ties with other states (Higgott 2004).

Japan's strengthening of bilateral alliance ties with the United States has not been unconditional and without hedging tactics, as shown by degrees of strategic divergence over North Korea; the minimalist Japan Self Defence Forces (JSDF) commitment in Iraq; and continued friction over the final settlement of the realignment of US bases in Japan (Hughes and Krauss 2007). Japan's temporary disengagement from the MSDF refuelling mission in support of Operation Enduring Freedom (OEF) in Afghanistan at the end of 2007—the result of strong resistance from the main opposition Democratic Party of Japan arguing for a less US and more UN-centred security policy—was another example of residual Japanese reticence to overly engage with US global security priorities. Although, of course, in the end Japan's Liberal Democratic Party (LDP) subsequently re-engaged with OEF with the passage of a new Replenishment Support Special Measures Law in January 2008.

Japanese policy-makers, despite their assertions that there is no fundamental incompatibility between bilateralism and multilateralism, are arguably aware that this strategy of re-strengthening ties with the hegemon carries opportunity costs in terms of limiting Japan's ability to engage in building regional multilateral security and political institutions that might help to constrain US power. Nevertheless, Japan's objective in the post-September 11 world has been to manage US hegemony chiefly through strengthened bilateralism in security, to portray itself as an indispensable ally, and through these means to hope to exert greater leverage over its ally's strategic orientation (Hughes 2008: 114–15).

Europe (defined here as the twenty seven European Union [EU] member states, but, as will be seen below, not always as necessarily coeval with the EU as an actor itself) has faced similar challenges to Japan in the face of often rampant US hegemony and unilateralism. Although the degree and finality of damage inflicted on the trans-Atlantic relationship should not be over-exaggerated as US–Europe relations still remain fundamentally strong in many security and economic aspects, disputes over trade, the global environment, and most prominently the Iraq war have certainly harmed ties. Europe—as is its wont as an actor of multiple identities, incorporating the EU as a collective actor, as well individual state diplomacies—has responded in different ways to the assertion of US hegemony. The EU on certain issues has collectively resisted the United States and utilized multilateral frameworks such as the World Trade Organisation (WTO) (Yoshimatsu 2007), as in the case of trade friction over steel and genetically modified (GM) foods. On other issues, particularly Iraq, but also missile defence (MD), Europe has experienced "disaggregation" (Peterson 2004: 620–21) between (in former Secretary of Defense Donald Rumsfeld's inaccurate phase) "Old and New Europe": the United Kingdom (UK) adhering to US hegemony; with France and Germany proving more obdurate in cooperating with US military "adventurism". The result has been a mix of cooperation and tension in US–Europe relations on a variety of levels, with the overall trend has perhaps being one of deterioration in trans-Atlantic ties, especially during the first term of the Bush administration; although relations have begun to recover in the latter stages of Bush's second term. This stands in sharp contrast to the general strengthening of US–Japan ties experienced in particular during the Koizumi administration, and might argue that Japan in the short term has been more successful than Europe in managing ties with the United States.

Japanese and European perceptions of and strategic responses to US hegemony post-September 11 clearly have much in common, because they stand as two important case studies that enhance comparative lessons for how key allies in different regions deal with US power on a range of political, economic and security issues. In addition, though, beyond the comparative aspect, Japanese and European responses to US hegemony have a common importance for understanding the management of US power because they are directly linked. This is due to the fact that Europe has often seen Japan as a key partner, with significant and compatible power resources, with which it can work in order to assist in the management of US hegemony, and the United States' perceived egregious tendencies towards serial bilateralism, "a la carte multilateralism" (Mack 2003; Berkofsky 2008: 25), and unilateralism. Hence, any move by Japan, as noted above, to strengthen its bilateral alliance with the United States and re-adhere firmly to US hegemony, to the possible detriment of other multilateral or regional options, carries important implications for the ability of Europe to fully engage Japan as a partner to deal with US power. Hence, the Japan–Europe relationship is important for the foreign policy of the EU and its individual member states in dealing with US power, and may have a significant impact on the opportunities and limitations for cooperation amongst US allies to utilize multilateralism and regional cooperation in order to constrain US hegemony.

The task of this chapter, therefore, is to consider the impact of a strengthened US–Japan alliance upon Europe's attempts to utilize enhanced cooperation with Japan as a means to respond to US hegemony; the ways in which closer US–Japan ties impose limitations, but also perhaps provide opportunities for new interaction, on specific international policy issues that are often bones of contention amongst the United States, Japan and Europe; and, based on the Europe–Japan example, the wider ramifications for US allies in seeking to work in tandem to address US power.

The chapter is organized into three sections. The first considers in more detail definitions of Europe as an international actor; European perceptions of US hegemony and the current challenges that it presents to Europe itself and its preferred view of the structuring of the international system and appropriate responses to extant economic and security issues; and Europe's preferred strategies in terms of "hard" and "soft" power and international frameworks to respond to the US challenge. The second section then examines European perceptions of Japan as an effective partner in the past and today in dealing with US power, in terms of complementary power capabilities, values, and common interests and views of the necessary structuring of the international system. The third section then evaluates the ways in which the deepening of US–Japan alliance ties has affected European approaches to managing the trans-Atlantic alliance, US hegemony in the international system, and related economic and security issues.

This chapter concludes that Japan's "hardening" of its international role through its enhanced military capabilities and strengthening of the US–Japan alliance, and its subsequent decreased emphasis on multilateral and intra- and inter-regional balancing against the United States, has indeed in many instances hindered European strategies to manage US hegemony. Although certainly not devastating for European strategies to collectively respond to the United States, Europe is finding it harder to find common ground with Japan on issues where it is diverging strategically from the United States but where Japan is showing greater strategic convergence with the United States. Examples of this in East Asia include European strategy towards the rise of China, and potentially the engagement of North Korea, and outside the region in Iraq.

However, this situation does not hold true for all European states individually, as those converging with the United States strategically, and most notably the UK, are finding grounds for deeper and more substantial cooperation with Japan. This is especially the case on "hard" security issues. Moreover, despite the increasing strengthening of the US–Japan alliance, there are still areas for possibly enhanced cooperation with EU as a collective whole. Japan continues to maintain a degree of strategic divergence from the United States on issues such as climate change, trade and the Middle East peace settlement, as do the EU and many individual European states, and thus there is scope for Europe–Japan cooperation on these issues. Furthermore, there are clearly areas of general convergence between the United States, Europe and Japan. Afghanistan is one illustration of this, and Iran may be another, if it continues with its nuclear programme. In this sense, a deepened US–Japan alliance may still provide opportunities for Europe–Japan cooperation and for moderating, whilst still generally cooperating with, US hegemonic behavior. Moreover, domestic political change in Japan, with the advent of the more internationally cautious Fukuda administration, made for retrenchment in ambitions for the US–Japan alliance, thus scaling back some of the growing hard power of Japan and opening up avenues for Japan–Europe cooperation. Hence, the chapter concludes that even though a changing US–Japan alliance poses difficult challenges for Japan–Europe cooperation and European approaches to US power and hegemony, nevertheless, depending on the specific issue, it may at the very least not hinder Japan–Europe cooperation, and even create promising new avenues for cooperation.

Europe and US hegemony: soft power versus hard power

European views of US hegemony are complex and prone to contradictions and ambivalence. Europe, on the one hand, has long enjoyed close and very cooperative ties with the United States in the international system. For many of the founders of the EU project and its antecedents, US federalism has served as a model for integration. For its part, the United States has generally sought to encourage European integration as a means to stabilize this region in the postwar and post-Cold War periods; although more recently it has shown concerns that European integration has reached the point that it may challenge US power (Peterson 2004: 616–17). The EU project has arguably only been made possible through a high degree of reliance on US military hegemony and leadership in the North Atlantic Treaty Organisation (NATO) for external protection; and, in the project's earliest stages, internal reassurance against the resurgence of German power—a process that can be termed as deepening European interdependence through dependence on the United States (Wallace 2002: 142). In turn, Europe and the United States have developed a sense of trans-Atlantic community (Hemmer and Katzenstein 2002) based on shared values of liberal democracy and an extraordinary degree of economic interdependence. In fact, the EU is perhaps already the "hegemonic" equal of the United States in terms of global economic size and influence (Baldwin, Peterson and Stokes 2003: 29).

On the other hand, though, European states have felt discomfort with dependence on US military power and hegemony, and their consequent relative political subordination, individually, or collectively in the guise of the

EU, to the United States in configuring the international system. The United States has always been the significant "Other" against which much of the construction of a European identity has taken place. During the Cold War, Europe at times attempted to portray itself as the "third force" in the international system to counter-balance US–Soviet bipolarity (Smith 2004: 19); and in the post-Cold War period, Europe has toyed with concepts of "trilateralism," that employ the EU and East Asia as regional entities hopefully capable of tying the United States into a tripolar international system and countering the US promotion of unipolarity (Hook, Gilson, Hughes and Dobson 2005: 73).

In order to promote this tripolar and multilateral vision, European states, and particularly through the agency of the EU, have sought to exploit a number of forms of power and multilateral frameworks for cooperation. The EU has developed a number of tools of "soft power", including the extensive provision of humanitarian aid and Official Development Assistance (ODA) and its self-promotion as a "development superpower" in the neighboring regions of North Africa, the Middle East, and further afield in the Caribbean, Sub-Saharan Africa and the Pacific. Europe's provision of ODA, although sharing with that of the United States an emphasis on good governance and clearly designed for strategic security purposes, has usually been characterized by conditionalities less "neo-liberal" in tone and thus promoting a more European-oriented model of economic development.

In a similar fashion, Europe has attempted to exert its "soft power" or "transformative power" (Maull 2005: 788–89) by standing as a model of liberal democracy and economy for states in Eastern and Southern Europe, and now also on the fringes of the Middle East and Europe in the shape of Turkey, seeking to accede to the EU. In part, it might be argued that Europe's development of "soft" power capabilities is a rationalization of its essentially still subordinate role to the United States and is not a real alternative to US hegemony which still deals in the real currency of military power (Smith and Steffenson 2005: 347). All the same, the European states, and the EU in particular, have laboured diligently to project an image of "civilian power" (Maull 1990/1991) to counter that of the United States as the quintessential military power.

At the same time, despite its play for civilian power status, Europe has also moved to try to augment its "hard" military power through the European Security and Defence Identity (ESDI) and St Malo process of 1998, under which the UK as the arch-"Atlanticist" and France as the arch-"Europeanist" military powers in Europe agreed that the EU should develop a "capacity for autonomous action, backed by credible military forces", and thus moved in the direction of beginning to reduce Europe's collective dependence on US military power (Smith 2002: 102; White 2001: 147–48). The EU has further boosted its potential military capabilities with the introduction of the Common Foreign and Security Policy (CFSP) and European Security and Defence Policy (ESDP). Clearly, though, Europe's collective military power capabilities outside NATO, and without the involvement of the United States, remain limited, and its chief power projection capabilities still lie with the individual state militaries of the UK and France. But even with these limited capabilities the EU has carved out an important military role in terms of conflict prevention, peacekeeping, post-conflict reconstruction, and "state-building". The EU has performed this role since 2003 in the Balkans in support of the originally US-led NATO operations, and independently on a small scale in the Congo, thus intimating an expanded, if still constrained, military role for the EU, and which has raised questions about the future viability of NATO as the chief provider of security for Europe (Menon 2004: 641–42).

In developing these forms of "soft" and "hard" power, the European states and the EU have sought to deepen their own further integration project so that Europe can stand more effectively as a collective political, economic and military pole vis-à-vis the United States (Maull 2005: 777), and also sought to reach out, in line with the tripolar and multipolar vision, to forge links with and support the region-building activities of other states as potential poles in the international system (Edwards 2005). Hence, the EU has established inter-regional relations with the Mediterranean countries though the Barcelona process since 1995, and with Asia through the Asia-Europe Meeting (ASEM) since 1996 (Gilson 2000; Maull 2005: 786). These dialogue forums have discussed a range of political and economic issues, and placed a notable emphasis on non-traditional security issues, including migration, drug trafficking, transnational crime and terrorism; and stressed cooperation to reinforce multilateral frameworks at the global level, including the UN.

Europe's strategy for augmenting its international presence, therefore, is seen to hinge upon the projection of predominantly "soft" power, with developing "hard" power components; a multi-dimensional view of security that stresses the interconnection between non-traditional security threats and traditional security, conflict prevention and state-building; and an emphasis on deploying power through the strengthening of Europe's own integration projects, the strengthening of other regional projects and inter-regionalism, and the strengthening of multilateral frameworks at the global level.

In practice Europe's aspirations do not always match its collective ability to act and the resultant policy outcomes. It is important to remember that Europe's will to act as a moderating influence on US hegemony has varied over time. The relationship experienced particular tensions in the "second cold war" of the late 1970s and 1980s when the Europeans increasingly looked for engagement with the Soviet bloc as against the hardened military posture of the Ronald Reagan administration; but then rebounded positively at the end of the Cold War; and has since dipped in the wake of September 11. Likewise, as noted earlier, European opinion over US hegemony is highly diverse. France's stance has traditionally remained aloof (in style, if not always in substance) from US hegemony, arguing strongly post-Iraq war for a multipolar world; the UK has argued the contrary case in favour of Europe aligning itself around the US pole; whilst Germany drifted closer to an anti-hegemonic position following events in Iraq. Moreover, it is clear that Europe has not always played the good multilateralist (Pollack 2004): for instance, seeking military intervention in the Balkans in the 1990s without seeking UN mandates, and thus acting in marked contrast to its later avowed "internationalist" position in the run-up to the Iraq war. Europe has also often found it difficult to discover true common ground with other regions in order to make its trilateral vision function: the ASEM process, for instance, has been greatly debilitated by friction between the EU and its Asian dialogue partners over questions of human rights and the inclusion of the Myanmar in the forum (Reiterer 2002: 75).

Still, despite these important provisos, it is clear that Europe's attempts to identify itself as a civilian power stand in contradistinction to the current character of US hegemony. This contrast is made all the sharper by the practices of the Bush administration which have tended to stress the pre-eminence of military-technical solutions in addressing multi-causal security issues such as transnational terrorism; the expression of US power through pre-emptive military actions and unilateralism; and selective multilateralism in the shape of "coalitions of the willing".

European views of Japan as a "civilian" power

Europe's status as a "civilian power" stands in contrast to and provides resources and frameworks to mediate the impact of US hegemony. At the same time, it provides a complementary basis for potential international cooperation with Japan, which also purports to share many of the same power traits as Europe.

For sure, Europe's relations with Japan have not always been cordial, or seemingly predisposed to close cooperation vis-à-vis US hegemony. In the early postwar period, Japan's client state-like association with the United States was perceived by European powers as a potential threat. Great Britain, for instance, strongly opposed the United States' sponsorship of Japan into the General Agreement on Tariffs and Trade (GATT) as endangering its textile industries. In much of the latter Cold War period, Japan's status as a "peril" to the European project was manifested in substantial trade friction. Japan was viewed as an economic threat due to its vigorous competition in areas of traditional European industrial strength, such as steel, shipbuilding and automobiles, and because of its tendency to negotiate bilaterally over trade with individual European Community (EC) member states rather than with the body collectively, thus indicating that it was practising a "divide and rule" policy (Hughes 2001: 61). Anti-Japanese sentiment reached a peak with accusations in the 1980s that it was using automobile production investment in the UK as a "Trojan Horse" to circumvent EC trade regulations, and the French Prime Minister Edith Cresson's extraordinary labelling in 1991 of the Japanese as "ants" and "outcasts".

Nevertheless, throughout the Cold War period, Europe and Japan began to establish the basis for closer economic and eventually political cooperation. The EC developed regular high-level consultations with Japan at the European Commission level, through parliamentary exchanges, and the establishment of the EC delegation to Japan in 1974. Japan and the EC also initiated a degree of political cooperation on issues around Europe's periphery with a joint statement in 1980s condemning Iran's seizure of the US embassy in Tehran, and shared strategic interests over Soviet intervention in Afghanistan and Poland. Europe–Japan relations then reached a new stage of maturity and "partnership" at the end of the Cold War. Japanese investment in Europe came increasingly to be seen as positive force supporting the revitalization of certain industries and furthering European integration, and the EU Commission's 1998 White Paper then argued for closer political and security relations with Japan. The EU–Japan Joint Declaration of 1991 stressed the two sides' shared principles of liberal democracy and economy; support for the UN and multilateral organization; and laid out specific areas for cooperation in the economic stabilization of post-Cold War Eastern Europe, the conservation of the environment, and tackling terrorism and transnational crime. All of these principles and issues were essentially "civilian" in nature, and promised the complementary interlocking of Europe and Japan's economic power and ODA resources, and a very different basis for cooperation from the respective military security relationships that each maintained with the United States (Gilson 2000: 121–65). Japan and Europe then reiterated these principles in the 2001 Action Plan, which further laid out a more specific agenda of cooperation in UN reform, human rights and democratization, conflict prevention and peace-building, and non-proliferation (Minstry of Foreign Affairs 2001).

In turn, this "civilian" power agenda has translated into significant policy initiatives by Japan and the EU in Eastern Europe, the Middle East and the Balkans. Japan was a founding member of the European Bank for Reconstruction and Development (EBRD) in 1990, and in the 1990s was a major donor of aid to Poland and Hungary, later to become EU accession and then member states. The EU and Japan became the major funders of the Palestinian Authority from the late-1990s onwards, thus finding common ground in their divergence from the United States' essentially "Israel-first" policy. Europe and Japan also found a common agenda for security cooperation through financial and technical support in the reconstruction of postwar Bosnia (Berkofsky 2008: 28–29).

For Europe, therefore, Japan has possessed the qualities to be an ideal "civilian power" partner to balance, if not explicitly, then at least implicitly, US dominance in the international system. This balancing role has largely taken the form of enabling Europe to engage in a number of important "civilian" political and security initiatives to strengthen its own regional integration project, to enhance its international presence around its periphery, and thus to stand more effectively as an alternative pole to that of the United States. Europe has also attached importance to Japan as a partner and anchor for its programme to support regionalism and the growth of a third pole in East Asia to provide for a more trilateral international system. The EU has often perceived of Japan as an important mediator in the ASEM forum between itself and the East Asian states, and especially on particular technical issues for cooperation. For instance, the EU viewed Japan as a key partner through which to channel its expertise on regional monetary cooperation to East Asian states in the wake of the East Asian financial crisis (Hook, Gilson, Hughes, Dobson 2005: 300–1).

Japan, for its part, has been careful not to alienate the United States by being seen to cooperate against it with the EU. Nevertheless, in the past, cooperation with the EU has been seen as a useful mechanism to channel its "soft power" for security ends, and "trilateralism" as a potential alternative or complement to exclusive reliance on the US–Japan bilateral relationship for the projection of Japan's international presence. For instance, even the arch-bilateralist Koizumi sponsored a so-called Task Force on Foreign Relations in 2002, which argued for closer ties with the EU as part of the diversification strategy of Japan's foreign policy away from over-reliance on the United States (Berkofsky 2008: 26).

Europe and the US–Japan alliance

If Europe has viewed Japan as a useful partner to construct Europe itself and other regions as countervailing poles to US hegemony, then the strengthening of Japan's alliance with the United States post-September 11, its declining status as a "civilian power", and its re-adherence to US unipolarity provides important challenges, but potential opportunities, for Europe–Japan international cooperation.

Europe and Japan have grounds for both divergence and convergence in their cooperation on the issue of the United States-led "war on terror" against transnational terrorism and WMD. Iraq has clearly been the most problematic issue for EU relations with the United States: the EU unable to articulate a collective and effective response to the initial US invasion of Iraq in 2003, and Europe splitting along lines of individual states' opposition to or support for the US military action. In contrast, Japan demonstrated greater strategic convergence with the United States on Iraq, expressing from the outset political "understanding", although not military support, for the invasion. Hence, in the early phases of this vital test of EU foreign policy and international cooperation outside the ambit of US bilateral alliance relationships to respond to US power, Europe and Japan found little common ground for substantive co-ordination of their diplomatic policies.

Likewise, Japan's shift towards a strengthened alliance with the United States to respond to WMD issues and its concomitant inability to more fully exploit its regional diplomatic options in East Asia has also created grounds for strategic divergence with Europe over its hopes for strengthening East Asia as an alternative regional pole. Europe since the start of the new century has largely sought to promote engagement with North Korea as the optimum approach to resolving the nuclear crisis and the domestic human security crisis inside the North. The EU has provided financial assistance for the Korean Peninsula Energy Development Organisation (KEDO), humanitarian assistance to respond to the North's domestic food shortages, and technical assistance to encourage economic reform; whilst a number of individual EU member states have normalized diplomatic ties with the North. Japan has clearly also sought to promote engagement with North Korea, demonstrated most dramatically by Koizumi's visits to the North in 2002 and 2004, and the stop–go persistence with normalization negotiations. However, Japan has gradually shifted to a more hard-line position on the North's nuclear programme and the issue of the abductions of Japanese citizens, and found it progressively more difficult to maintain effective engagement options with the North, culminating in its imposition of sanctions in reaction to the July missile tests and October nuclear test (Hughes 2006). In the meantime, Japan has strengthened its "hard power" to respond to the North through the upgrading of its national military capabilities, and through the enhanced operability of the US–Japan alliance, as seen in Japan's 2004 National Defence Programme Guidelines (NDPG), the conclusion of the 2005 bilateral Defence Policy Review Initiative (DPRI) (Hughes 2005; Hughes 2004), and acceleration of Ballistic Missile Defense cooperation with the United States (Hughes and Krauss 2007; Hughes 2009). Europe certainly shares Japan's and the United States' concerns over the North's threat of nuclear proliferation and has been generally supportive of scaling back engagement with the North since 2002. Nonetheless, Japan's conversion to a more "hard power" stance over the North Korea issue, coupled with the effective demise of KEDO since 2003, has narrowed the scope for Europe and Japan acting in concert as "civilian powers" to provide an alternative engagement policy to counter or complement the United States' shift to strengthened containment under the Bush administration. Indeed, the United States and Japan have at times berated Europe for what has been seen as its overly "soft" engagement with North Korea.

Europe and Japan face similar difficulties in constructing mutually supportive policies to respond to the rise of China. Certainly, Europe and Japan share strong common interests in seeking to support the peaceful political and economic integration of China into the regional and global political economies, a concern for the protection of human rights in China, and their respective foreign policies are predominantly geared towards China's engagement. Japan and the EU also launched in September 2005 a "strategic dialogue on East Asia's security environment", including discussion of China-related security matters (Berkofsky 2008: 30).

All the same, Europe and Japan have shown increasing signs of divergence in their perception of China's rise and the appropriate means with which to respond. Europe, clearly perceiving China as more an opportunity than a potential threat, given its lack of geographical proximity but deepening economic ties, has put forward since 2003 a programme of "comprehensive strategic partnership" with China (Commission of the European Communities 2003: 3). This involves an emphasis on cooperation for the implementation of WTO agreements in China; the promotion of human rights, democracy and good governance; and environmental protection. Much of this European agenda overlaps with that of Japan, and its concern with economic cooperation and environmental ODA in China. But it is clear that Japan in recent years has found it harder to pursue this type of "civilian power" agenda towards China, and has turned increasingly to military options in order to hedge against the security risks of China's rise, and once again this has involved re-adherence to US hegemony and US military strategy in the East Asia region. Japan's strengthening of its bilateral alliance with the United States over the issue of China, therefore, creates little positive impetus for joint Europe–Japan cooperation, and in fact has actually created grounds for open discord. In June 2005, at the annual EU–Japan summit, both sides declared their common interest in developing China as a responsible and global partner, but the Japanese side also inserted in their communiqué their outright opposition to any move by the EU to lift its embargo on arms sales to China, in place since Tiananmen Square in 1989 (Ministry of Foreign Affairs 2005). Japan had taken particular umbrage at this potential EU initiative, believed to have been sponsored by France, as a threat to Japanese and East Asian regional security. Japan was successful, in conjunction with US protests and internal European dissension, in using the "strategic dialogue on East Asia's security environment" to convince the EU not to lift the embargo. Nonetheless, the issue demonstrated the potential divergence in approach between Europe on the one hand, and Japan and the United States on the other, vis-à-vis China (Serra 2005: 33). Moreover, the issue of the arms embargo still contains the potential to blow EU–Japan strategic cooperation wide open, if, as it seems rumoured, the EU moves to re-export arms to China in such as way that does not "upset the strategic balance in East Asia".

At the same time as potential gaps between Europe and Japan have opened up on the question of joint cooperation in responding to the US "war on terror", WMD and China, it is clear that the Europe–Japan relationship is strong enough, at enough levels, for both sides to still find areas for continued or new cooperation. Hence, the EU and Japan have found common grounds for cooperation in the reconstruction of postwar Iraq; the EU currently serving as the second largest donor after Japan to the International Reconstruction Fund Facility for Iraq (IFFRI) (European Commission 2005). Europe's multiple identities as a diplomatic and security actor have also meant that Japan's shift to a more "hard power" international character has created new opportunities for cooperation with some European states in Iraq. The UK in particular has been able to forge still closer security ties with Japan through the role of its forces in providing protection for the deployment of Ground Self-Defence Forces (GSDF) around Samawah in the UK-administered zone in Southern Iraq.

Europe–Japan cooperation has faced selective strategic divergence and constraints in responding to Iraq, North Korea and China. Nevertheless, these problems have not derailed joint cooperation in other areas of common interest and in reaction to the assertion of US hegemony. Europe and Japan have shown considerable and continued strategic convergence with each other, and divergence with the United States, over the issue of climate change. Europe and Japan argue strongly that their joint cooperation was in large part responsible for the Kyoto Protocol coming into force despite the US disownment of it under the Bush administration. Europe and Japan have also found common, if not wholly co-ordinated cause, in successfully opposing the United States over its imposition of protectionist steel tariffs in 2002 and over food standards for imports of beef and genetically modified (GM) foods (Yoshimatsu 2007).

Moreover, on certain issues there is also a general convergence of European, Japanese and US interests, making for strong trilateral cooperation. Although the United States' interest in state-building in Afghanistan has not been entirely consistent, it has been in strong accord with the EU, individual European allies and with Japan on the need for the reconstruction of the Afghan state and the need to employ military and economic power in this endeavour. Hence, the hope is that Afghanistan may serve as the site for the interaction of the United States', the EU's and Japan's "soft" and "hard" power capabilities. Indeed, Afghanistan might even serve as the site for the interaction of European and Japanese "hard" power if Ozawa Ichirō, the leader of the opposition Democratic Party of Japan (DPJ), were to have his way, and convert the JSDF mission to support OEF to become one supporting the International Security Force Afghanistan (ISAF) through a military ground presence engaged in reconstruction missions. Japanese policy-making opinion was clearly heavily divided over a possible Afghan mission for the JSDF. Since early 2008, Japanese government officials inched towards the possibility of enacting a permanent law for JSDF dispatch which would obviate the need for separate time-bound laws for each overseas mission, and thus avoid lengthy and divisive Diet discussions relating to Japan's international security contribution. In June 2008, Prime Minister Fukuda appeared to lean towards this option, but was hesitant fearing opposition from its own New Kōmeitō partner. But if Japan did enact such a law it could at very least lead to a new JSDF mission flying in logistical support to NATO and European military forces for peace maintenance activities.

The same story of possible strategic convergence may also apply to their reaction to Iran over the longer term. Up until early 2007, the EU—represented by France, the UK and Germany—and the United States have pursued a "good cop–bad cop" approach to Iran's nuclear programme, holding out the possibility of both diplomatic and economic incentives and military pressure as means to force it to desist. Japan has walked a middle and not entirely ingenuous line: indicating its shared desire with Europe and the United States for Iran to submit its programme to the appropriate international safeguards, but still moving ahead with deals to exploit the Azegedan oil fields in Iran (even though it has recently cut its stake in the old field under US pressure, it still maintains a foothold in the project) (Heginbotham and Samuels 2002). If the Iran issue comes to a head, with the failure of diplomacy and increased pressure from the UN Security Council, then this may be an important issue to make or break trilateral cooperation amongst Europe, Japan and the United States. Europe in this instance may find itself closer to the United States having attempted but exhausted diplomacy with Iran. Japan may find itself isolated from both the Europeans and the United States, thereby undermining the prospect for Europe–Japan cooperation to counteract the United States' potential willingness to use force against Iran, and loosening any alliance leverage that Japan has over the United States. In the final calculation, Japan will line up with Europe and the United States to exert diplomatic pressure on Iran, but the issue will be a crucial test of the limits of Japan–Europe cooperation and Europe's ability to construct itself and others as alternate poles to US hegemony.

Conclusion: Japan and Europe talking and moving past each other?

Europe has long eyed Japan as a potential "civilian" partner with which to augment its own regional integration designs and to boost the integration plans of other states and regions in order to provide some form of counter to unchecked US hegemony. The extent of Europe–Japan cooperation should not be over-exaggerated: this bilateral partnership and broader trilateralism have never been seen as a full substitute for the trans-Atlantic relationship but rather as a useful partial counterweight and alternative only on certain issues. Japan's reaction to the aggressive reassertion of US hegemony post-September 11 by strengthening its "hard" and bilateral alliance ties with the United States has had important implications for European strategy with regard to Japan, and, in turn, with regard to the United States. Japan's new "hard power" and strong support for the United States has created a number of difficulties for Europe–Japan cooperation in Iraq, North Korea and, perhaps most importantly over the longer term, China. But it has to be acknowledged that these difficulties are not universal for all of Europe, as other individual states can see new opportunities for cooperation with a Japan that is gradually becoming a more important military player and visible US ally. In other areas, and chiefly those that are less strictly related to military security cooperation, the strengthened US–Japan is not necessarily a bar on Europe–Japan cooperation. European and Japanese cooperation has remained strong on climate change and the management of the international trading system, and in large part this is a result of the need to cooperate in the face of US intransigence. In yet other areas, Europe–Japan–US cooperation remains strong in spite of, or because of, the strengthened US–Japan alliance, as in the case of Afghanistan.

Europe's policy-makers were most recently given a portent of one potential future course of Japan as a potential partner for international cooperation with the then Prime Minister Abe Shinzō's visit to Europe in January 2007. In the wake of North Korea's missile and nuclear tests, Abe's visit focused very much on security issues, with the new prime minister emphasizing a new Japanese willingness to cooperate with European states on security in the Middle East and Afghanistan. Abe on this trip became the first Japanese prime minister to address NATO's North Atlantic Council, and hinted that as Japan continued to investigate the implementation of a permanent law on international peace cooperation and constitutional revision it would seek to enhance its military cooperation with NATO (Ministry of Foreign Affairs 2007a). Japan and the UK reconfirmed their burgeoning security cooperation originating in the Iraq conflict (Ministry of Foreign Affairs 2007b). But in contrast to previous Japanese leaders who had visited Europe, Abe also conveyed much stronger ambitions for European states to reciprocate in assisting Japan's security agenda, thus adding a stronger undertone of conditionality to relations. Abe insisted on extracting promises of cooperation from European leaders in the UK, France, Germany and NATO to assist in a resolution to North Korea's abductions of Japanese citizens, and that all European states should actively implement sanctions against the North. Abe further stressed continually to European states concerns about the rise of China militarily, and that Japan would renew its quest for a permanent seat on the UN Security Council.

Hence, European states in January 2007 encountered a more "muscular" Japan, perhaps moving in directions with its security policy that Europe would find hard to follow fully in the future. Abe's resignation in September 2007 and his replacement by the more pragmatic Fukuda precipitated some rowing back on Japanese security ambitions and plans for the expansion of the US–Japan alliance, thus perhaps delivering a softer edge to Japan's international role. Certainly Fukuda's agenda up until the G-8 held in Japan in July 2008 focussed on cooperation with Europe in the area of climate change. Fukuda also showed a greater willingness to engage China and to mitigate security tensions, as well as to extricate Japan from its diplomatic bind over North Korea. However, Japan is unlikely to move off its long-term incremental trajectory towards "normalization" as a more assertive military power.

The key to understanding this mixed pattern of cooperation between Japan and Europe now and in the future consists of two variables. The first is the nature of European and Japanese power resources. The degree of cooperation between the two appears reliant in part on the commensurability of their "soft" and "hard" power portfolios. Europe is moving to acquire both, with still a greater emphasis on economic power. Japan, by contrast, is perhaps placing greater emphasis currently on augmenting its military capabilities. These changing power resources may create complementarities for post-conflict reconstruction and state-building, but as Europe and Japan begin to emphasize different "soft" and "hard" power resources their abilities to act in concert may actually begin to bypass and drift past each other. Hence, Japan's increasing interest in acquiring "hard power" may unbalance the triangle of US–Europe–Japan relations, and strengthen the US–Japan side rather than strengthening the counteracting Japan–Europe side.

The second key variable is simply the nature of overlap in their common interests vis-à-vis US hegemony and the geographical proximity to their own regions. Europe and Japan have found it easier to cooperate on issues of common concern where it does not impact directly on their security, as in the Middle East or on the periphery of Europe. However, when the issue directly affects Japan's security and involves potential military conflict, then Japan has usually chosen to fall back on the alliance relationship with the United States and the prospects for Europe–Japan cooperation remain constrained, as in the case of China. It would seem that the further Japan pushes its military role and more it becomes preoccupied with its security vis-à-vis China, then this can only further limit its options to break out of this cycle by seeking cooperation with Europe as an alternative expression for its political and security identity. Similarly, Europe's options to deal with US hegemony will on the whole be constrained by the strengthening US–Japan military alliance.

References

Allin, Dana, Andréani, Gilles, Errera, Philippe and Samore, Gary (2007) *Repairing the Damage: Possibilities and Limits of the Trans-Atlantic Consensus*, Adephi paper 389, Oxford University Press/IISS.
Baldwin, Matthew, Peterson, John and Stokes, Bruce (2003) "Trade and economic relations", in John Peterson and Mark A. Pollack (eds.) *Europe, America and Bush: Transatlantic Relations in the Twenty First Century*, London, Routledge, pp. 29–46.
Berkofsky, Axel (2008) "True strategic partnership or rhetorical window dressing? A closer look at the relationship between the EU and Japan", *Japan aktuell*, February: 22–37.
Commission of the European Communities (2003) *A Maturing Partnership: Shared Interests and Challenges in EU-China Relations*, Brussels, European Commisssion, http://europa.eu.int/comm/external_relations/china/com_03_533/com_533_en.pdf.
Edwards, Geoffrey (2005) "The pattern of the EU's global activity", in Christopher Hill and Michael Smith (eds.) *International Relations and the European Union*, Oxford, Oxford University Press, pp. 39–63.
European Commission (2005) *Reconstructing Iraq: State of Play and Implementation to Date*, Brussels, European Commission, http://europa.eu.int/comm/external_relations/iraq/doc/assist_2005.pdf.
Gilson, Julie (2000) *Japan and the European Union: A Partnership for the Twenty-First Century?* Basingstoke, Macmillan.
—— (2002) "Asia Meets Europe: Inter-Regionalism and the Asia-Europe Meeting", Cheltenham, Edward Elgar Publishing.
Heginbotham, Eric and Samuels, Richard J. (2002) "Japan's Dual Hedge", *Foreign Affairs*, 81 (5): 110–21.

Hemmer, Christopher and Katzenstein, Peter J. (2002) "Why is there no NATO in Asia? Collective identity, regionalism and the origins of multilateralism", *International Organization*, 56 (3): 575–607.

Higgott, Richard (2004) "US foreign policy and the securitization of globalization", *International Politics*, 41 (2): 147–75.

Hook, Glenn, Gilson, Julie, Hughes, Christopher W., Dobson, Hugo (2005) *Japan's International Relations: Politics, Economics and Security*, London, Routledge.

Hughes, Christopher W. (2001) "Japan in Europe: Asian and European perspectives", in Glenn D. Hook and Hasegawa Harukiyo (eds.) *The Political Economy of Japanese Globalization*, London, Routledge, pp. 56–70.

—— (2004) *Japan's Reemergence as a "Normal" Military Power*, Oxford, IISS/Oxford University Press.

—— (2005) "Japanese military modernization: in search of a 'normal' security role", in Ashley J. Tellis and Michael Wills (eds.) *Military Modernization in an Era of Uncertainty*, Washington DC, National Bureau of Asian Research, pp. 105–36.

—— (2006) "The political economy of Japanese sanctions towards North Korea: domestic coalitions and international systemic pressures", *Pacific Affairs*, (7) 3, Fall: 455–81.

—— (2008) "Igirisu no tai Bei izon no daishō", *Asuteion*, 68, 102–15.

—— (2009) "Supersizing the DPRK threat: Japan's evolving military posture and North Korea", *Asian Survey*, 49 (2) March/April, 2009: 291–311.

Hughes, Christopher W. and Krauss, Ellis S. (2007) "US–Japan alliance futures: Koizumi"s legacy, Abe's security policies, US challenges", *Survival: The IISS Quarterly*, vol. 49, no. 2, Spring: 157–76.

Johnson, Chalmers (2004) *The Sorrows of Empire: Militarism, Secrecy and the End of the Republic*, London, Verso.

Krauss, Ellis S., Hughes, Christopher W. and Blechinger-Talcott, Verena (2007) "Managing the MedUSA: comparing the political economy of US–Japan, UK–German and US–UK relations", *The Pacific Review*, 20 (3), September: 257–71.

Lind, Michael (2005) "How America became the world's dispensable nation", *Financial Times*, 25 January.

Mack, Andrew (2003) "The United States and the Asia-Pacific: bilateralism plus 'multilateralism à la carte'", in David M. Malone and Yuen Foong Khong (eds.) *Unilateralism and US Foreign Policy: International Perspectives*, Boulder, Colorado: Lynne Rienner Publishers, pp. 375–98.

Malone, David M. and Khong, Yuen Foong (2003) "Resisting the unilateral impulse: multilateral engagement and the future of US leadership", in David M. Malone and Yuen Foong Khong (eds.) *Unilateralism and US Foreign Policy: International Perspectives*, Boulder, Colorado: Lynne Rienner Publishers, pp. 421–29.

Maull, Hans W. (1990/1991) "Germany and Japan: The New Civilian Powers", *Foreign Affairs*, 69 (5): 91–107.

—— (2005) "Europe and the new balance of global order", *International Affairs*, 81 (4): 775–99.

Menon, Anand (2004) "From crisis to catharsis: ESDP after Iraq", *International Affairs*, 80 (4): 631–48.

Ministry of Foreign Affairs (2001) "An Action Plan for EU–Japan Cooperation", http://www.mofa.go.jp/region/europe/eu/summit/action0112.html#future.

—— (2005) "14th EU-Japan Summit Joint Press Statement", http://www.mofa.go.jp/region/europe/eu/summit/joint0505.pdf.

—— (2007a) "Speech by Prime Minister Shinzo Abe at the North Atlantic Council ? Japan and NATO: Toward Further Collaboration'", 12 January, http://www.mofa.go.jp/region/europe/pmv0701/nato.html.

—— (2007b) "Japan–UK Joint Statement: A Framework for the Future", 9 January, http://www.mofa.go.jp/region/europe/uk/joint0701.html.

Peterson, John (2004) "America as a European power: the end of empire by integration?" *International Affairs*, 80 (4): 613–29.

Pollack, Mark A. (2004) "Unilateral America, multilateral Europe?", in John Peterson and Mark A. Pollack (eds.) *Europe, America and Bush: Transatlantic Relations in the Twenty First Century*, London, Routledge, pp. 115–27.

Reiterer, Michael (2002) *Asia-Europe, Do They Meet? Reflections on the Asia-Europe Meeting*, Singapore, Asia-Europe Foundation.

Serra, Régine (2005) "L'evolution stratégique du Japon: un enjeu pour l'Union", Occasional Paper no. 59, European Union Institute for Security Studies, Paris.

Smith, Hazel (2002) *European Foreign Policy: What it is and What it Does*, London, Pluto Press.

Smith, Michael E. (2004) *Europe's Foreign and Security Policy: The Institutionalization of Cooperation*, Cambridge, Cambridge University Press.

—— (2005) "The EU and the United States", in Christopher Hill and Michael Smith (eds.) *International Relations and the European Union*, Oxford, Oxford University Press, pp. 343–63.

Smith, Michael and Steffenson, Rebecca (2005) "The European Union and the United States", in Christopher Hill and Michael Smith (eds.), *International Relations and the EU*, Oxford: Oxford University Press, 2005, pp. 343–63.

Wallace, William (2002) "US unilateralism; a European perspective", in Stewart Patrick and Shepard Forman (eds.) *Multilateralism and US Foreign Policy: Ambivalent Engagement*, Boulder, Colorado: Lynne Rienner Publishers, pp. 141–64.

White, Brian (2001) *Understanding European Foreign Policy*, Basingstoke, Palgrave.

Yoshimatsu, Hidetaka (2007) "Japan's management of trade frictions over steel with the United States: a comparative analysis", *The Pacific Review*, 20 (3): 273–300.

Conclusion

Tsuneo Akaha

The preceding chapters have examined the evolving hard power and soft power of Japan and the United States, and the resulting changes in the balance between the two forms of power in the security alliance between the two countries. They have also analyzed how the changing power relations undergirding the trans-Pacific alliance has affected the other major powers' assessment of their security interests and their views of the bilateral alliance. The conceptual discussion of the hard–soft power relationship in the United States and Japan and in their alliance in Chapters 1, 2, and 3 revealed the disparate levels of the hard and soft power of the allies and their relatively successful – but far from entirely trouble-free – efforts to adjust their alliance missions and responsibilities in response to both the changing security environment at the regional and global levels and the changes to their respective power capacity. Their periodic assessment of the security environment and power capabilities resulted in changes in the allies' contributions to the overall alliance.

Over the postwar decades, the overall mission of the alliance has changed from the lop-sided one of ensuring Japan's physical security with the overwhelming hard power of the United States to a less unequal – yet still uneven – sharing of power for regional peace and stability. Under the global Cold War structure the one-sided alliance was politically sustainable and strategically meaningful. With the end of the Cold War, however, the bilateral alliance's strategic rationale came under increasing scrutiny in both countries. The emergence of the United States as the sole remaining "superpower" would likely have extended the life of the uneven alliance across the Pacific had it not been for several significant changes to the regional and global security environment.

Clearly the most important change in the regional environment has been the rise of China as a political and economic power, with growing military muscle. How the United States and Japan should adjust their respective policies toward China and their alliance in the face of this change has become a topic of heated debate in both countries, with voices of engagement and containment being heard in nearly equal volume on both sides of the Pacific. The discussion is likely to continue as long as the two allies' strategic assessments of China and its role in the region and in the world remain indefinite. The net effect of China's rise, in both hard and soft power terms, has been to boost both the hard power and the soft power of the United States and Japan and to encourage greater cooperation to bulk up their combined hard power. At the same time, Japan has made some efforts to expand its economic, social and cultural ties with China. On the social and cultural front, Japan's soft power has generated some goodwill among Chinese citizens, who are visiting Japan in increasing numbers. Japan's renewed effort in environmental cooperation with China has also borne some fruit. However, the legacies of history continue to cast a shadow over Japan's soft power appeal to China. Whether Tokyo will be able to overcome its soft power deficit vis-à-vis Beijing will be increasingly complicated as its alliance relations with Washington are likely to demand greater hard power contribution by Japan to both its own security and to the stability of the region. From Beijing's perspective, As Yuan contended in Chapter 4, Beijing's relations with Washington and Tokyo, particularly with the former, will be the most important factor in China's assessment of how, where, and to what extent the US–Japan alliance will affect its security interests negatively. As a result, unstable and indeterminate political calculations are likely to characterize Beijing, Tokyo, and Washington for the foreseeable future.

Another important change affecting the US–Japan alliance has been the nuclear and ballistic missile development in North Korea and Pyongyang's unpredictable behavior in the face of international efforts to contain its proliferation threats. While the United States and Japan, as well as the other major powers, are in complete agreement on the goal of securing a non-nuclear Korean peninsula, the concerned powers are divided on how best to achieve that goal. Further complicating the US–Japan policy coordination, both bilaterally and within the framework of the Six-Party Talks, is the issue of the North Korean abduction of Japanese citizens, an issue that has had more political traction in Japan than the nuclear issue. The uncertain future of the North Korean issue has boosted the call for further building up Japan's hard power among both nationalists and those who support a strong US–Japan security alliance. Of particular note has been Japan's visible hard-power exercise in securing the UN Security Council's condemnations and sanctions against North Korea's nuclear weapons development and ballistic missile launches, the latest missile launch being in April 2009.

A global issue that has also tipped the hard–soft power balance toward the former in Japan's security policy as well as in the US–Japan alliance has been the global terrorist threats following the September 11, 2001 attacks in the United States. Japan has responded with a significant amount of contribution in hard power, such as its SDF presence in Iraq, refueling mission in the Indian Ocean, and financial and logistical participation in the international efforts to stabilize Pakistan and Afghanistan. Here again, the US–Japan alliance has been instrumental in encouraging Japan to boost its hard power. In particular, Tokyo's determination not to repeat the "pocket book diplomacy" criticism it had suffered in the Persian Gulf War ensured that Japan would "show its flag," albeit still in a constitutionally circumscribed manner, in the international counter-terrorist efforts post-9/11.

How will the United States and Japan improve the alliance's effectiveness in stabilizing the regional security environment and in countering global security threats? The preceding chapters have demonstrated the difficult task of finding an optimal balance between hard and soft power in pursuit of what Nye calls "smart power." Conceptually, we know every country has both hard power and soft power and that it should seek the most effective combination of the two forms of power. We also know that hard power can at times contribute to soft power and at other times erode soft power. Equally importantly, we understand that soft power can compensative for inadequacies in hard power for certain purposes but soft power is no substitute for hard power for other purposes. The preceding analyses have also shown that the sources of soft power are often beyond the control of policymakers because they are the creation of the culture and society rather than a product of political design. They have also shown that soft power is ultimately in the eyes of the beholder and that an actor's intention to exercise its soft power may have the unintended or even reverse effect as far as the target of that power is concerned. Hence, soft power as an instrument of policy in Japan, in the United States, or in their alliance, clearly has its limitations.

While recognizing the above difficulties and limitations, we can see that soft power is preferable to hard power on both moral grounds and in terms of cost effectiveness. Soft power, defined as attraction or appeal, requires neither the investment in "carrots" nor the expenses of "sticks". From this perspective, we are hopeful that the new US administration under President Barack Obama will shift its hard–soft power priorities toward the latter, making a clear break with the George W. Bush's Administration. As Meeks documents in Chapter 1, in constant 2005 dollars, the United States spent $7.7 trillion on national defense between 1992 and 2006, or 16.1 percent more than the next ten largest spenders combined, or 316 percent more than Japan. On the other hand, Japan's defense spending has been limited to under 1 percent of GDP and its net ODA in 2006 was $11.6 billion or 0.25 percent of GDP, making military expenditure to ODA ratio about 4 to 1. The grants and loans that ODA represents are, in our definition, "hard power," but they can generate and contribute much more to soft power. On the other hand, military spending is more costly and is clearly seen as "hard power" by both the allies who share it and those against whom it is exercised.

The United States must restrain its exercise of hard power, which remains the strongest in the world, and restore and expand its soft power, which has been tarnished under the previous administration. The Bush Administration's approach to international terrorism was often seen as a unilateral exercise of hard power and eroded its soft power appeal, as evident in world public opinion surveys. While the United States was immersed in its long presidential campaign, Washington was unable to take bold foreign policy initiatives, including toward China or North Korea, the two most important security concerns for the US–Japan alliance. With the Obama Administration now in place, Washington has begun the urgently needed task of restoring the international confidence in the United States as a reliable partner in multilateral efforts to combat the international terrorism, slow the global warming, and now end the global economic and financial crises. The new administration's first priority is to get the country out of its economic difficulties, but it will not succeed without the cooperation of other major powers, including Japan and China.

Japan, for its part, must invest in necessary hard power capabilities within its constitutional limits and also learn to exercise its substantial soft power more effectively. Domestic problems prevent optimistic prospects in this regard, however. Japan has seen a succession of short-lived administrations, under Abe and Fukuda, and now Aso, whose alarmingly low public approval is threatening to end the rule by the LDP–Komeito coalition. The opposition Democratic Party of Japan, under Ichiro Ozawa, gained the upper hand in public approval for a brief period but is now struggling to maintain its viability as an alternative to the current coalition government. With the unprecedented level of political uncertainty, Japan is not in a position to take bold foreign policy initiatives to remove its security threats. Japan, in other words, will have to rely on the United States, China, and other powers to contain the most immediate threat to its security, i.e., North Korea. Incremental changes are likely to characterize its efforts to boost its hard power and also sustain its soft power in the international arena. As Arase (Chapter 2) observes, Japan's current soft power policy lacks coherence and its hard power policy is not enhancing its soft power. In other words, great expectations are unwarranted.

Under these circumstances, the United States and Japan should exert greater efforts to strengthen multilateral institutions and processes to deal with regional and global issues. In addition to the issues mentioned in the preceding paragraphs, the two countries also need to cooperate with the international community in combating piracy and the proliferation of WMD, democracy promotion, post-conflict reconstruction and development, poverty reduction, and UN reform. These moves are likely to be welcomed by European powers, which have shown much concern about the United States' hard power policy post-9/11 and its tendency to impose its priorities on its allies. As Hughes observes in Chapter 7, European countries have also noticed Japan's recent efforts to augment its hard power capabilities.

Clearly, the United States and Japan must find a more effective balance between their hard power and their soft power, both individually and collectively. As far as the nature of the US–Japan alliance is concerned, as Arase notes, Japan's desire for an independent great power status and its continued need to rely on the United States for its own security are contradictory. As long as these competing forces are in play, it will be difficult for the alliance to find a comfortable and sustainable balance between hard and soft power. Moreover, as Hughes maintains, depending on what sources of soft and hard power

Europe and Japan will emphasize, their ability to act in concert may suffer. This is particularly likely in policies toward China, where Europe's security interests are less pronounced than Japan's and the latter works more closely with the United States.

Neither South Korea nor Russia is likely to fundamentally influence the balance of soft and hard power in Japan, in the United States, or in the US–Japan alliance. As Pinkston observes in Chapter 5, Koreans see little of Japan's soft power, so Tokyo's efforts do not reassure them about Japanese intentions. On the other hand, they see in the US–Japan security alliance an important constraining effect on Japan's growing hard power capabilities. The United States and Japan have been able to use their collective soft power to contain North Korea's bellicose behavior, but the latter's inability to exercise soft power is largely its own fault. According to Sevastyanov, Russia understands and accepts Japan's desire to boost its hard power, but Moscow's view of the US–Japan alliance is largely a function of its relations with Washington. With the territorial dispute between Moscow and Tokyo preventing any dramatic change in their bilateral relations, it is unlikely that Japan's independent hard–soft power balancing act will either threaten or promote Russia's security interests in the region in any major way. Two developments that could pose significant difficulties for Russia are the US–Japan development of a TMD system in Northeast Asia and a Japanese decision to acquire nuclear weapons in order to eliminate the security threat from North Korea. Obviously, the two developments depend heavily on US policy and power in the region.

Index

acts, laws, pacts, treaties: Anti-Ballistic Missile (ABM) Treaty 89, 90 (abrogation 131, 135–36, 147); Anti-Terrorism Special Measures Law 42, 52, 91, 122; ASEAN Treaty of Amity and Cooperation 102; Basic Policy for National Defense 38; Basic Space Law 97; International Peace Cooperation Law 40–41; Law Concerning Special Measure on Humanitarian and Reconstruction Assistance in Iraq 67; Law Ensuring Peace and Security in Situations in Areas Surrounding Japan 41; Mutual Security Assistance Pact 36–37; Nuclear Nonproliferation Treaty (NPT) 69, 70, 72, 79; Replenishment Support Special Measures Law 152; San Francisco Peace Treaty 36; Six-Party Talks 70–71, 73–74, 78, 106, 127, 132, 144, 148, 170; Special Situations Law 42, 54; Taiwan Relations Act 97, 100; Taiwan Security Enhancement Act (1999) 98; Treaty on Conventional Armed Forces in Europe 136, 144; US–DPRK–ROK Joint Declaration on the Denuclearization of the Korean Peninsula 125–26; US–Japan Defense Guidelines 41, 88; US–Japan Security Treaty (1960) 37, 38, 40, 41, 68, 77; War Contingencies Laws 42–43

Afghanistan 1, 22; hard power 5–6; Japan 1, 42, 45, 121, 152, 155, 164, 165 (Japanese Self Defense Forces (SDF) 122, 152, 163, 170); soft power 5–6; South Korea 121; Soviet invasion of 39; United States 1, 23; US–Japan alliance, European views 155, 163, 164, 165; *see also* Japanese Self Defense Forces (SDF); US–Japan alliance, European views

Akaha, Tsuneo 13, 58–79, 169–73; China 62–66, 74–75; hard power 13, 53, 66, 69–74; Japan 5, 13, 58–79; North Korea 13, 64, 69–74; soft/hard power balance 58–79; soft power 5, 12, 13, 58–74 (dilemma 13, 66–67, 172); South Korea 62–66, 74–75; US–Japan alliance 13, 63, 66–69; *see also* Japan; Japanese hard power; Japanese soft power; North Korea; US–Japan alliance

Arase, David 1–15, 35–57, 169, 172; hard power 2–3, 5, 9–10, 11, 13, 35, 37, 46, 53, 172; Japan 1–15, 35–55; Japanese security policy 35–57; soft power 2–15, 172 (official development assistance (ODA) 23); US–Japan alliance 1, 3–4; *see also* Japan; Japanese security policy; soft power; US–Japan alliance

Asia Pacific Economic Cooperation (APEC) 50, 132

Asian Financial Crisis (AFC) 50, 103, 160

Association of Southeast Asian Nations (ASEAN) 49–51; ASEAN + 3 6, 50, 51; ASEAN Regional Forum (ARF) 50, 102, 103, 105, 132, 149; Asia Pacific Economic Cooperation (APEC) 50; Asian Financial Crisis (AFC) 50, 103; China 7, 50–51, 102–4, 105 (ASEAN Treaty of Amity and Cooperation 102; China–ASEAN Comprehensive Economic Cooperation Agreement 6);

Index 175

East Asian Summit (EAS) 51; Japan 49–51; Russia 132, 148–49; Treaty of Amity and Cooperation (TAC) 7, 102; US–Japan alliance 49–51; *see also* Southeast Asia

Chicago Council on Global Affairs 8, 9, 105

China xii, 13–14, 62–66, 74–75, 83–116; Chinese Communist Party (CCP) 2, 36; economic growth, superpower xii, 1, 7, 29, 32, 46, 61, 62, 86, 87, 101, 106, 107, 122, 123, 154, 169; Hu Jintao 64, 65, 108; human rights 7, 61, 161–62; military issues 2–3 (military expenditure 46, 66, 86; rapid development 2, 46, 69, 101, 123); Nationalist Party (KMT) 2, 36, 47, 48, 53; nuclear weapons 1, 41, 69, 123; People's Liberation Army (PLA) 1, 3; US–Japan alliance 3, 4, 26, 33, 46–47, 68, 74, 169–70, 172 (containment 26, 46, 47, 68, 88, 122, 125, 169; economic growth, power 32, 62, 101, 106, 107, 169); US–Japan alliance, European views 151, 152, 154, 161–63, 164, 165, 166; Wen, Jiabao 64, 103, 108; *see also* China, foreign policy; Japan; Japan, foreign policy; Taiwan; US foreign/security policy; US–Japan alliance; US–Japan alliance, Chinese perspective

China, foreign policy 85; Association of Southeast Asian Nations (ASEAN) 7, 50–51, 102–4, 105 (ASEAN Regional Forum (ARF) 102, 103, 105; ASEAN Treaty of Amity and Cooperation 102; China–ASEAN Comprehensive Economic Cooperation Agreement 6); 'Beijing consensus' 104; image 8; Japan 2, 41, 42, 46–47, 51, 53, 62–66, 69, 85–86, 122, 123, 162, 165, 166, 169–70 (anti-Japanese demonstrations (2005) 47, 63; Chinese power growth 32, 61, 62, 86, 87, 101, 122, 123; commercial realism/reluctant liberalism 85–86; East China Sea 47, 65, 95, 100; economic assistance to China 60, 61, 76, 86, 162; island sovereignty issues 2, 64, 95, 100, 122; Japanese perceptions of China 46, 65–66, 86; power growth 32, 61, 62, 86, 87, 101, 122, 123); multilateralism 7, 14, 51, 102, 104, 106; North Korea 71, 78, 106–7; Russia 2, 142; soft/hard power: Beijing's balancing act 14, 84, 101–7 (hard power 101, 106; 'New Security Concept' (NSC) 14, 102, 103; Shanghai Cooperation Organization (SCO) 102; soft power 103–6, 109; US/China soft power comparison 104); soft power 2, 6–8, 9, 20, 104; Southeast Asia 6–7, 14, 84, 102–3, 105; Taiwan 1, 3, 41, 46, 47–48, 97–101; United States 30, 32, 41, 74, 101; *see also* China; Japan; Japan, foreign policy; Taiwan; US foreign/security policy; US–Japan alliance; US–Japan alliance, Chinese perspective

democracy: democratic peace theory 119; Japan 37, 38, 60, 100, 119; soft power 11–12, 32; South Korea 119; Taiwan 97, 99, 100; United States 11–12, 29, 32, 85, 105, 134, 155

East Asia xii; hard power 6; international relations xii (confrontational relations xii); multilateral management of regional security relations 6; power shift 86–87; soft/hard power balance xii, 5; soft power 2, 6–8 (growing attention paid to soft power 5); US–Japan alliance 4; *see also* China; China, foreign policy; Japan; US–Japan alliance; US–Japan alliance, Chinese perspective

Europe/European Union xii, 4, 5, 153; Afghanistan 155, 163; Asia 154, 156, 160 (Asia-Europe Meeting (ASEM) 157, 158, 160); China 154, 161–63, 164, 165, 166; democracy, liberal 155, 156, 159; economy, economic power 30, 155, 156, 159 (European-oriented model 156; 'hegemonic' US equal 155); foreign policy 157; France 156, 157; Germany 153, 158, 163, 165; hard power 156–57 (Common Foreign and Security Policy (CFSP) 156; European Security and Defence Identity (ESDI) 156; European Security and Defence Policy (ESDP) 156); human rights 158, 159, 161–62; Iraq 153, 154, 155, 158, 160, 162; multilateralism/'trilateralism' 4, 153, 156, 157, 158, 159, 160; North Atlantic Treaty Organization (NATO)

157; North Korea 154, 161 (Korean Peninsula Energy Development Organisation (KEDO) 161); official development assistance (ODA) 156, 162; 'Old/New Europe' 153; soft power 5, 156–57 ('civilian power' 156, 158; predominance 157; 'transformative power' 156); terrorism 157, 158, 159; United Kingdom 153, 156, 157–58, 163, 165; *see also* US–Japan alliance, European views

Germany 9, 155

hard power xii, 5–6, 35, 37, 46, 53, 127, 172; ballistic missile defense 2; East Asia 6; economic hard power 20–21; hard power model 5; North Korea 117, 119; nuclear weapons 20; poor countries 21; primacy of 2–3, 5; soft/hard power balance xii, 5–6, 53–54, 67, 75, 134, 169, 170, 171, 172; soft/hard power, China 14, 84, 101–7 (hard power 101, 106); soft/hard power continuum 21; soft/hard power interaction 9–10, 11, 21, 134, 171; South Korea 124, 125–27; United States 3, 14, 23, 24, 135, 136, 147, 156, 169, 171, 172; US–Japan alliance 2, 3, 33, 66, 170, 172 (Japanese/US asymmetry 33, 105, 169); world military expenditure 21, 22; *see also* Japanese hard power; nuclear weapons; US military issues/hard power; US–Japan alliance, Chinese perspective; US–Japan alliance, European views; weapons of mass destruction (WMD)

Hughes, Christopher W.: US–Japan alliance, European views 14, 151–68, 172–73; *see also* Europe/European Union; Japan; United States; US foreign/security policy; US military issues/hard power; US–Japan alliance; US–Japan alliance, European views

human rights: China 7, 61, 161–62; Europe 158, 159, 161–62; Japan 60, 61, 65, 127, 159; soft power 11–12, 60, 128, 134; United States 11–12, 134

international relations: alliance theories 24–28, 124 (balance of interest model 28, 31; balance of power/balance of threat model 25, 28; functional categories 124; identity perspective 25–27); alliances, identity and international relations theories 24–28; Asia-Pacific (bilateral military alliances 105; common security and multilateralism 105; multipolarization 105); constructivist approaches 10, 120; democratic peace theory 119; liberal/neoliberal theories 10, 24, 119; realism/idealism dichotomy 27; realist theories 10, 24–25, 28, 67, 119, 126, 148; soft power xii, 10–11, 58, 67; utility maximization 10–11; *see also* hard power; multilateralism; power; soft power; US–Japan alliance

Iran 20, 28, 31, 136, 155, 159, 163–64

Iraq: hard power 5–6; International Reconstruction Fund Facility for Iraq (IFFRI) 162; Japan 1, 42, 45, 121, 160 (Japanese Self Defense Forces (SDF) 67, 77, 122, 144, 152, 162, 170); soft power 5–6; South Korea 121; United States 1, 23, 32, 66–67, 135; US–Japan alliance 66–67; US–Japan alliance, European views 151, 152, 153, 154, 158, 160, 162, 163, 164, 165

Japan: Constitution (1946) 3, 36, 37, 38, 40–41, 53, 58 (Article 9 3, 11, 36, 37, 40, 41, 42, 44, 51, 52, 53, 54, 55, 62, 72, 73, 95, 96, 144; nuclear weapons 71, 78; revision 11, 13, 35, 37, 41, 43, 49, 51, 52, 54, 62, 63, 68, 83, 91, 144); cultural insularity 12–13; democracy 37, 38, 60, 100, 119; economic power 4–5, 11, 29, 30; Emperor 37, 38; Japanese miracle 12, 19; human rights 60, 61, 65, 127, 159; national identity 26–27, 38, 43, 87, 108; nationalism 27, 42, 63, 64–65, 87, 98; oil 31, 40, 47, 62, 65; Westernization 26–27; World War II 11, 27, 35, 42, 49, 141; Yasukuni Shrine 12, 46, 48, 49, 63, 64, 75, 106, 108, 127; *see also* Japanese foreign policy; Japanese hard power; Japanese politics; Japanese security policy; Japanese Self Defense Forces (SDF); Japanese soft power; US–Japan alliance

Japanese foreign policy xiii, 3, 31–32, 35, 127, 141, 147–48, 152–53, 160, 172; Afghanistan 1, 42, 45, 121, 152,

155, 164, 165, 170; Association of Southeast Asian Nations (ASEAN) 49–51; China 2, 41, 42, 46–47, 51, 53, 62–66, 69, 85–86, 122, 123, 162, 165, 166, 169–70 (commercial realism/reluctant liberalism 85–86; East China Sea 47, 65, 95, 100; economic assistance to China 60, 61, 76, 86, 162; Japanese perceptions of China 46, 65–66, 86; power growth 32, 61, 62, 86, 87, 101, 122, 123); criticism 64, 106, 127; factions 31–32 ('middle power internationalists' 31, 32; 'neo-autonomists' 31, 55; 'normal nationalists' 31, 32, 55; 'pacifists' 31–32); 'Fukuda Doctrine' 32, 50; international cooperation 59–60, 66; Iraq 1, 42, 45, 67, 77, 121, 160, 162; island sovereignty issues 2, 14, 49, 64, 65, 95, 100, 122; Japanese image 8, 46–47, 54, 61, 62, 63, 141; Middle East 62, 63, 91; Ministry of Foreign Affairs (MOFA) 12, 54 (*Gaiko Forum* 12); North Korea 1, 4, 5, 14, 39, 41, 42, 48–49, 51, 53, 54–55, 66, 69–74, 78, 144, 152, 161, 165, 172; official development assistance (ODA) 4, 12, 23, 39, 50, 91, 108 (Japanese soft power 59, 60–61; ODA Charter 60–61); Russia 137–38 (Russian perception of 141–42, 147, 148); soft power 60–66, 74; South Korea 14, 39, 49, 53, 62–65, 121–25, 145; Taiwan 41, 45, 47–48, 92, 98–101; Task Force on Foreign Relations (2002) 160; United Kingdom 158, 162, 165; United Nations 52 (UN Security Council 32, 33, 64, 105, 106, 145, 165); 'yen diplomacy' 21, 27; *see also* China, foreign policy; Europe/European Union; Japan; Japanese hard power; Japanese politics; Japanese security policy; Japanese Self Defense Forces (SDF); Japanese soft power; North Korea; Russia; South Korea; Taiwan; United States; US foreign/security policy; US military issues/hard power; US–Japan alliance; US–Japan alliance, Chinese perspective; US–Japan alliance, European views; US–Japan alliance, Korean views; US–Japan alliance, Russian perspective

Japanese hard power 2–3, 4, 5, 9–10, 11, 13, 33, 35, 37, 46, 53, 66, 69–74, 84, 90–97, 105, 106, 108, 121, 123, 127, 170, 172; missile defense development and deployment 83, 84, 89–90, 92, 94–95; North Korean threat and Japan's tilt toward hard power 13, 41, 42, 48–49, 53, 54–55, 64, 69–74, 93, 94, 121–25, 161, 170; nuclear debate 92–94; Nuclear Nonproliferation Treaty (NPT) 72, 79; nuclear weapons 48–49, 71–73, 78, 105, 106, 108, 173 (virtual nuclear weapons 125–26); search of hard power 4–5, 106, 108; Six-Party Talks 70–71, 73–74, 78; soft/hard power balance xii, 5–6, 53–54, 67, 75, 134, 169, 170, 172 (China 14, 84, 101–7); Three Non-Nuclear Principles 48, 71, 72, 92, 93, 105, 108; US–Japan alliance 72, 75, 170–71; US–Japan alliance, European views 154, 155, 161, 162, 164, 165; US nuclear umbrella 72, 94, 108; *see also* Japanese foreign policy; Japanese security policy; Japanese Self Defense Forces (SDF); Japanese soft power; North Korea; US–Japan alliance

Japanese politics 172; 2009 election xii; Abe, Shinzō 4, 12, 13, 31, 32, 48, 51–53, 71, 72, 74, 78, 93, 100, 108, 140, 147–48, 152, 165, 172 (nationalist political agenda 64–65); Asō, Tarō 4, 61, 65, 152; Democratic Party of Japan (DPJ) 43, 44, 45, 46, 51, 52, 98, 152, 163, 172; 'Fukuda Doctrine' 32, 50; Fukuda, Yasuo 4, 32, 53, 65, 74, 78, 152, 155, 163, 165, 172; Kishi, Nobusuke 37, 51–52, 78; Koizumi, Junichirō 4, 29, 31, 32, 42, 43, 59, 98, 108, 139, 152; Liberal Democratic Party (LDP) xii, 12, 13, 35, 39, 40, 43–44, 51–53, 93, 96, 98, 100, 152 (corruption 54; formation 36, 37; members 37, 55; right wing 37, 40, 41, 42, 44, 51–52); Ozawa, Ichirō 52, 53, 71, 163, 172; 'reluctant realism' 62, 76; security policy 35, 36–37, 38, 39, 40, 43–44, 45, 46, 51–54, 55, 62, 64–65, 71, 78; Sino–Japanese relations 87, 98, 108; Yoshida, Shigeru 36–37, 121 (Yoshida Doctrine 36–37, 38, 39, 40, 121); *see also* Japanese hard power; Japanese security policy; Japanese Self Defense

Forces (SDF); Japanese soft power; US–Japan alliance
Japanese security policy 4–5, 35–57, 84, 91–92, 95, 152–53; 1951–89: resistance to rearming 35–39, 43 (crisis, change, and the role of the US 38–39; international structure 35–36, 38, 39; national institutions 36–37, 38; normative factors 37–38); 1989–99: reluctant accommodation to new realities 40–42, 43 (international structure 40, 41–42; national institutions 40; normative factors 40); 9/11: a new role after 42–46, 74 (administrative, election reforms 43–44; the US alliance factor 44–46); basis 38; concerns 62; defense doctrine 38, 39, 41, 49, 72, 91; 'Higuchi Report' 58; Integrated Security Strategy 59–60, 66; 'normal' country status 4, 5, 27, 31, 62, 83, 88, 89, 91, 92, 94, 105, 107, 109, 121, 122, 131, 144, 148; North Atlantic Treaty Organization (NATO) 163, 165; Occupation policy 11, 35–37; official development assistance (ODA) 60–61; pacifism 31–32, 39, 40, 51, 58, 60, 67, 106, 121; political developments 51–54 (hard/soft power 53–54); regional outlook 46–51; soft power 53–54, 58–63 (soft power as instrument of security policy 66, 74, 75); terrorism 29, 59, 60, 62, 91, 159; Tokyo War Crimes Tribunal 11, 64; US–Japan alliance 35, 38, 39, 40, 44–51, 68 (Japan's strengthening of alliance ties with US 152–54, 164, 166); Yoshida Doctrine 36–37, 38, 39, 40, 121; *see also* acts, laws, pacts, treaties; China; Japan; Japanese foreign policy; Japanese hard power; Japanese politics; Japanese Self Defense Forces (SDF); Japanese soft power; US foreign/security policy; US military issues/hard power; US–Japan alliance; US–Japan alliance, Chinese perspective; US–Japan alliance, European views; US–Japan alliance, Korean views; US–Japan alliance, Russian perspective
Japanese Self Defense Forces (SDF) 1, 2, 3, 5, 12, 38–39, 40, 41, 42, 43, 58, 73, 83, 88, 91–92, 96, 122, 137, 144–47, 148, 163; Afghanistan 122, 152, 163, 170; Anti-Terrorism Special Measures Law 42, 52, 91, 122; civilian control 38, 58; Defense Agency/now Ministry of Defense 38, 52, 68, 90, 92, 94; Defense Policy Review Initiative (DPRI) 161; disaster relief and humanitarian assistance 12, 43, 67, 77, 122; integration with US Forces 1, 3, 43, 45–46, 91, 94–95, 109; Iraq 67, 77, 122, 144, 152, 162, 170; Maritime Self-Defense Force (MSDF) 137, 144–45, 152; militarism 1, 2, 37, 38, 58; military expenditure 23, 58, 86, 88, 91, 94, 144, 171; military space policy 95–97; multi-functional 12, 43, 91; National Defense Program Guidelines (NDPG) 12, 43, 88, 91, 122–23, 161 (national defense objectives 123); National Defense Program Outline (NDPO) 39, 41, 42, 43, 69, 91, 137; origins 38; past mistakes 1, 12, 54, 58, 63, 64–65, 90, 106, 124, 141; remilitarization, rearmament 13, 33, 37, 41, 46, 47, 54, 62, 66, 72, 73, 79, 83, 84, 88–89, 107, 109, 120–21, 122, 124–25, 127, 131, 144–45, 173; Replenishment Support Special Measures Law 152; Self Defense Forces Law 38; Taiwan 100; theater missile defense (TMD) system 89, 132, 133, 136, 143, 144, 148, 173; US–Japan alliance as cover for Japanese remilitarization 13, 83, 84, 88–89, 90–97, 107, 109, 124–25, 127, 173; *see also* Japan; Japanese foreign policy; Japanese hard power; Japanese politics; Japanese security policy; Japanese soft power; US foreign/security policy; US military issues/hard power; US–Japan alliance
Japanese soft power 4, 6, 8, 14, 23, 33, 74, 123, 127, 172; activities 123; challenges 62–63; China 60, 61, 170; 'The Council on Security and Defense Capabilities Report: Japan's Visions for Future Security and Defense Capabilities' 12; cultural appeal 14, 20, 54, 58, 62; 'cultural diplomacy' 61–62; deficit: China and South Korea 62–66, 74–75, 170; dilemmas 11–13, 66–67, 172; European views of Japan as 'civilian'

power 154, 158–60, 164; Integrated Security Strategy 59–60, 66; international cooperation 59–60, 66; Japanese foreign policy 60–66, 74; Japanese image 8, 46–47, 54, 61, 62, 63, 141; Japanese security policy 53–54, 58–63 (soft power as instrument of security policy 66, 74, 75, 171); official development assistance (ODA) 59, 60–61; pitfalls 12–13; resources 58, 62, 108–9, 123, 131–32, 141–43, 149; search of soft power 4–5; soft/hard power balance 53–54, 67, 75, 169, 170, 171, 172; strategy 50; US–Japan alliance 63, 66–69, 108; *see also* Japan; Japanese foreign policy; Japanese hard power; Japanese politics; Japanese security policy; US foreign/security policy; US military issues/hard power; US–Japan alliance
Jordan 21, 22, 23

Meeks, Phil 15–16, 19–34, 169, 171; alliances, identity and international relations theories 24–28; classic realist theory 14–15, 19, 24–25; hard power 20–21, 33; Machiavelli's soft power dilemmas 19–24; soft power 15, 19, 23–24, 33; US–Japan alliance 15–16, 26, 28, 33 (balance of interest model 15, 28; balance of power/balance of threat model 15, 28); US and Japanese interests 24, 28–31; US–Japan rivalry 15, 30–31; *see also* international relations; US–Japan alliance
Middle East 155, 159, 165, 166; Europe 156; Japan 62, 63, 91; United States 27, 31, 32, 33
military issues *see* hard power; Japanese hard power; Japanese Self Defense Forces (SDF); US military issues/hard power
multilateralism 152, 153, 158; Association of Southeast Asian Nations (ASEAN) 102, 105; China 7, 14, 51, 102, 104, 106; East Asia 6; EU-US–Japan multilateralism/'trilateralism' 156, 157, 158, 159, 160, 164; United States 4, 172 (unilateralism 14, 153, 158); US–Japan alliance 66, 172; *see also* international relations

non-governmental organizations (NGOs) 59, 125, 142
North Atlantic Treaty Organization (NATO): enlargement 131, 134, 135–36, 147; Japan 163, 165; US–Japan alliance, European views 14, 155, 157, 163, 165; *see also* US–Japan alliance, Russian perspective
Northeast Asia 105; China 68, 105; Japan 4, 32, 53; primacy of hard power 2–3; Russia 14, 132–33, 143, 144, 148–49, 173; South Korea 49; theater missile defense (TMD) system 89–90, 132, 133, 136, 143, 144, 148, 173; United States 4, 8; US–Japan alliance 1, 4, 14; wars 2; *see also* Japan; North Korea
North Korea (Democratic People's Republic of Korea-DPRK) 13, 20, 69–74, 173; ballistic missile defenses (BMD) 69, 73, 123; China 71, 78, 106–7; hard power 117, 119; image 117–18; inter-Korean competition 117; Japan 1, 4, 5, 14, 39, 41, 42, 48–49, 51, 53, 54–55, 66, 69–74, 78, 144, 152, 161, 165, 172 (abduction of Japanese citizens 72, 73, 74, 106, 127, 161, 165, 170; trade 119); Korean War 2, 38, 120; national division 117; national unification policy 117–18; North Korean threat and Japan's tilt toward hard power 13, 41, 42, 48–49, 53, 54–55, 64, 69–74, 93, 94, 121–25, 161, 170; Nuclear Nonproliferation Treaty (NPT) 69, 70, 79; nuclear weapons 1, 5, 13, 41 48–49, 51, 53, 54, 55, 64, 69–70, 71, 74, 78, 161 (emergence of the DPRK threat 121–25); Russia 132, 144; sanctions against 4–5, 51, 69, 70, 71, 72, 74, 78, 106, 119, 128, 161, 170; Six-Party Talks 70–71, 73–74, 78, 106, 127, 132, 170; soft power 14, 117–18, 173 (coercive 127–28; media 118; resources 118); South Korea 71 (North Korea's armed provocations 126); United States 41, 48, 70, 71, 127; US–Japan alliance 4, 14, 48–49, 69–71, 170, 172; US–Japan alliance, European views 152, 154, 161, 163, 164, 165; weapons of mass destruction (WMDs) 5, 62, 69, 123; *see also* Japanese hard power; Japanese soft

power; US–Japan alliance, Korean views
nuclear weapons: China 1, 41, 69, 123; Japan 48–49, 71–73, 78, 105, 106, 108, 173 (virtual nuclear weapons 125–26); North Korea 1, 5, 13, 41 48–49, 51, 53, 54, 55, 64, 69–70, 71, 74, 78, 121–25, 161; Nuclear Nonproliferation Treaty (NPT) 69, 70, 79; Taiwan 1, 45; *see also* hard power; North Korea; weapons of mass destruction (WMDs)
Nye, Joseph: power 20; 'smart power' 11, 171; soft power xii, 5, 9, 10, 127, 134; *see also* soft power

oil 65, 164; Japan 40, 47; North Korea 70, 71; Persian Gulf 31; Russia 14, 133, 135, 138, 140; United States 133, 135; US–Japan interests 30–31
Organisation for Economic Cooperation and Development (OECD) 22

Pakistan 21, 22, 23, 27, 28, 170
Palestine 22, 23, 159
Pinkston, Daniel A.: US–Japan alliance, Korean views 14, 117–30, 170, 173; *see also* North Korea; soft power; South Korea; US–Japan alliance; US–Japan alliance, Korean views
power 25–26; 'compulsory' power 26; 'great/minor' powers 25; 'institutional' power 26; power alliance 33; 'productive' power 26; Russell, Bertrand 10; 'structural' power 26; US hegemony 2, 19–20, 23–24, 26, 83, 88, 104, 119, 122, 151–66, 169; *see also* hard power; international relations; soft power; US–Japan alliance, European views

Russia xii, 4, 14, 105; ASEAN Regional Forum (ARF) 132, 149; Asia Pacific Economic Cooperation (APEC) 132; China 2, 139, 142, 145, 148; Cold War 132, 138, 146; economic power 29–30, 135, 140; foreign policy 135; Gorbachev, Mikhail 28; island sovereignty issues 2, 14, 131, 132, 136–41; Japan 137–38 (Russian perception of 141–42, 147, 148); Northeast Asia 14, 132–33, 143, 144, 148–49, 173; Putin, Vladimir 135, 136, 138, 139, 140, 147; Russian Far East 14, 132–33, 138, 140–41, 142, 146, 147–48; security policy 134; Six-Party Talks 132, 144, 148; Soviet Russia 25, 26, 35, 39, 87, 121, 139, 140, 157, 159; terrorism 132, 133; *see also* Northeast Asia; US–Japan alliance, Russian perspective

Sevastyanov, Sergey: US–Japan alliance, Russian perspective 14, 131–50, 173; *see also* Japanese Self Defense Forces (SDF); Northeast Asia; Russia; US–Japan alliance, Russian perspective
soft power 5, 8; and hard security 2–3 (primacy of hard power 2–3, 5); China 2, 6–8, 9, 20, 104; concept 5, 9–11, 19, 20, 127, 134, 142–43, 147, 171 (constructivist approach 10; liberal model of international relations 10; neo-liberal model 20; realist model of international relations 10, 14, 19, 24; utility maximization 10–11); cultural appeal as source of 5, 9, 14, 20, 58, 134, 141, 171; difficulties, limitations 171; East Asia 5, 6–8; economic power 19, 20; Europe 5, 156–57 ('civilian power' 156, 158; predominance 157; 'transformative power' 156); international relations xii, 10–11, 58, 67; Machiavelli's soft power dilemmas 19; North Korea 14, 117–18, 127–28, 173; Nye, Joseph xii, 5, 9, 10, 20, 127, 134 ('smart power' 11, 171); official development assistance (ODA) 23; persuasion 20, 51, 117, 127–28, 134; resources 9, 11, 19, 58, 118, 134, 141, 171; social basis 10–11, 12, 171; soft/hard power balance xii, 5–6, 53–54, 67, 75, 134, 169, 170, 171, 172; soft/hard power, China 14, 84, 101–7 ('charm offensive' 84, 102–3; 'New Security Concept' (NSC) 14, 102, 103; soft power 103–6, 109; Southeast Asia 14, 84, 102, 105; US/China soft power comparison 104); soft/hard power continuum 21; soft/hard power interaction 9–10, 11, 21, 134, 171; South Korea 117, 118–19, 123–24; United States 1, 6–8, 9, 11–12, 24, 32, 33, 171 (cultural appeal 20, 24; declining 2, 6, 7, 24, 32; East Asia 6–8; US/China soft power comparison 104); World War II 11; *see also*

international relations; Japanese soft power; US–Japan alliance, Chinese perspective; US–Japan alliance, European views
Southeast Asia 6–7, 49–51; China 6–7, 14, 84, 102, 105 ('charm offensive' 84, 102–3; soft power 6–7, 14, 105); Japan 8, 65, 87; *see also* Association of Southeast Asian Nations (ASEAN)
South Korea (Republic of Korea-ROK) 14, 39, 49, 53, 62–65, 173; Cold War 121; Grand National Party (GNP) 123; hard power 124, 125–27; image 118–19; inter-Korean competition 117; island sovereignty issues 2, 49, 64, 123, 124; Japan 14, 39, 49, 53, 62–65, 121–25, 145; Japan-Korean relations 119–20, 121, 123–24; Lee Myung-bak 49, 118, 123, 124; Kim Dae-jung 63; Korean War 2, 38, 120; Korean wave of pop culture 118–19; national division 117; national unification policy 117–18; Northeast Asia 49; North Korea 71 (North Korea's armed provocations 126); Park Chung-hee 126; Roh Moo-hyun 49, 64, 118, 121, 124, 126; 'self-reliant national defense policy' 126; soft power 117, 118–19, 123–24 (resources 118); Taiwan 126; US–Japan alliance 4, 49; US–Japan/US-ROK alliance imbalance 124; US-ROK alliance 119, 121, 124, 126; *see also* US–Japan alliance, Korean views

Taiwan: Chen Shui-bian 97, 99; China 1, 3, 41, 46, 47–48, 97–101; democracy 97, 99, 100; independence 97, 122; island sovereignty issues 2, 64, 95, 100, 122; Japan 41, 45, 47–48, 92, 98–101 (closer Japan-Taiwan relationship 98–100); Lee Teng-hui 47–48, 99; nuclear weapons 1, 45; 'One China' 97, 98, 99; sea lines of communication (SLOC) 3, 99, 100; South Korea 126; United States 97–98 (closer security cooperation 98; closer US-Taiwan relationship 97, 98; US arms sales to 85, 97–98); US–Japan alliance 47–48, 64, 68–69 (as factor interfering with China's policy toward Taiwan 13, 83, 84, 85, 89, 90, 92, 95, 97–101, 105, 107, 109); *see also* China; China, foreign policy; Japan; US–Japan alliance; US–Japan alliance, Chinese perspective
Taiwan Strait 1, 2, 45, 47, 53, 89, 92, 95, 97–101, 109; *see also* China; China, foreign policy; Taiwan; US–Japan alliance, Chinese perspective
terrorism: 9/11 4, 13, 21, 22, 29, 42, 84, 85, 108; Anti-Terrorism Special Measures Law 42, 52, 91, 122; definition 28–29; Japan 4, 13, 29, 42–46, 54, 59, 60, 62, 91, 159; hard power 171; Russia 132, 133; Spain 29; United Kingdom 29; United States 3, 28–29, 84, 134, 151, 160, 171, 172, 173 ('War on Terrorism' 27, 29, 53, 85); US–Japan alliance 28–29, 31, 42–46, 84, 85, 106, 151, 157, 158, 160, 170; US–Japan alliance, European views 151, 157, 158, 160; *see also* US foreign/security policy

United Kingdom 29, 42, 158; European union 153, 156, 157, 163, 165; Japan–UK relations 158, 162, 165; US hegemony 153, 154, 156, 157–58; *see also* US–Japan alliance, European views
United Nations: Japan 52 (seat on UN Security Council 32, 33, 44, 47, 64, 105, 106, 145, 165); Persian Gulf War 40; UN Charter 72; UN Security Council 70, 74, 164, 170
United States xii; Bush Jr., George 24, 29, 32, 42, 53, 84–85, 90, 97–98, 105, 124, 127, 132, 136, 147, 151, 152, 153, 158, 161, 163, 171–72; Clinton, William 41, 97, 151; democracy 11–12, 29, 32, 85, 105, 134, 155; *Economist* 23–24; economy, economic power 1, 30; hegemony 2, 19–20, 23–24, 26, 83, 88, 104, 119, 122, 151–66, 169; human rights 11–12, 134; image 8 (unpopularity 23); Nixon, Richard 38, 84, 126; Obama, Barak 54, 171, 172; official development assistance (ODA) 22–23; Reagan, Ronald 157; *see also* China; China, foreign policy; Japan; US foreign/security policy; US military issues/hard power; US–Japan alliance; US–Japan alliance, Chinese perspective; US–Japan alliance, European views; US Japan alliance, Russian perspective

Index

US foreign/security policy: Afghanistan 1, 23; Anti-ballistic Missile (ABM) Treaty, abrogation 131, 135–36, 147; China 30, 32, 36, 41, 74, 101; foreign policy 12, 27, 32, 89, 134–35; Iraq 1, 23, 32, 66–67, 135; Middle East 27, 31, 32, 33; Northeast Asia 8; North Korea 41, 48, 70, 71, 127; rogue state 28; security policy 35–36, 89–90 (China 36; global security strategy 3, 54, 107, 108, 152; Japan 35–41, 44–46, 93–94; Korean War 38; Vietnam War 38); soft power 1, 6–8, 9, 11–12, 24, 32, 33, 171 (cultural appeal 20, 24; declining 2, 6, 7, 24, 32; East Asia 6–8; US/China soft power comparison 104); Taiwan 85, 97–98; terrorism 84, 85, 134, 151, 160, 171, 172, 173 (9/11 21, 22, 29, 84, 85, 108; 'War on Terrorism' 27, 29, 53, 85); unilateralism 14, 153, 158; United Kingdom 153, 154, 156, 157–58; US–ROK alliance 119, 121, 124, 126; *see also* China; China, foreign policy; Japan; United States; US military issues/hard power; US–Japan alliance; US–Japan alliance, Chinese perspective; US–Japan alliance, European views; US–Japan alliance, Russian perspective

US military issues/hard power 1, 2; ballistic missile defense (BMD) 89; Cold War 3, 25, 26, 28; hard power 3, 14, 23, 24, 135, 136, 147, 156, 169, 171, 172; Korean War 38; MacArthur General, Douglas 36, 38; military aid 21–22; military expenditure 21, 23, 86, 171; National Missile Defense (NMD) system 131, 135–36, 143–44, 147; NATO enlargement 131, 134, 135–36, 147; new goals 3; Persian Gulf War 11; theater missile defense (TMD) system 132, 133, 136, 143, 144, 148, 173; Vietnam War 38, 126; weapons of mass destruction (WMD) 151, 160; *see also* hard power; United States; US foreign/security policy; US–Japan alliance; US–Japan alliance, Chinese perspective; US–Japan alliance, European views; US–Japan alliance, Russian perspective

US–Japan alliance 1, 3–4, 13–15, 26, 33, 63, 66–69, 105, 169–73; Armitage Report 42, 45, 90; Association of Southeast Asian Nations (ASEAN) 49–51; balance of interest model 15, 28, 31; balance of power/balance of threat model 15, 28; balancing domestic/foreign interests 24, 28–31; Bush Jr., George 84–85, 90, 97, 98, 105; changing alliance 1, 3–4, 11, 62, 88, 169 (implications for Japan 3, 4; implications for the region 4); changing international identities 24–28; China 3, 4, 26, 33, 46–47, 68, 74, 169–70, 172 (containment 26, 46, 47, 68, 88, 122, 125, 169; economic growth, power 32, 62, 101, 106, 107, 169); hard power 2, 3, 33, 66, 170, 172 (Japanese/US asymmetry 33, 105, 169); Iraq 66–67; Japan: contributing alliance partner to the US 1, 3, 42–46, 66; Japanese security policy 35, 38, 39, 40, 44–51, 66, 68, 169; militarization 13, 14, 35, 42–46, 66, 73, 79, 83, 84, 88–89, 90–97, 107, 109, 124–25, 127 173; North Korea 4, 14, 48–49, 69–71, 170, 172; Nye Report 41, 122; Persian Gulf War 11; popularity, support 32, 68, 77; regional outlook 46–51; soft/hard power balance 67, 75, 169, 170, 171, 172 (soft power 15, 33, 66, 106, 172; dilemma 66–67; Japanese soft power 63, 66–69); South Korea 4, 49; strategic divergence 152, 155; Taiwan 47–48, 64, 68–69; terrorism 28–29, 31, 42–46, 84, 85, 106, 151, 157, 158, 160, 170; US–Japanese interests 24, 28–31 (energy 28, 30–31; MNCs 28, 30, 31; terrorism 28–29, 31; trade 28, 30, 31); 'US–Japan Alliance: Transformation and Realignment for the Future' 45; US–Japan Joint Security Consultative Committee (JSC) 45–46, 100; US–Japan rivalry 15, 30, 40; *see also* acts, laws, pacts, treaties; international relations; Japan; Japanese foreign policy; Japanese hard power; Japanese security policy; Japanese Self Defense Forces (SDF); Japanese soft power; United States; US foreign/security policy; US military issues/hard power; US–Japan alliance, Chinese perspective; US–Japan alliance, European views; US–Japan alliance, Korean views; US–Japan alliance, Russian perspective

US–Japan alliance, Chinese perspective 3, 4, 13–14, 26, 33, 46–47, 83–116, 170; alliance as cover for Japanese remilitarization 13, 83, 84, 88–89, 90–97, 107, 109 (Japan's military space policy 95–97; nuclear debate 92–94); alliance as factor interfering with China's policy toward Taiwan 13, 83, 84, 85, 89, 90, 92, 95, 97–101, 105, 107, 109 (closer Japan–Taiwan relationship 98–100; closer US–Taiwan relationship 97–98; 'One China' principle 97, 98, 99); alliance's scope and missions 13, 83–84, 87–90; Chinese attitudes toward US–Japan alliance 87–88; containment of China 88; missile defense development and deployment 83, 84, 89–90, 92, 94–95 (theater missile defenses (TMD) 89–90; theater missile defenses (TMD) R&D 89–90, 95; United States–Japan Roadmap for Realignment 94); Sino–Japanese relations 13–14, 83, 85–87, 98, 108, 109 (ambivalence 85; end of the Cold War/Soviet Union's disintegration 87; generational leadership changes 87, 98; international security environment changes 87, 90; power shift in East Asia 86–87; rivalry 85–86, 87, 96, 107); Sino–US relations 13–14, 83, 84–85, 97, 98, 107–8, 109 (Bush Jr., George 84–85, 97, 98, 105; common interests 107; communication channels 84; differences 84, 85, 105, 108; objectives for post-Cold War Asia 85; terrorism 84, 85; US global strategy 107, 108); soft/hard power: Beijing's balancing act 14, 84, 101–7 (Association of Southeast Asian Nations (ASEAN) 102–4, 105; 'charm offensive' 84, 102–3; hard power 101, 106; 'New Security Concept' (NSC) 14, 102, 103; Shanghai Cooperation Organization (SCO) 102; soft power 103–6, 109; Southeast Asia 14, 84, 102, 105; US/China soft power comparison 104); *see also* China; China, foreign policy; Japan foreign policy; Japanese security policy; Japanese Self Defense Forces (SDF); Taiwan; United States; US foreign/security policy; US–Japan alliance

US–Japan alliance, European views 4, 14, 151–68, 172; Afghanistan 155, 163, 164, 165; China 151, 152, 154, 161–63, 164, 165, 166, 173; Europe, European Union 153; Europe–Japan relations 153–54, 155, 158–60, 161–62, 164–66 (convergence 159, 160, 163, 164, 166; divergence 160–63; power resorces 165–66, 172–73; rivalry 158); Europe–US hegemony: soft power/hard power 154, 155–58 (EU strategies to balance US hegemony 153, 154, 156, 157, 158, 159, 164, 166); Europe-US–Japan alliance 14, 154, 155, 160–64, 166 (convergence 155, 163–64; divergence 163); Europe–US relations 155 (ambivalence 155–56; disputes 153, 154); European/Japanese responses to US hegemony 151–55, 163, 166 (deterioration in Europe-US ties 153; Japan's strengthening of alliance ties with US 152–54, 164, 166); European views of Japan as 'civilian' power 154, 158–60, 164 (Action Plan (2001) 159; common principles 159; EU–Japan Joint Declaration (1991) 159); Iran 155, 159, 163–64; Iraq 151, 152, 153, 154, 158, 160, 162, 163, 164, 165; multilateralism/'trilateralism' 156, 157, 158, 159, 160, 164; North Atlantic Treaty Organization (NATO) 14, 155, 157, 163, 165; North Korea 152, 154, 161, 163, 164, 165; terrorism 151, 157, 158, 160; United States (Bush Jr., George 151, 152, 153, 158, 163; unilateralism 14, 153, 158); weapons of mass destruction (WMD) 151, 160; *see also* China; China, foreign policy; Europe/European Union; Japanese foreign policy; Japanese security policy; US foreign/security policy; US–Japan alliance

US–Japan alliance, Korean views 14, 117–30, 170, 173; Bush Jr., George 124, 127; hard power (Japan 121, 123, 127, 170, 173; South Korea 125–27); Japan-Korean relations 119–20, 121, 123–24 (resentment (*han*) 120); Japan's virtual nuclear weapons 125–26; North Korea 4, 14, 48–49, 69–71, 117–18, 173 (emergence of the DPRK threat 121–25); Nye Report 41, 122; soft power 14, 117–19, 123–24

(Japan 123, 127, 173); soft power: persuasion/coercion 127–28; South Korea 4, 14, 49, 117, 118–19, 121, 123–24, 173; United States 122; views of the US–Japan alliance 4, 119–21, 123–25, 127–28 (alliance as cover for Japanese remilitarization 124–25, 127, 173; constructivist approaches 120; containment of China 122, 125; fears/han 120–21; liberal/neoliberal theories 119; realist theories 119); *see also* Japanese foreign policy; Japanese security policy; North Korea; soft power; South Korea; US–Japan alliance

US–Japan alliance, Russian perspective 4, 14, 131–50, 173; Russian–American global 'coopetition' 131, 133–36, 148 (abrogation of the ABM Treaty 131, 135–36, 147; Bush Jr., George 132, 136, 147; Europe 133–34; hard power 135, 136, 147; Kosovo crisis 134; military cooperation 133, 134; misinterpretation 134–36, 147; National Missile Defense (NMD) system 131, 135–36, 143–44, 147; NATO enlargement 131, 134, 135–36, 147; theater missile defense (TMD) system 132, 133, 136, 143, 144, 148, 173); Russian–Japanese relationship 131 (bilateral military cooperation 137; controversy 131, 136–37; economic ties 138–39, 140, 147–48; peace treaty 139–40, 145, 147, 148; territorial dispute 2, 14, 131, 132, 136–41, 142, 145, 145, 147, 148, 173); Russian security interests and threat perception in Northeast Asia 14, 132–33, 143, 144, 148–49, 173 (main threats 132–33; paramilitary threats 132–33); soft power concept 134, 142–43, 147; sources and effectiveness of Japanese soft power 131–32, 141–43, 149; US–Japan alliance 14, 132, 143–47, 148, 173 (decommissioned Russian Pacific Fleet nuclear submarines 146, 148; Japanese Self Defense Forces (SDF)

137, 144–47, 148; Russia–Japan–USA triangle 145, 146, 148; US as leading partner 131, 148, 173); *see also* Japanese Self Defense Forces (SDF); Northeast Asia; Russia; United Sates; US foreign/security policy; US–Japan alliance

war: China 2; Cold War 1, 3, 5, 121 (conventional interpretation 24–25; Russia 132, 138, 146; South Korea 121; United States 3, 25, 26, 28); Korean War 2, 38, 120; Northeast Asia 2; Persian Gulf War 11, 40, 42, 170–71; Soviet Russia 25, 132, 138, 146; United States 3, 11, 25, 26, 28, 38, 126; Vietnam War 2, 38, 126; World War II 1, 2, 11, 120 (Japan 11, 27, 35, 42, 49, 141); *see also* Afghanistan; hard power; Iraq; nuclear weapons; weapons of mass destruction (WMD)

weapons of mass destruction (WMD) 59, 62, 132, 135; ballistic missile defenses (BMD) 69, 89; intercontinental ballistic missiles (ICBMs) 78, 143, 144; North Korea 5, 62, 69, 123; Taiwan 45, 89; theater missile defenses (TMD) 89–90, 132, 133, 136, 143, 144, 148, 173; United States 152 (National Missile Defense (NMD) system 131, 135–36, 143–44, 147; theater missile defense (TMD) system 89–90, 132, 133, 136, 143, 144, 148, 173); *see also* hard power; North Korea; nuclear weapons

Weber, Max 10

World Trade Organisation (WTO) 153, 162

Yuan, Jing-dong: US–Japan alliance, Chinese perspective 13–14, 83–116, 170; *see also* China; China, foreign policy; Japanese Self Defense Forces (SDF); Taiwan; US–Japan alliance; US–Japan alliance, Chinese perspective

CPSIA information can be obtained at www.ICGtesting.com
Printed in the USA
BVOW041223150212

282943BV00002B/3/P